2ND EDITION

LIVING A LIFE
I LOVE™

HEALING SEXUAL COMPULSIVITY, SEXUAL ADDICTION, SEXUAL AVOIDANCE *and* OTHER SEXUAL CONCERNS.

WESTON M. EDWARDS, PH.D.

Your Name_____

If found, please return by calling_____

D1314258

Copyright
Living a Life I Love™: Healing sexual compulsivity, sexual addiction, sexual avoidance and other sexual concerns. 2nd Edition.

SERIES: Living a Life I Love™

© 2012 Weston Edwards

Please don't make illegal copies. This workbook represents thousands of hours of effort over decades of work. I am only compensated for my time and effort when you purchase the workbook.

For additional copies, or discounted bulk orders, of this workbook, please visit or email:

> Weston Edwards, PhD
> request@sexualhealthinstitute.org
> www.livingalifeilovebooks.com

ISBN-13: 978-1466209053
ISBN-10: 1466209054

Disclaimer. This information provides accurate and authoritative information regarding sexuality; the information is for education purposes only. The publisher and author are not engaged in providing professional services. You should seek the services of a trained professional if you need expert assistance or therapy services.

Dedication

To those seeking hope:

My prayer is this workbook will be a source of healing to help you find the courage to live with freedom.

Acknowledgments

I choose first to acknowledge the clients in my practice, workshops, and treatment programs. My life coaching and therapy clients continue to be the source of inspiration in my commitment to courage, healing and freedom. Over the past four years, previous versions of this book have been piloted with clients' generous acceptance (tolerance) of changes, edits, updates, corrections, rewrites and drafts. Their feedback has been vital to this version.

The resources noted in the bibliography reflect the major sources I used in writing the book and rounding out material gathered through my work. With the exception of a few endnotes, I don't include references within the text due to the nature of the book. In an academic text, or in conference presentations, I include the parenthetical citations per the APA writing manual (a PDF file with detailed citations is available upon request); however, this is not such a book. I am grateful to my colleagues, known and unknown, who have taught me so much. Two mentors, Eli Coleman and Simon Rosser, have profoundly shaped my work.

For the organization and design of the workbook, I thank Rachel Stockert, my editor for this edition. When you find an amazing editor, they really do take the material to a whole new level. Rachel works freelance—please considering hiring her (rachel.stockert@gmail.com). Rhonda Freshwater at www.rhondafreshwater.com out did herself with the cover design. (A hint to the meaning of the cover is Part 2, Stage 2, Section 8). Also, thanks to Timothy State for permission to use the picture on the back cover. More of his pictures can be seen at: www.flickr.com/photos/timothystate/.

Finally, I acknowledge the amazing people in my life. To my husband, Luis (yes, we were married [in Canada] in July 2011): Thank you for your generosity of time to write this workbook when you'd much rather be the focus of my attention. And a shout out of acknowledgement to the other amazing people in my life including Mark, Larry, David, Peter, Timothy, Amanda, and Stephanie. Thank you for being part of the reason I can say, "I'm Living a Life I Love."

Weston Edwards
Dec 16, 2011

Welcome and Introduction

Take a moment to think about living a life you love. What would such a life be like? Many of us don't know what life we would love to live if we had the opportunity. This is often due to a lack of self-knowledge. We don't know our true selves and therefore don't know what those selves need and want. In addition, it's difficult to love and nurture that which we don't know. One of the most common realms in which the self hides (or is hidden) is that of sexuality. Through this book, I'll help you recognize the role of sexual health in creating personal fulfillment and encourage you to discover, accept, and care for your true sexual self.

For many people, delving into the realm of sexuality is very painful. Due to the nature of the healing process, however, we have to experience and confront this pain in order to work through it. In addition to pain, addressing sexual issues often stirs up shame, guilt, fear, and embarrassment. This is completely normal; if you experience these emotions it's a good sign that you're moving in the right direction! All of these painful emotions are the consequences of repressed sexual energy. By acknowledging and accepting your true sexual self—and being gentle with yourself—you can learn to express this energy in healthy ways.

If you're reading this, certain sexual behaviors are probably interfering with your life and/or the life of someone you care about. In order to prevent more damage from being done as you work through this treatment process, you need to stop any immediately problematic behaviors *now*, which is why I've included an *Immediate Short-Term Prevention Plan* assignment shortly into Part One of the book. In addition to stopping immediately problematic behaviors, the longer-term goals I want for you are to reduce and stop problematic sexual behaviors while developing and learning to maintain healthy ones. In order to accomplish this, however, you'll need a solid understanding of the concepts and terms involved. After all, how can we think or talk about "problematic sexual behavior" if we don't know what this means to us? How can we stop problematic behavior without understanding what's motivating us to do it in the first place?

In Part One, I introduce concepts and definitions that are both necessary and useful to understand as you move through the treatment process presented in Part Two. For example, you'll learn about the ten components of sexual health—a list of topics around which the work in the book is structured. As you contemplate the material in Part One, you'll begin to make connections between these concepts and your own life. One of your first assignments, then, will be to start a journal (to be used throughout the book) in which you'll record the connections you make while reading. I have provided several prompt assignments to assist you with this.

In Part Two, you'll apply the concepts you learned in Part One to your own experiences. This part of the book is presented in three stages – *Problem Identification*, *Primary Treatment*, and *Groundwork for Completing Treatment*. In *Stage One: Problem Identification* you'll examine your own sexual behaviors through a series of assignments, pinpointing and ultimately prioritizing problem areas in order to build a personalized structure for treatment. In *Stage Two: Primary Treatment*, you'll work to address the issues identified in Stage One. The topics in this stage reflect the ten components of sexual health discussed during Part One. This second stage is where you'll learn to stop unhealthy patterns and build healthy ones to replace them. Through a variety of carefully selected assignments, you'll examine the behaviors, thoughts, values and circumstances that define your life. In *Stage Three: Groundwork for Completing Treatment* you'll review what you did and learned in the first two stages, using this information to develop a *Continuing Care Plan* to serve as a guide for you to reference and revise as you work toward living a life you love. Finally, the *Personal Definition of Sexual Health* generated through the last assignment will serve as the roadmap for your journey into the future you create. It's the tool you'll take with you as you continue past the assignments of this book.

NOTE: As you begin the work in this book, carefully consider what information to share, with whom to share it, and how and when to do so. In addition, be sure to keep the workbook in a secure location since you'll be filling it with a bounty of personal information. See "Caution: Risks of Disclosure" on page 5 for important additional information concerning confidentiality.

Things to Know as You Begin

What you must understand before you go is this: the air is cold, the sky is dark, the trees are thick, the path is winding, and at the end awaits a field of light. (Anonymous, unknown source)

This section of the book is dedicated to 1) helping you curtail immediately problematic behaviors, and 2) providing you with a map of what lies ahead as you work toward improved sexual health.

Healing and Hope

The purpose of this workbook is healing. Yes, it's about addressing sexual compulsivity, sexual avoidance, and many underlying issues, but even those issues are focused on healing and hope. My experience suggests, more than anything else, that people are seeking hope—hope to step beyond fear, paralysis and pain. In my work, I am constantly inspired by the positive energy coming from other people. Simply having a place to talk about their experience of pain can create the energy a person needs to start the healing process. My hope is that you will find the resources in this workbook helpful in your healing journey.

The Pain of Sexuality

Many people experience pain in the realm of sexuality. Too often, we're stuck in the pain of sexuality. We often focus on internal causes such as abuse, shame, or fear, but other sources of pain can include social, familial, cultural or religious messages. A major problem occurs when painful external messages become internalized and the individual replicates and reinforces the painful messages in a tighter and tighter circle within him or herself. Once this pattern begins, the pain takes on a life of its own, leading to feelings of hopelessness, desperation and profound isolation. For me, this is the saddest part of the pain.

As you begin your journey, I can't take away the pain. You can't avoid the pain—a fact that only intensifies it. Instead, I encourage you to feel the pain. Paradoxically, the only way to resolve the pain is to go through it. In a recent encounter, I worked with someone through the healing process. At one point, the release of the pain resulted in a surprisingly intense sobbing session. The level of wailing can best be described by imagining a 4-year-old toddler wailing after his/her finger has been accidentally slammed in a car door. Witnessing this from a normally stoic grown adult highlighted the pain encountered in the realm of sexuality. Once the pain is acknowledged and experienced, it can be transformed into something profound and healing. You're probably familiar with this common saying in the workout-gym-weightlifting community: No pain, no gain. Not so surprisingly, this saying also applies to healing the pain of sexuality. When this process is complete, you can experience peace and acceptance—and you have the potential for great love.

Sex, shame, fear, recovery, hope, and life

The first steps for many individuals in discussing sexual issues are often shaped by shame, embarrassment, fear and guilt. I can't stress enough how *normal* these feelings are when opening up a new area of growth. Even though these reactions are normal, it's important to start the process of talking about your sexual health concerns. While it may seem easy for someone else to say it, many of these thoughts and feelings are irrational—based in cultural messages that sex is bad and in a general aversion to addressing sexuality. My experience suggests that sexuality is at the core of many of the most important aspects of our life. For many people in recovery, sexuality is the last issue to be addressed. Unfortunately, it's often the last issue counselors want (and, in some cases, are trained) to address as well.

In almost every situation, when you start the process of addressing sexuality, the reaction is eventually positive. The energy protecting the shame is released, allowing that energy to be directed toward life-giving actions. New possibilities are created, allowing you to live a new life.

Sexual repression as a form of passive death

Repression is to live a life that you were not meant to live. Repression is to do things you never wanted to do. Repression is to be a fellow that you are not. Repression is a way to destroy yourself. Repression is suicide – very slow of course, but a very certain slow poisoning. (OSHO)[1]

The last line of this quote struck me. "Repression is suicide – very slow of course, but a very certain slow poisoning." This is no truer than in the realm of sexuality. I can't remember how many times I've worked with people who are experiencing a slow death because of the repression of their sexual energy. Shame, fear, hurt, and guilt are the consequences of this repression. What would it look like if you ended your own repression regarding your sexuality? How might life be different? How might you be different? How would your relationships be different?

One of the best interventions is to simply affirm the possibility that you can be the person you are—your true self. You have within yourself (as does everyone else) the inherent permission to be alive in the realm of sexuality. Sexual health is about accepting the responsibility to live a life you love. It's stepping beyond repression to affirm your wants, needs, and desires. Sometimes this is easy; often it takes a bit of work.

Sin is doing something wrong; hell is staying in something wrong.

There is no greater hell than to be a prisoner of fear. (Ben Johnson)

In spiritual/religious language, we might recognize we did something wrong, label it as sin, and feel the need to seek forgiveness. What I also find occurring in the realm of sexuality is tremendous shame creating a personal definition of hell. If sin is doing something wrong, hell is staying in something wrong. When a person realizes s/he did something wrong, the individual enters into shame spirals, emotionally abuses the self, and forever puts the self in a negative place. The isolation and alone-ness is paralyzing. Many of these individuals punish themselves much more than anyone else could ever punish them. They are in a self-imposed hell distinguished by helplessness, frustration, and hopelessness.

If you exist within this self-imposed hell, I encourage you to work towards self-forgiveness—and to be gentle with yourself. This isn't about letting yourself off the hook, but rather, treating yourself with the level of compassion every individual (including you) deserves. Developing sexual health requires accountability that's respectful and leads toward forgiveness and healing versus shame, fear, and the ongoing experience of a personal hell.

Caution: Risks of Disclosure

The work you will do throughout this book is both personal and powerful. As you begin, there are a few things you should know about the potential consequences of what you reveal to others through writing and/or conversation.

Primary Partner(s): The material in this book—as well as the simple fact that you are reading and working on it—is likely to have a significant impact on your primary sexual partner(s). As a result, it's critical that any information you disclose to your partner be done so with the utmost care. Please read "Talking About Sex" in Part One before discussing this work with your partner.

Therapists/Other Professionals: In any therapeutic relationship, confidentiality limits what a professional can disclose to others. Depending on where you live, however, there are limits to this privilege. Be sure you understand these before sharing information with your therapist. Again, be sure to read "Talking About Sex" before revealing information to anyone.

Journal/Workbook Security: As you progress through the book, you are encouraged to write in it as well as keep a journal (page 12). Pay attention, however, to where you leave the workbook and journal. Consider who might have access to it.

Immediate Short-Term Prevention Plan

Often what brings a person to therapy is the fact that there are immediate behaviors interfering with that person's life. These behaviors need to be stopped immediately—before any additional consequences occur. In medical triage, the most important issues are treated first. When someone is bleeding, medical providers don't worry about a temperature until they've first stopped the bleeding. Likewise, if you're reading this book, you're probably concerned in some way about specific sexual behaviors (or someone you care about is concerned). The focus of the *Immediate Short-term Prevention Plan* is identifying these critical behaviors and finding temporary strategies to help you address them as you start the process of enacting more lasting change. Let's stop the bleeding first!

Abstinence as Strategy

For obvious reasons, the most effective prevention strategy is *abstinence*. Many people think abstinence has to mean never having sex, masturbating, or logging onto the Internet again as long as you live. For most people, this is neither realistic nor healthy. Sometimes, however, individuals *do* find that taking a short break from problematic behavior—a day, a week, a month, or a couple months—can be helpful. Abstinence can be a great strategy for getting a handle on how out-of-control your sexual behavior really is—and containing potential damage while you find long-term strategies. If your sexual behavior is out of control, it will become clearer during the abstinence period. So, while you won't stop having sex forever, consider a period of abstinence to get yourself focused. During an illness, the patient may not be able to eat. Once stable, the patient is re-introduced to solid food in a planned and careful manner. In the same way, you will reintroduce healthy sexuality into your life—with planning and care.

Abstinence as Starvation

The human mind is constructed in such a way that when you tell yourself *not* to think about something, it becomes all you think about. For example, I want you to think about your favorite dessert or meal. Seriously, think about enjoying this dessert. Can you feel your mouth watering simply with the thought of it? Now, tell yourself to *stop* thinking about it. *Stop* thinking about it! You probably can't. In a similar way, telling yourself you will never have sex or won't think about sexuality only reinforces the pattern of thinking about sex. Attempting to avoid addressing sexuality through abstinence or force of will is called "white-knuckling." Eventually, your level of exhaustion will overcome the force of your will and you will revert to patterns of unhealthy sexual behavior. A person with unhealthy eating behaviors can't simply stop eating—they would starve! They have to develop *healthy* eating habits to take the place of the unhealthy ones. Sexual behavior works in the same way, which is why this workbook encourages you to engage in *healthy* sexuality rather than trying to starve yourself.

Other Potential Strategies

Two other strategies to possibly integrate into your Immediate Short-term Prevention Plan include harm-reduction and moderation management. An example of *harm reduction* is using the Internet for sexual release by masturbating to sexually explicit material rather than hiring a prostitute in real time. While still risky, the online behavior might be *less* harmful. Limiting the time you use to engage in a particular behavior is *moderation management*. This might mean limiting your viewing of sexually explicit material to two hours a day as a step toward moderating your behavior.

Your Immediate Short-term Prevention Plan

In the following assignment you will create a list of the problematic behaviors you feel you need to stop immediately. Once you have generated the list, keep it handy—you may discover/remember more as you continue through the workbook. Read over the list slowly and carefully; this is the first step in stopping your detrimental behaviors. Remember that these behaviors don't define who you are, they are simply things you do. Just like any other change, it won't be easy to change these behaviors, but you can celebrate the fact that you're getting a handle on the problem.

Next, you'll come up with immediate plans (think in terms of the coming week) to address each of the problems you identified. What strategies will work best for you, even in the face of your own self-sabotage? Even if your plans aren't 100% successful, you'll be further ahead than when you started. If a plan works, great; if not, regroup and figure out how to improve it. A behavioral analysis can help determine the best new path if you need one (see Behavioral Analysis on page 75). Don't be discouraged if a strategy doesn't seem to work—you'll be able to learn from the process regardless, uncovering the unique characteristics of your own acting-out cycle (page 56) in order to strengthen your plans.

ASSIGNMENT: Immediate Short-term Prevention Plan

Review the following questions, first completing a list of behaviors/problems and then indicating immediate prevention strategies to address each.

- What sexual behaviors prompted you to open this book? What are your short-term plans to address those behaviors?

- Are any of your sexual behaviors considered illegal? Are you worried you might get arrested? What are your short-term plans to address this?

- Which sexual behaviors would you never want anyone else to know about? These are often behaviors that require immediate attention. If so, what are your short-term plans to address them?

- Are you spending too much money, time and/or energy looking for or trying to arrange sex? What are your short-term plans to address this?

- Are you unable to stop your sexual behaviors despite negative consequences? What are your short-term plans to address this?

- Can you think of strategies that have worked for you in the past? Can you use any of those strategies now?

As your awareness of your behavior grows, so, too, will your awareness of concerns that lead to acting-out behaviors. The assignments throughout the book are designed to build on the Immediate Short-term Prevention Plan, which eventually serves as a foundation for the Continuing Care Plan in Part 2: Stage 3.

Goals of the Workbook

When you start a marathon race, your focus is not on the first mile. Rather, it's on completing the entire race and planning how you'll survive all 26 miles. In the same way, it's important to have the end of therapy in mind. I not-so-jokingly start initial therapy sessions by telling the client our mutual goal is to work me out of a job. I ask them to think about what it would look like to be done with treatment. Often, people don't have an answer, which is okay at this point. The question, nevertheless, frames the therapeutic relationship as time-limited, goal-focused and ever-conscious of the client's goal(s). Although formal therapy might be complete, the life process has only begun.

As in any treatment program, you must understand what the end goals are in order to achieve them. In this case, there are two goals I want you to achieve:

Reduce/Stop Your Unhealthy Behaviors

The first goal is to help you understand the cycle that feeds your problematic sexual behaviors (this is referred to as your *acting-out cycle*—page 56). By identifying primary high-risk situations, feeling triggers and thinking errors, you can reduce the raw number of compulsive behaviors you engage in. Through a variety of topics and assignments, I'll explain the concepts and help you apply them to your experience. In addition to eliminating unhealthy behaviors, the material will address related risk factors that may be relevant to your sexually compulsive patterns. As a note of caution, you may experience various levels of personal distress while working on the assignments; this is typical in any personal growth process. As you move through the workbook, I recommend that you cultivate a support system to help smooth the progress of your work (the assignment on page 61 will help you do this).

Develop/Maintain Healthy Sexual Behaviors

Eliminating unhealthy behaviors creates a void. To maintain long-term health, you'll need to fill this void by practicing healthy sexual behaviors. The workbook will walk you through a process during which you'll discover and declare a Personal Definition of Sexual Health for yourself. This is what *you* think is healthy in *your* life. Discussions about sexuality so often focus on what you shouldn't do that many people have never really thought about what is healthy. The assignments in the workbook follow a sexual health model (adapted from the culmination of several) to help you understand yourself better, provide extensive information that encourages healthy sexual choices, and facilitate your journey to define appropriate sexual behaviors—all of which will enable you to live a life you love.

In order to achieve these goals, you must gain a deep understanding of what the concept of *sexual health* means in general, and even more importantly, for *you*. This can only be achieved through both learning *about* sexual health and gaining knowledge *through the experience of* sexual health.

What You Will Learn: Five Core Tasks

While it's important to identify clear goals to work towards, it's sometimes easier to talk about goals in more tangible terms. In other words, in working toward the goals described above, what will you actually learn? My expectation is that when you complete the workbook, you'll have learned the following five core tasks:

> *Identify and clarify your sexual needs.* Sexual needs are defined as desire, appetite, biological necessity, impulse, interest, and/or libido with respect to sex. How much sex do you want? What are your levels of interest? And so forth.

Identify and clarify your sexual values. Sexual values are defined as moral evaluations, judgments, and/or standards about what is appropriate, acceptable, desirable, and innate sexual behavior. You are the ultimate judge of what is healthy in your life.

Describe what you like. You'll be able to describe what you like about sexuality and sexual expression. You'll be able to identify the behaviors you like to engage in, as well as your motivations relating to or based on sexual attraction, sexual arousal, sexual gratification, or reproduction (e.g., fantasy, holding hands, kissing, masturbation, sexual intercourse).

Describe whom you are attracted to. You'll be able to identify whom you like in all realms of intimacy. What are the physical, emotional, intellectual, interpersonal, economic, spiritual, or other attributes that attract you to a sexual partner?

Let others know. This involves developing skills for letting others know your responses to the previous four tasks. Communication can occur via assertive communication, or learning other healthy and effective ways to express what you want in your life.

Everything in the book revolves around helping you learn these five core tasks. The following section describes how the structure of the book helps you accomplish this.

Structure of the Book

Returning to the image of the marathon race, the goal is to complete the race. The actual path to the goal, however, may be a route through places you've never seen. This book is structured to ensure you don't get lost on your way to the goals noted above. This structure is your map through the difficult terrain that follows.

A glance at the *Table of Contents* will reveal two clear but interconnected parts. *Part One: Understanding the Concepts* introduces ideas, theoretical models, and terms that are necessary to understand as you move through *Part Two: Applying the Concepts to Your Life*. Likewise, *Part Two* helps you understand the concepts in *Part One* more deeply by applying them to the context of your own experiences. Throughout the book you'll find assignments complimenting this interconnectedness with both conceptual and experiential work. *Part Two*, as a workbook of sorts, is compiled mostly of these assignments. This "workbook" is presented in three stages: *Problem Identification*, *Primary Treatment*, and *Groundwork for Completing Treatment*. Each of these stages is briefly described below.

Stage 1 - Problem Identification

During this stage, you'll have opportunities to examine your sexual behaviors and assess your level of compulsiveness. You'll complete a number of assignments examining your sexual history and your acting-out cycle. The objective in this stage is for you discover and label many of the problematic behaviors in your life. You'll also gain initial insight into the relationships between many of these behaviors. Based on your findings, you'll identify major topics to address in your journey toward improved sexual health.

Stage 2 - Primary Treatment

Once you identify the acting-out cycle in *Stage 1*, the second stage helps you begin your work on the treatment topics most relevant to this cycle. You'll do this by completing assignments and discovering resources for the most frequently identified topics. In reviewing the topics, you may identify additional, previously unrecognized topics that contribute to your acting-out cycle. By the end of this second stage, you'll be able to identify your sexual needs and values, develop the necessary skills to build the type of intimacy and relationships you want, and assertively express what you want regarding type, frequency, and variety of sexual expression.

Stage 3 - Groundwork for Completing Treatment

Stage 3 attempts to stabilize the growth and movement toward sexual health you began in Stage 2. Here you'll continue to reach out to others, obtain support and encouragement, and increase accountability. This accountability and support will also help you honestly discover your true core. From this core you'll complete your "Continuing Care Plan" and "Personal Definition of Sexual Health." You'll also evaluate your Personal Definition of Sexual Health based on the values you find most important in your life. These values will express and protect what you believe is appropriate, acceptable, desirable, and respectful of your innate sexual energy. You are the ultimate judge of what is healthy in your life, and once you define that you can move toward agreement between your sexual values and behaviors.

And then... Repeat

Unlike a marathon, life is an ongoing journey. As humans, we need to constantly update our path, make sure we're aware of our goals, and be aware of possible barriers. In this life journey, it's important to occasionally rethink where you're heading in terms of your sexual health. As you read and work through the book—and into the future beyond that—I encourage you to occasionally review the material and repeat the relevant assignments. In fact, part of *Stage 3: Groundwork for Completing Therapy* includes assignments aimed at exactly that. Many of the questions in the workbook are evocative—designed to help you dig deeper into self-awareness. We seldom have the same response to the same question all the time, and new discoveries about ourselves loop us back through a never-ending process of realization and change. See *The Role of Inquiry* (page 30) and *The Stages-of-Change Model* (page 44) for further elaboration on this.

Keeping a journal throughout the process of reading and completing the assignments in this book is an invaluable activity. The following assignment will get you started. As you write in your journal, try to avoid making judgments; the journal is a place to record your feelings and thoughts, not beat yourself up.

ASSIGNMENT: Start a Journal

Create a journal in which you can make notes for yourself about reactions, thoughts, emotions, and things you want to remember. Your journal might be a cheap spiral notebook or a fancy leather-bound diary; it might be a secure word document (or series of documents) or a manila folder full of daily printouts. Use whatever format is most appealing to you. Remember to make sure your journal is secure (not accessible to others). Also, consider the format you choose in the context of your issues. In other words, if you have a compulsive Internet problem, it might be wise to use a notebook that will keep you away from the computer (rather than journaling in Word and finding yourself unable to stay off the Internet).

Write in your journal on a regular basis. Throughout the book there are prompts to draw your attention to topics that are particularly useful to journal about; however, you should take the initiative to write in your journal whenever you find yourself making connections or noting specific topics that speak to you. I recommend you write in your journal at least once a week. Here are a few questions to get you started:

- What thoughts have been prominent in your mind since you began reading *Living a Life I Love*?

- What feelings have been prominent?

- Reflect on the experience of generating an Immediate Short-term Prevention Plan. Was it difficult? What thoughts and feelings did it provoke?

Theory behind the Structure

The workbook is organized in a way that could be used by you alone or in conjunction with formal therapy. If you look carefully, you'll see several standard therapeutic models within the structure, topics, and assignments. Stage 1, for example, reflects the data collection often completed in early therapy. In the clinic I supervise, for example, we use an interview process where a therapist and client complete a bio-psych-social assessment. The topics and assignments in Stage 1 are based on the concepts of developing rapport (*Talking about Sex, Journal Assignments*), short-term treatment plan/what brought you to treatment (*Immediate Short-term Prevention Plan, Prompts for Coping Plans and Revisions to Prevention Plan*), and data collection (*Sex History, Sexual Behavior Timeline, Logging Sexual Behaviors, Your Acting-Out Cycle, and Behavioral Analyses*). In the therapeutic setting, once data is collected, a client will collaborate with the clinician to complete a treatment plan. The treatment plan is where the client tells the clinician what the most important issues are; in the workbook, this corresponds to the "Prioritization of Issues" section you complete at the end of Stage 1. The list of issues provided for you to prioritize mirrors the topics presented in Stage 2.

In therapy, after the completion of the treatment plan, the client starts the work corresponding to the client-defined priorities. In this case, you begin addressing these priorities in Stage 2. The organization of this stage is based on the ten components of sexual health I believe are most important in this context. If additional material on a topic is needed, I encourage you to go beyond the workbook; in many cases, specific resources for doing so are suggested. The topics and assignments in this stage reflect an integration of two important theoretical models (*Cognitive Behavior Model and Health Promotion Model*) commonly used in a formal therapeutic setting.

In the therapy process, there comes a time when both the clinician and client recognize the process is nearing an end. Stage 3 reflects this ending (or decreasing) of formal therapy through two major assignments. First, the Continuing Care Plan prompts you to clarify the major issues you'll continue to address after treatment. The assignments in this stage represent the integration of an effective therapeutic technique (*Motivational Interviewing*) and another theoretical model (*Stages-of-Change Model*). Second, the Personal Definition of Sexual Health provides you with an opportunity to demonstrate and document your progress during the treatment process, in addition to helping you define long-term sexual health for yourself. As in a formal therapy setting, your values as "the client" shape what you think is most important and, therefore, confirm what you're willing to commit to continuing into the future. In other words, *you* set the primary agenda, define what sexual behaviors are healthy for you, and develop strategies for attaining and maintaining those behaviors.

As the reader of this book, whether client or professional, I encourage you to adapt the structure as needed to meet your individual needs. Please use the workbook in a way that makes sense to you. The implicit structure is what makes sense to me, but in the end, a Personal Definition of Sexual Health requires each of us to define what is right within our own world. My hope is that you find the workbook helpful in whatever way you choose to use it. The following section presents some specific suggestions on this subject.

How to Use this Book

This is a guidebook for you to use on your journey toward sexual health. At times, the journey will be painful and challenging as you go through areas you might rather avoid. Sometimes it will be like a roller-coaster ride—an exhilarating (and possibly frightening) experience. Sometimes it will be like doing dishes—simply something that needs to be done. The journey is a process of self-discovery and reflection. It requires you to be completely honest with *your* truth versus what you think others want. After moving on from certain topics, you'll return to discover a deeper level of truth within it as a result of your additional learning. In some cases, a later topic might lead you to reexamine an earlier assumption or belief. This process of change is a dynamic process; being open to the fluidity of the process is difficult, but necessary and extremely empowering.

The tone of this workbook is conversational, as if you and I were sitting together discussing the topics contained within it. Each section presents clear-cut questions and assignments designed to help increase your sexual health. As you read and work through the various sections, remember that there's no right or wrong response, simply *your* response. You may find that some assignments don't apply to you, so please adapt the process to your particular needs. I encourage you to review each assignment, asking yourself, "How does this particular topic apply to me?" If the topic fits, you'll need to follow up as necessary. In some sections, there are experiential assignments for you to complete; these are designed to bridge the knowledge of a concept with an opportunity to experience it. This will enable you to experience sexual health versus simply reading about it.

Your role in all of this is to discover how your problematic behaviors present themselves, and how you'll change them into healthy ones.

How *NOT* to Use this Book

If you chose to, you could rush through this workbook in a few hours (or even less) by simply writing down quick responses to the questions. That approach, however, isn't likely to be very productive. The workbook is designed for reflection. Pay attention to the concepts of discernment and integrity. Be honest and thorough. Don't edit your responses—simply write. If issues arise as you answer the questions, know that you'll have plenty of time and help in addressing them. Space is available throughout the workbook, although in some cases you'll need to use your journal or additional paper. It's hard to say how long you should review each topic. On the one hand, I've moved through a topic each week in focused groups. On the other hand, individuals often take one or two months to complete the sex history and time-line. A significant amount of time may be necessary if you continue to remember important items as you go. The amount of time you'll need to work through this process, then, will vary depending on who you are. I've seen people complete the entire process in as few as 9 months, and others in longer than 24 months. In a few cases, I've worked with clients who came back for periodic "refreshers" or "check-up sessions" when they encountered bumpy parts of the journey. One measure you can use to determine whether or not you're "done" with a specific section is to gauge your ability to talk about the content with your support network (page 61). If your thoughts and feelings about a topic overwhelm you when you try to talk about them, you're probably not ready to move on. If you can talk about it as though you're talking about the weather, you can probably start the next section. When your work is done, you should be able to look yourself in the mirror and say, with integrity, "This is re-solved."

Part One: Understanding the Concepts

This part of the book is dedicated to familiarizing you with the concepts and definitions necessary to move toward the longer-term goals of stopping problematic sexual behaviors and developing and learning to maintain healthy ones. As you move through *Part One*, you'll begin to see connections between the material and your own thoughts and experiences. Your journal will grow as you reflect on the thoughts, memories, experiences and feelings that pop up. Assignments are provided periodically to prompt you to stop and reflect, but you should record anything noteworthy in your journal, whether or not there's an assignment. By the time you reach *Part Two*, your journal will contain a wealth of material for you to look over as you identify, explore, and address the way these concepts apply to your movement toward living a life you love.

Problematic Behavior

This section jumpstarts your understanding of what "problematic" means in the context of sexual behaviors and, in particular, your own life. Before we dive into the meat of this definition, the following assignment will start you along a journey of identifying and reflecting on your behaviors.

ASSIGNMENT: Weekly Journal Questions

Stopping the cycle that fuels problematic behavior requires that you identify, on a regular basis, any sexual thoughts, feelings or behaviors you experience. In your journal, write your answers to the following questions. Pay attention to the last 7 days only. Revisit these questions on a weekly basis.

NOTE: When you first encounter these questions, you may not be sure exactly how to interpret them. Simply answer the questions as best you can without worrying about the exact meaning of terms. As you move through the book, your understanding of these questions and how they apply to your life will become increasingly clear.

• Describe any sexualizations and/or sexual fantasies.

• Describe any masturbation behaviors. Include details such as where, with whom, how much, the situation, thoughts, and fantasies.

- Describe any Internet, other technology, and/or phone use for sexual stimulation and/or behaviors.

- Describe any sexual intercourse (e.g., oral/anal/vaginal sex).

- Describe any use of sexually explicit material.

- Describe any other types of sexual behavior.

What makes behavior problematic?

What does the word *problematic* even mean? When a particular behavior or set of behaviors interferes with other aspects of your life, psychologists, psychiatrists, and counselors call it *problematic*, meaning these behaviors are causing problems and jeopardizing important areas of your life. It's not unusual for people to be unaware of the consequences their actions have on their own and other people's lives. When isolated consequences occur, they're probably not an indication of a problem. However, if consequences continue or increase, it may be a signal that you need to pay more attention to what's happening. As these behaviors expand and you become aware of them, you may try to avoid or minimize consequences by attempting to control the problematic behavior. Unfortunately, during this time it also becomes more difficult to see what's happening and to control our behaviors.

Indicators of Problematic Behavior

The following criteria are indicators of problematic behavior: compulsivity, continuation despite adverse consequences, and obsession. Here are explanations of each:

Compulsivity

Compulsivity is the loss of the ability to choose whether or not to stop a behavior. In our daily lives, we establish habit-forming routines. We often get up at the same time every day, brush our teeth in the same way, keep a work area arranged in a particular order, put the same arm into a shirt first when getting dressed, and shop at the same grocery store week after week. We repeat many behaviors, often to the point they become habits. Habits serve a useful function—they free us from having to actually think about what we're doing all the time. Imagine how difficult it would be if every time you began to put on your shirt or brush your teeth, you had to think about how to do these tasks! Another term to describe this is *automaticity*. In contrast to this, compulsive behavior is altogether different from routine habits. It's out-of-control behavior marked by deeply entangled rituals and obsessions, along with overwhelming feelings of frustration, self-blame powerlessness, and hopelessness.

Continuation Despite Adverse Consequences

All behaviors have consequences. It's common for people to continue compulsive behavior despite adverse consequences, such as loss of health, job, relationships, marriage, or freedom. Most of the time, we're able to look at our behavior and make the appropriate changes to reduce negative consequences. Unfortunately, when *compulsive* behavior is involved, this isn't the case. Attempts to control the behavior—and its potentially dire consequences—don't work. We want to stop, but feel as though we can't. Other people may see the direct and indirect negative consequences of our behavior even though we may not see them ourselves.

Obsession

Obsession is when we're so preoccupied with something (in this case, sex) we focus on it exclusively and at the expense of other parts of our lives—without care for the consequences. You know you're obsessed with something when you just can't stop thinking about it; it occupies much of your mental energy most of the time.

What is *Sexual Compulsivity*?

When it comes to the field of problematic sexual behavior, coming up with a universal term is a challenge. The nature in which the problem appears is diverse, resulting in a range of accepted terms. Previous and current terms used to describe problematic sexual behavior include: *sexual compulsivity, sexual compulsion, sexual addiction, sexual impulsivity, sexual obsession, sexual anorexia, out-of-control sexual behavior, sexaholism* and *love addiction*. Recent research focuses on the term *hyper-sexuality*, but this term misses the struggle of those who avoid sex. Generally, I use the term *sexual compulsivity* to describe out-of-control sexual behaviors. This workbook focuses on the subject of general sexual compulsivity.

Within the larger category of general sexual compulsivity, there exist specific ways that compulsivity shows up. In order to understand this, imagine looking at a playing die. Although there is only *one* die, it has six different sides and therefore appears to be different depending on which side is facing up. In the same way, sexually compulsive behavior can show up in many different ways. In addition to behaviors such as picking up sexual partners at bars or strip clubs, having multiple affairs, or spending money on pornography, sexual compulsivity may show up as sexual avoidance and/or Internet-based sexual compulsivity. Initially, it may seem like these are completely different, but once you examine the patterns underlying the behaviors, it's easy to see that they overlap significantly.

Sexual Avoidance

One side of sexual compulsivity is *sexual avoidance*. This is also known as *sexual anorexia* and describes the state of depriving oneself of sex. Thoughts and feelings of shame, fear, and hopelessness can lead us to avoid sexual contact. One of the more difficult aspects of sexual avoidance is recognizing the problem. "How can I have a sex problem if I don't have sex?" We know when we're not having sex, but we may not recognize that *not* having sex can mean we're out of control, just as *having* sex can mean we're out of control. Sexual avoidance is a less recognized and, as a result, less treated condition. Understanding the motivating factors underlying the lack sex is what's important. Often the underlying cause of sexual avoidance is similar to the cause of other types of sexual compulsivity. It's important for you to assess the presence of sexual avoidance as part of your sexually compulsive behavior. Returning to the metaphor of the die: a period of avoidance can turn into a flood of active sexually compulsive behaviors, which eventually turns into a period of avoidance again. Just as a person with anorexia might sometimes engage in binging behaviors—both of which are sides on the compulsive eating disorder die—so, too, a person who compulsively avoids sex may engage in other unhealthy sexual behaviors when the die turns. The underlying issue remains the same although it manifests in different behaviors at any given moment. Because of the cumbersome nature of writing "sexual compulsivity/sexual avoidance" throughout the workbook, I use the term "sexual compulsivity" to encompass both.

Cybersex

The term *cybersex* has become a catchall to describe a variety of computer- or technology-based sex-related behaviors, including accessing pornography (audio, video, text, online) and engaging in sexual chat with others. As with other sexual behaviors, cybersex is not, by definition, an unhealthy or compulsive behavior. It's only when cybersex behavior interferes with other important aspects of life that it becomes problematic. While this book can be used to address Internet sexual compulsivity, a similar workbook is available specifically addressing the unique aspects of problematic Internet sexual behavior. *Cybersex Unplugged*, co-authored with Dr. Delmonico and Ms. Griffin, presents specific discussions and reflection questions that address the nuances of this specific type of sexual compulsivity. Please visit www.livingalifeilovebooks.com for more information.

What behavior is problematic in *your* life, and how do you know?

There exists a range of intensity with regards to problematic behaviors. What's problematic behavior for one person may be perfectly fine for another. The intensity of your problem will depend on the presence of consequences, your values, and your relationship agreements with others (e.g., your marriage/partnership).

It will be most helpful for you to pay attention to whether or not there is a repetitive and consistent pattern to your behavior, and how the consequences of your behavior are affecting your life and relationships. A bit further into the book, you'll learn about *acting-out behaviors*—behaviors that seek an outcome or payoff that doesn't actually get you what you really want (page 56). Doing the same thing over and over again, knowing beforehand that it won't work, is *acting-out*. In my opinion, any and all types of acting-out behavior are problematic by definition.

In thinking about your sexual behavior to determine the level of your problem or the degree of out-of-control behavior in your life, it's important to realize that you may not be the first person to recognize the problem. There are two basic ways a person learns a problem exists:

Subjective Realization – This is when, on some level, you recognize your sexual behavior is a problem. Sexual compulsivity includes many sexual behaviors or thoughts that violate your personal values and boundaries. These behaviors often lead to feelings of guilt, shame, and self-recrimination. In psychology, we call this *ego-dystonic*. In other words, you're thinking: "I know I did something I didn't want to do." The vast majority of people seeking help realize they need help to address the *why, what, who, when* and *where* of their problem. This is the focus of Part Two.

Objective Notification – This is when you haven't realized there's a problem on your own, but some form of external feedback has presented itself, bringing the situation to light. This feedback can come in the form of a legal consequence (such as an arrest), a financial consequence (money spent on the Internet, or termination from a job), a health consequence (a sexually transmitted illness, or assault), or damage to a relationship (often due to the violation of boundaries). All of these are examples of consequences of acting-out behavior. For some people, the objective component of sexual compulsivity may not always be present. There may not be an external factor helping to clarify the presence of sexual compulsivity. In other cases, an external factor is useful (such as when there is a high level of denial by an individual regarding the impact of his/her behavior).

What is not *sexual compulsivity?*

There are a few behaviors that are sometimes confused with *sexual compulsivity*, but which are actually very different. It's important for us to distinguish these before moving on.

Sexual Promiscuity

Sexual compulsivity is *not* the same as sexual promiscuity. Having a lot of sex in and of itself is not a problem. It's the context of the sexual behavior that helps an individual discern whether the behavior is healthy or not. As noted above, sexual compulsivity can occur in the absence of sexual behavior, as in the case of sexual avoidance. Other examples of sexual compulsivity that occur in the absence of sex are obsessive thoughts or fear of sex.

Pedophilia and Ephebophilia

Sexual compulsivity is also *not* the same as pedophilia (defined as an attraction to pre-puberty children) or ephebophilia (defined as attraction to post-puberty children/adolescents who are not adults). While these problems may overlap with sexual compulsivity in some ways, the issues are separate therapeutic concerns. While much of the material in this workbook can be adapted to work with pedophilia and ephebophilia, these issues require specialized training, treatment, and supervision. If you find this relevant to your experience, please be sure to seek the help you need in order to ensure your process of growth is healthy and successful.

Other Compulsive Behaviors

When examining your acting-out cycle—which you must do in order to stop problematic behaviors and develop healthy ones—it's important for you to recognize related behaviors. Problematic sexual behavior is rarely a self-contained problem; rather, it's usually the culmination of a number of behavior cycles. A number of classic forms of compulsive behavior are briefly examined below. Once you review each, determine whether or not you should seek additional assessment. Should you find that any of these forms compulsive behavior are relevant to your life, keep them in mind as you work through *Part Two* and be sure to include them in discussions with your support network.

Chemical Dependency

The use of chemicals—and alcohol in particular—is considered perfectly acceptable within many segments of our society. While the use of alcohol in and of itself may not be problematic, a large percentage of people who use alcohol do so to the detriment of their well-being or the well-being of others. The same is true for other types of chemical use. The link between chemical use and sexual behavior is well documented; therefore, as we address sexual behaviors it's critical to assess any chemical dependency problems early on.

There is, of course, a distinction between chemical use, chemical abuse and chemical dependency. For example, if a person drinks alcohol and believes there's nothing wrong with doing so, this is *use*. There might be times, however, when the person engages in unhealthy, risky or unwise behaviors while drinking. If this happens rarely, these occasions represent *abuse*. If this abuse occurs regularly, the person engages in a high number of risky behaviors, and/or several of the symptoms noted below are present, this probably qualifies as *chemical dependency*.

When clinicians interview people for indicators of chemical dependency, they typically look for the following signs:

- Problems completing responsibilities at work, school or home as a result of chemical use.
- Using chemicals when it's physically hazardous (while driving, for example).
- Recurrent substance-related legal problems.
- Continued substance use despite having persistent negative consequences.
- Tolerance, as defined by either of the following: (a) a need for markedly increased amounts of the substance to achieve intoxication or the desired effect; or (b) markedly diminished effect with continued use of the same amount of the substance.
- Withdrawal, as manifested by either of the following: (a) the presence of a characteristic withdrawal syndrome for the substance; or (b) the same (or closely related) substance is taken to relieve or avoid withdrawal symptoms.
- The substance is often taken in larger amounts, or over a longer period of time, than intended.
- There is a persistent desire or unsuccessful effort to cut down or control substance use.
- A great deal of time is spent on activities necessary to obtain, use, or recover from the effects of the substance.
- Important social, occupational or recreational activities are given up or reduced because of substance use.
- The substance use is continued despite knowledge of a persistent physical or psychological problem most likely caused or exacerbated by the substance.

ASSIGNMENT: Initial Assessment—Chemical Use

It's important for you to identify your level of chemical use so treatment options can be determined, as needed. The more severe the level of use, the more intensive the treatment will need to be. A helpful tool is the classic alcohol-screening CAGE questionnaire, derived from the following four questions:[2]

- Have you ever felt you ought to cut down on your drinking? (Cut Down)
- Have people annoyed you by criticizing your drinking? (Annoyed)
- Have you ever felt badly or guilty about your drinking? (Guilty)

- Have you ever had an eye-opener (a drink first thing in the morning) to steady your nerves or get rid of a hangover? (Eye-opener)

Give yourself one point for each "yes" answer. A total score of two or more is generally considered clinically significant and warrants further assessment. A similar drug screen questionnaire can be found at: www.counsellingresource.com/quizzes/drug-abuse/index.html. If your scores indicate a potential problem, I strongly recommend you seek additional assessment and treatment, if necessary.

Eating Disorders

When the topic of eating disorders is raised, the image that often comes to mind is an adolescent female or young woman throwing up to reduce her weight because of poor body image. Although women account for the majority of eating disorder cases, the number of men with eating disorders is growing. This is particularly true in the gay community.

Typically, eating disorders fall into three conditions: *Anorexia Nervosa, Bulimia Nervosa* and *Eating Disorder-- Not Otherwise Specified.* Anorexia Nervosa is typically exhibited through the failure to eat or maintain proper nutrition. Bulimia Nervosa is typically exhibited through purging behaviors such as throwing up or laxative use. Most often, however, there isn't an either/or diagnosis, hence the combined diagnosis of Eating Disorder--Not Otherwise Specified, which is a sort of catchall diagnosis. Symptoms of an eating disorder include:

- Significant changes in weight.
- Eating more than a typical person does during a typical meal.
- Constantly thinking about food.
- Constantly thinking about body image.
- Constantly thinking, "I'm fat."
- Purging after eating.
- Over-exercising.
- Excessive use of laxatives.

ASSIGNMENT: Initial Assessment—Eating Behaviors

Although it's difficult to accurately diagnose eating disorders, there are assessment tools available. One researcher identified four questions that may be helpful.[3] If you answer, "yes" to three of the questions below, she recommends you seek further assessment.

- Do you worry you've lost control over how much you eat?
- Do you make yourself throw up when you feel uncomfortably full?
- Do you currently suffer, or have you ever suffered, from an eating disorder?
- Do you ever eat in secret?

Gambling

Another related area of concern for some individuals is their gambling behavior. It's important to identify any problematic gambling behaviors as they may be related to sexually compulsive behaviors.

ASSIGNMENT: Initial Assessment—Gambling Behaviors

In order to determine the severity of a gambling problem, Gamblers Anonymous asks its new members to answer the following "20 Questions.[4]"

1. Have you ever lost time from work due to gambling?
2. Has gambling ever made your home life unhappy?
3. Has gambling affected your reputation?
4. Have you ever felt remorse after gambling?
5. Have you ever gambled to get money to pay debts or solve financial difficulties?
6. Has gambling ever caused a decrease in your ambition or efficiency?
7. After losing, do you feel you must return as soon as possible to win back your losses?
8. After winning, do you have a strong urge to return and win more?
9. Do you often gamble until you run out of money?
10. Have you ever borrowed money to finance your gambling?
11. Have you ever sold anything to finance your gambling?
12. Are you reluctant to use "gambling money" for normal expenditures?
13. Does gambling make you careless of the welfare of yourself and your family?
14. Do you ever gamble longer than planned?
15. Have you ever gambled to escape worry or trouble?
16. Have you ever committed or considered committing an illegal act to finance gambling?
17. Has gambling ever caused you to have difficulty sleeping?
18. Do arguments, disappointments or frustrations create within you an urge to gamble?
19. Do you ever get the urge to celebrate any good fortune with a few hours of gambling?
20. Have you ever considered self-destruction as a result of your gambling?

If you answered "yes" to seven or more of these questions, you may have a gambling problem and I strongly recommend you seek further assessment. A more in-depth gambling addiction self-test is the South Oaks Gambling Screen.[5]

Spending

Spending behavior can be related to sexual behavior. Like many of the similar cross-compulsive behaviors, each of these issues may require treatment in its own right. Behaviors that suggest spending is compulsive include:

- Shopping or spending money as a result of feeling disappointed, angry or scared.
- Shopping or spending habits are causing emotional distress.

- Arguing with others about your shopping or spending habits.
- Feeling lost without credit cards.
- Buying items on credit that you aren't able to buy with cash.
- Feeling a rush of euphoria and anxiety when spending money.
- Feeling guilty, ashamed, embarrassed or confused after shopping or spending.
- Lying to others about your purchases or spending.
- Thinking excessively about money.
- Spending a lot of time juggling accounts or bills to accommodate spending.

ASSIGNMENT: Initial Assessment—Spending Behaviors

One researcher highlights the following five factors that may suggest compulsive spending behavior.[6] If two or more of these relate to your experience, I recommend you seek additional assessment.

- A tendency to shop and spend in binges or buying episodes.
- Preoccupation, compulsion, and/or impulsiveness in shopping and spending patterns.
- Excessive spending due to enjoyment of the shopping and spending activity.
- Significant life-functioning problems surrounding and/or resulting from shopping and spending behavior.
- Feelings of remorse, regret, and shame.

Compulsive Working

Due to the fact that our culture over-values hard work in many ways, it's difficult to assess compulsive work behaviors. As with many of the other compulsive behaviors, the degree of the problem often exists on a continuum of severity. In some cases, the reality is that we simply don't recognize compulsive patterns. Unfortunately, there's not much academic research in this area. The following assignment is intended to help you determine whether or not compulsive working is an issue you may need to address.

ASSIGNMENT: Initial Assessment—Work Behaviors

Here are some basic questions for your consideration:[7]

- Do you treat your home as your second office (do you regularly take work home)?
- Do you use hard work to justify behaviors that may not be healthy?
- Do you take office work with you on vacation? Do you take smart devices (laptop, cell phone, pager, and so forth) with you to keep in touch with your work life?
- Do you prefer being isolated and buried in your work to all forms of social activity? Do you brush social activity aside as trivial?

- Do you fail to enjoy the returns of hard work (i.e., professional success, money) because you're too busy working?
- Are you physically run down because of overwork and stress? Do you feel you can't be bothered?

Upon reviewing these questions, if you believe you may have a problem with compulsive working, I recommend you seek further assessment.

Abuse/Trauma

The impact of abuse/trauma on sexuality is significant. Two brief examples may be helpful at this point. A person who was abused may avoid sexual contact with any other person. I've worked with individuals who "turn off" and avoid sexuality. Then, these individuals will use chemicals as a form of courage to help them overcome the thoughts surrounding the abuse. In a different way, a person who was abused may believe the only way the ever get attention is through sexual contact. Thus, sexual compulsive behaviors may be attempts to gain a sense of affirmation.

(More detailed information about specific kinds of abuse and the impact of these on sexual behaviors is presented in *Types and Impact of Abuse/Trauma* on page 131.)

Indicators of Abuse

Below are typical symptoms experienced by individuals who have been abused and/or neglected. These symptoms aren't necessarily associated with abuse in every instance, but they *are* the early warning signs professionals look for.

Physical Indicators of Abuse

- Displays agitation or anger, uncontrollable behaviors, tantrums.
- Displays anxious behaviors (nail biting, teeth grinding, rocking, etc.).
- Often belittles self ("I'm bad" or "I'm evil," for example).
- Resists authority or desperately tries to please because of fear of repercussions.
- Exhibits excessive guilt.
- Shows fear of a particular person or place.
- Thoughts involve themes of sexual acts, torture, bondage, humiliation and/or abuse.
- Hurts others sexually or physically.
- Acts aggressively around pets.
- A child mimicking adult sexual behavior (such as intercourse, kissing with tongue, etc.).
- A child having age-inappropriate sexual knowledge.
- Increased chemical use.
- Increased sexual behavior.

Emotional Indicators of Abuse

- Develops lots of new fears.

- Shows inappropriate emotions or no emotions at all.
- Fearful that others hate, are angry with, want to hurt, will punish, or will kill them.
- Fearful that someone is "after them" or going to hurt them; wary of strangers.
- Has low self-esteem.
- Is unable to form friendships.
- Is self-destructive; intentionally inflicts harm on self.
- Appears to be "in a fog."
- Has excessive mood swings.
- Has suicidal thoughts, statements or gestures.

ASSIGNMENT: Initial Assessment—Abuse

Review the above indicators of abuse. Consider whether or not any of these indicators are present. Might there be a particular event or source behind the indicators? In order to recover from abuse, it's important for you to work with a therapist specifically trained to address these issues.

Guiding Principles

What follows are a series of guiding principles that are important to keep in mind as you start this process. These are tools to frame the conversation so you can start and stay in it. They're suggestions to support your journey toward sexual health—ways to be gentle to yourself, make sense of the struggle, and cope with challenges as they occur.

Experiencing Sexual Health

Much of this workbook is about providing basic education regarding sexual health. I'm always impressed by how much individuals want to achieve sexual health. A colleague and I have a running debate concerning the need to learn about sexual health versus the need to experience sexual health. While we might argue the nuances, we agree that both are important. A true understanding of sexual health requires not only learning *about* sexual health, but also gaining knowledge through the *experience of* sexual health.

Here are some thoughts on how to move forward in your *experience* of *sexual health:

- Give yourself permission to be a sexual being. Sexuality is a normal, vital, and positive aspect of your life.
- Ask: "Says who?" One of the earliest questions a child learns is "Why?" Plenty of stories are available in which an exhausted parent eventually says, "Because I said so—and eat your carrots!" The question of "why" applies in the realm of sexuality as well, and often the answer we've been provided with is: "Because I said so."
- Challenge most (if not all) of the messages you've heard about sexuality. This doesn't mean you have to discard your beliefs. Instead, understand both the letter and spirit of

the messages. Much of our sexuality discussion is based on "you should," or more often, "you shouldn't."

- Sexual health is a journey. Today's thoughts are for today. What you like today is for today. What you want is for today. Too often we lose sight of today and catastrophize every sexual experience.

- Reach out for support. Using your support network best facilitates this process. Your network may include friends, family or professionals such as your therapist, spiritual guide, or other providers.

- Balance is important in the journey. Too often we seek perfection, and if perfection isn't possible (it never is), we consider the experience bad, sinful, or unhealthy. Sexual health involves many variables. For example, I place good- and bad-feeling sexual experiences on a different continuum from healthy/unhealthy experiences. You can have a sexual encounter that feels good but is unhealthy. For example, I frequently work with clients who experience a great deal of sexual pleasure while under the influence of crystal methamphetamine. You can also have a bad-feeling experience that's healthy. An example is when you try to be sexual but are too tired to function sexually, then end up using the moment to connect in other intimate ways.

- Experiment. When you watch a child in a playground, s/he meanders through all of the play areas—stopping at the swings or the merry-go-round, then checking out the slide, and perhaps building something in the sandbox. When the child likes something, s/he stays in that area. If a bully or some equally unpleasant thing happens along, the child moves on. It's important for you to experiment within the realm of sexuality in the same way. Check out what you like or don't like. Enjoy the positive experiences and let go of the unpleasant ones.

ASSIGNMENT: Experiencing Sexual Health

- What is one belief about sexuality that would be helpful to challenge?

- Identify one person who could be a support for you.

- Identify a time when you had an experience of sexual health.

Life's Pivot Points

Throughout life, there are moments when what was ceases to be any longer. These incidents occur all the time and lead to a new sense of self. I refer to these moments as *pivot points*. When a pivot point occurs, the trajectory of your life pivots, and you change direction. You experience something that expands your identity. In some cases, a pivot point is big and affects a lot of people; in other cases, the pivot point is seemingly minor and unique to you. Sometimes the change seems positive; other times the change seems negative. Here are some examples:

- Many individuals in the United States see 9/11 as a pivot point. It changed the trajectory of the country and people argue about whether or not the country's response was the right one.

- Any moment in your personal experience when you decide to start or end a relationship is a pivot point. While the relationship process may take a while, there is often a moment when you know something has changed.

- Ever been so angry with someone that you hold a huge grudge, finally gather the courage to confront the person, and then find the individual doesn't even remember the incident? This is an example of a pivot point in *your* life that was of little consequence to the other person.

- Ever have someone apologize to you for something you don't remember? That incident was a pivot point for *them*.

- Sometimes pivot points are about self-awareness. For example, recognizing how you engage in disrespectful behaviors toward yourself or others. Becoming aware that you're attracted to someone of the same sex is another example.

- Some pivot points are spiritual. In the 12-step AA tradition, Step 1 reflects the moment when an addict surrenders to the powerlessness of the addiction/compulsivity—a pivot point. Being reborn within a religious tradition is another example.

The key to self-growth is increasing your awareness of not only the large, but also the small, pivot points in your life. Too often, we simply focus on "major" pivot points. Many pivots occur on a daily basis, however; consider these the small, daily self-corrections in your life (much like the continual corrections you make when driving a car). By sitting back and reviewing the pivot points, you create an opportunity to examine the underlying issues, leading to awareness and transformation. Your response to pivot points demonstrates what is key in your life.

The Role of Inquiry: Why does a person stop at a stop sign?

One philosophical branch of study is epistemology, which essentially asks, "How do we know what we know?" This has a direct application to the field of sexual compulsivity. Specifically, "How do we know what we know about sexuality?" For me, this raises an implicit question: "How do we know whether 'it' is healthy or unhealthy?" My emphasis is to integrate a healthy dose of skepticism into the discussion. The key is challenging the assumptions an individual has regarding any belief, value, opinion, thought, or conclusion. Throughout my work with clients, I ask: "Says who?" "What's underneath/before that?" "What else could it be?" and "What about…?" The goal of these questions is to challenge the absolutism that exists in the current culture regarding sexuality. In my opinion, nowhere else do we still have such a dichotomy of "right" and "wrong" putting external pressure on individuals to conform.

One of my favorite exercises involves asking: "Why does a person stop at a stop sign?" After a moment of confusion (often caused by the thought, "What is the purpose of this stupid question?"), the client usually responds with a nice answer, sometimes punctuated with a "that's so obvious" attitude (and for drama, a nice roll of the eyes). I enjoy following up with: "Why else might a person stop at a stop sign?" The exercise continues until the client exhausts all of his/her responses (there are usually about two or three responses), at which point I ask the person to think of funny, silly, stupid, or absurd reasons. In one group session, the group eventually identified 67 reasons (the record so far) that a person might stop at a stop sign, demonstrating my points that: 1) Until we think outside the box, our options are limited; 2) There's more than one reason a person stops at a stop sign; and 3) Ultimately, it doesn't matter *why* the person stops, it matters *that they actually do stop.*

So often in the realm of sexuality, society tells us we should already know the answer to the question of what is right or wrong. We've been taught, told, indoctrinated with, forced to accept, or otherwise encouraged to believe the "right" answer to such a great extent that we haven't thought about our individual response to the question, "What is sexually healthy for me?" The movement toward sexual health is a process of discovery and thinking outside the box. Your purpose in this process is to ask: "Why do I think this? What else might be an answer, response, thought, issue, or concern associated with the topic?" This process of inquiry is about unfolding, uncovering, and discovering. In the end, you are a sexual being who chooses (for yourself) how to be sexually healthy.

The role of inquiry also supports ongoing review of the process, as discussed in the "And then… Repeat" section above. This review occurs during the process of working through the workbook as you examine your previous responses. Ongoing review might also include revisiting the material annually once you've completed the workbook. This process of inquiry reflects the fact that life is an ongoing task, and the self is always evolving.

We are the source of our own pain and joy, simultaneously.

In a given situation, the individual's point of view or frame of reference is either a source of pain or joy. This is one of the foundational beliefs/approaches in my work. An individual often experiences pain as a result of attachments, expectations, desires or thoughts (such as, "I think I need 'this'" or "this needs to be a certain way"). Different traditions and theories have different words for essentially the same concept. I use the word "thoughts" to integrate many of these approaches. Thoughts are often unconscious, hidden, or habitual patterns of thinking. They are always occurring, and individuals/societies know how to manipulate them. The pattern goes something like this: On some level, you have a thought that having a car, house, partner, relationship, job or something will lead to feelings of happiness. When this need or desire remains unmet, you experience feelings of pain (sadness, loneliness, incompleteness, etc.). It's easy to see how these perceptions are the source of your pain. When the need *is* met, you might feel a type of happiness, but it's often temporary (followed by a return to pain).

Recognizing these thoughts for what they are (that is, just thoughts) allows you to reshape your view of the world and respond in different ways. You can change your point of view, and in doing so, you can change your response to the thought. Avoiding the pain or otherwise suppressing the feeling will only lead to more pain. As part of your growth, you'll have to find ways to address your pain. Sometimes the pain doesn't really exist (see "Existential Fear" on page 40). Sometimes you simply need to learn how to cope with painful feelings and thoughts. What works for one person doesn't necessarily work for others. Taking a big picture view, recovery is an individual approach and reflects your personal journey toward finding meaning in your life. Finding the crucial elements underlying these experiences is the key to healing. When you live a life that connects you to these values, you experience the transformation of pain into joy.

The Reverse-Golden-Rule

Treat others, as you would like to be treated. (Luke 6:31)

A guideline I want to introduce as you move forward in your journey of sexual health is the *reverse-golden-rule*. We've all heard of "The Golden Rule" (see quote above). It's pretty straight forward, and most people get it. But have you ever heard of the reverse-golden-rule? Here it is: *Treat yourself as you would treat others.*

Many times in my work, I watch clients treat themselves poorly. They emotionally berate themselves, sometimes even expressing the self-hate and shame out loud. Statements such as, "I'm so stupid," "I'm a fuck-up," and "I deserve shit" are not uncommon. When I hear these, I simply ask: "Would you treat others the way you treat yourself?" Almost always, the response is "no." Hence, the reverse-golden-rule. Treat yourself the same way you would treat others. For individuals early in the sexual health journey, this is often the only way to learn self-care, self-respect, and self-love. Treating yourself with care will allow you to explore what it means to be a sexually healthy person without shame and guilt. Some individuals simply don't know how to do self-care. Treating yourself as you would treat others may be a way to internalize self-respect, self-care, and self-love. Simple questions to ask include, "What would you say to another person?" "How would you treat others?" "Would you say to others what you're saying to yourself?" Ultimately, your recovery and healing will require compassion for the self. If you don't know how to be compassionate to yourself, the reverse-golden-rule is a place to start.

Discernment

A hurricane wind ripped through the mountains and shattered the rocks before God, but God wasn't to be found in the wind; after the wind an earthquake, but God wasn't in the earthquake; and after the earthquake fire, but God wasn't in the fire; and after the fire a gentle and quiet whisper. When Elijah heard the quiet voice, he muffled his face with his great cloak, went to the mouth of the cave, and stood there. (1 Kings 19:11-13)

Discernment is the exercise of discovering and revealing the quiet whisper of truth within you. Discernment is a process. Although your first response to a question might seem like the "correct" one, discovering your personal truth occasionally requires additional time. We often edit or limit our thoughts, beliefs and desires. Discovering your deeper self requires you to challenge the thoughts, beliefs and values you assume to be true. Discernment is the journey of self-discovery. The role of inquiry is related to discernment in that discernment is the application of inquiry. Self-discovery is about integrating results from that inquiry, including many trials and errors, experiments, successes and failures.

Discernment is also about responsibility. It requires you to step up and say, "This is important. This is what I believe." Too often, people avoid this responsibility for any number of reasons, including fear of judgment or disapproval. Paradoxically, when you step up and take responsibility for your journey, freedom is possible, resulting in a feeling of empowerment to say, "Yes, this is me!"

The process of discerning your values, and the behaviors consistent with those values, is the process of discovering your truth. It's ultimately up to you to determine what behaviors are sexually healthy. In other words, what behaviors help you grow as an individual, foster respect in your life and the life of your partner, and contribute positively to the health of your community? It's a process to discover the behaviors that reflect and protect the values you use to shape your life. All the work you do in this book is culminated with the development of your Personal Definition of Sexual Health, which helps you discern your truth regarding sexuality. My experience suggests that you'll be much more successful in your work toward sexual health if that work reflects your truth. What do you really want in your life?

Integrity and Authenticity

Sexual health is neither good nor bad; it's simply authentic. Focus on *your* authenticity, not what you believe others think should be authentic to you. I often find clients worrying so much about what family, friends, partners, and others think is important, they lose their own voice on the subject. *Authenticity* is more than simply doing what you want when it comes to sexuality; it's engaging in behaviors that express the core of who you are. The key is your core—your heart of hearts. From that core, sexual health is authentic.

Many people want their clinician to be in charge. I can't tell you how many times I've heard, "Tell me what to do," "Is this OK?" or "What should be my bottom-line behavior?" As a clinician, I provide feedback and suggestions, but impose very few behavioral restrictions. When I do, the restrictions are usually around legal, ethical or health consequences. I might say, "Engaging in anonymous sex with individuals isn't consistent with what you say you want," or "Using the work computer to look at porn may get you fired." To fall into the trap of telling you right from wrong sets up the therapist as the external control. In motivational psychology, a long-term consequence of external control is a decrease in compliance with external limits. Slowly, resentment builds as the individual fights with those external limits. Eventually, a total break may occur when the other person's resistance causes a rupture in the therapeutic relationship.

The same holds true here. In other words, this workbook will not tell you what to do or suggest you follow predetermined rules or patterns. Rather, the approach here emphasizes integrity and authenticity, implying an internal source of control. Research in motivational psychology has repeatedly demonstrated that individuals will create profound changes and new possibilities when internally motivated. They will, for example, run marathons because they want to make a difference in the world. Think for a moment about someone who inspires you; this person's source of motivation is probably internal. By fostering a source of control *within you*, this book best sets you up to be successful as you work to identify behaviors, attitudes and goals that lead to wholeness, completeness and unity.

This approach helps you create *integrity* in your life. However, it also requires more work than simply following a list of rules. It requires some trial-and-error that will likely result in a reassessment of how you want to live your life. Following this approach, you can create an internal moral code of sexual health. You'll be happier, more effective and, ultimately, whole. In the end, this requires from you a transformation rather than mere compliance. In this transformation, unlimited possibilities are achievable, including living a life you love.

A person living in integrity has a number of important, identifiable characteristics:

Honesty

You say what you mean and you mean what you say. When someone asks, "How are you today?" you don't respond with a bland autoreply. You respond with integrity by saying what is true: "It's a good day," or "It's a bad day," or "I don't really know at the moment."

Completeness

Your responses are complete. You share everything as appropriate versus disclosing only certain pieces of information strategically. When something happens, you're thorough in your reporting of what occurred. You actively volunteer all information, versus playing a cat-and-mouse game by holding back things that might get you into trouble. A lie of omission is as damaging as a lie of commission.

Assertiveness

You speak your opinion and beliefs. If your friend, partner, support network, group or therapist wants you to do something you don't want to do, you are assertive in your communication. You say what you want and need. When I see a client struggling with a goal, I ask, "Are you sure this is *your* goal? Are you ready to put in the work toward reaching this goal?" For example, "Do you really want to lose five pounds, or are you simply bowing to the pressures of a culture that tells you to be skinnier? Do you *want* to do what's necessary regarding diet and exercise, or do you think you *should*?" Another example is a man who won't try to stop viewing pornography because that isn't *his* goal—it's his wife's goal *for* him. While this means the couple has to find another way to resolve their issues, the man's integrity in this regard is a critical ingredient in their recipe for a lasting solution.

Balance

Integrity reflects balance, and it's something we know intuitively. You'll know when you are or are not in balance. If something feels right, you know it. If something feels out of whack, you generally know it. When you ride a bicycle, for example, you know when you're in balance (or not). The same is true for the realm of integrity. You know intuitively when you're in balance.

Endurance

Living with integrity is tough; it requires the energy to keep going when you feel like giving up. When you're in conflict, the desire to run away is normal; integrity requires you to find the endurance to stay in the conversation even when you're anxious or fearful.

The Power of Thought

We are what we think. All that we are arises with our thoughts. With our thoughts, we make the world. (Buddha)

A lot of the emphasis in this treatment approach focuses on helping you understand your thinking patterns and, in particular, your thinking errors. In order to do so, I first need to discuss an important concept: *the power of thought.*[8] The basic premise of this concept is that all aspects of our existence are based on thought. Thought shapes our feelings, our interactions with others, and how we perceive and examine life events. This section discusses why I believe thought is so powerful.

The Experience of Each Moment

Your thoughts shape both your worldview and your experience of each moment. Within each moment, your awareness and knowledge are based on perceptions, and through the almost instantaneous analysis of these perceptions, you arrive at a conclusion (i.e., a thought) that guides your feelings, choices and behaviors. This is a bit different from conventional wisdom, which often dictates that feelings come first.

Consider the following situation and alternate scenarios:

You've parked your car on the street. As you return from the store, you find your car is gone. The awareness is that your car is missing. The feelings you experience are the result of conclusions based on various thoughts. Depending on the thought, your feelings might be different. Consider the difference between the following:

Scenario #1: You've read in the newspaper about car thefts in the neighborhood. The conclusion you arrive at is: "My car has been stolen." You probably experience feelings of anger toward the thief, of having been violated, or both.

Scenario #2: You notice a sign reading: "No Parking 4-6 p.m." You realize it's now after 4pm and your car was parked illegally. You think: "My car has been towed." You might feel anger at yourself, embarrassment, frustration, or shame because you think you should have known better. Notice that your feelings depend on your thoughts.

Scenario #3: You're talking on your cell phone when you get to where you think you parked your car. You think, "My car is gone." As with Scenario #1, you experience anger, violation, and/or frustration. Then you notice your car is parked six spaces up (you were distracted and went to the wrong spot). Now you think, "Oh, there it is!" The corresponding feelings might be embarrassment, relief, and/or humor as you realize how you overreacted. Notice how a change of thought changes the feelings you experience.

These three scenarios help demonstrate how thoughts shape your feelings and subsequent behaviors. Much of our thought is actually automatic and can occur in the blink of an eye.[9] Sometimes, you simply don't realize how many different thoughts you have in a particular moment. Not true, you say? Let's revisit the idea of driving a car. Think about how many complicated tasks, thoughts and attention to stimuli occur while you drive. Yet, you never *think* about driving. You simply drive. In treating sexual compulsivity, the treatment process is about helping individuals realize how ritualized the acting-out cycle is.

The Power of Story

When you think about who you are, you essentially come up with a story. When you string enough of these stories together, you develop a sense of self. These stories are simply thoughts. Some of our stories have a profound role in shaping our identity, while others have minimal impact. Sometimes there's a story you want to deny, avoid or otherwise minimize. Sometimes you simply forget your stories. In some cases, you've never thought about a particular storyline, even though you were a major actor in it. When prompted, however, uncovering the story can lead to profound change. All of our beliefs about sexuality are based on these stories. Later, I'll talk about the importance of story in the development of spirituality. For now, know that story helps us understand what is most important in our life. Story is what explains why we do what we do.

I encourage you to think of all the stories you have about yourself and others. One place to look for your stories is in the language of your thoughts and statements. What tends to follow when you use the word, "because"? The stories that shape your life often begin with phrases such as: "I do that because…," "I'm that way because…," and "This is important because…" In some cases, you might put a lot of emphasis on other people's assumption of what your story should be. You might experience significant pressure to conform to another person's story. You might tend to go along with their version of your story versus creating your own.

As you'll find, some of the stories may be helpful, others may be unhelpful. Some stories may suggest topics to review with your support network or therapist. A few of the stories may be a source of profound joy or emotional pain. As you understand the stories, remember that there are no "right" or "wrong" stories. What is important is that this is *your* story.

Believe it or not, it's possible to change the story. This is a process of growth and development. Taking a new perspective on a story can lead to new insights. Gaining additional information changes the content of the story. Feedback from peers can facilitate a reframing of the story. This process of change requires you to know and understand the stories in your life. The movement toward sexual health is the process of discovering your stories of sexuality. The workbook is designed to help you rewrite and update these stories.

- Identify one "because" about why you picked the current (or last) job you had.

- Identify one "because" about the last time you had sexual contact.

Mindfulness

Two strategies to use at this point for increasing awareness of the power of your thoughts are *mindfulness* and *transference*. Both are powerful tools that give us insight into the power of thought. They are related. Mindfulness of the thoughts allows us to because mindful of the transference.

Mindfulness is an awareness of your current thoughts, feelings, body state and surroundings achieved by paying attention to your reactions, motivations and actions. Our minds are so full of ongoing chatter. To increase your ability to be mindful, I encourage you to become aware of your inner conversation. When someone walks into the room, you may say to the person next to you, "She's attractive." But your inner conversation is what you have with yourself when no one is around. Someone might walk into the room, and you say to yourself, "I want to have sex with her" or "She won't like me." Various meditation techniques can be helpful in increasing your mindfulness. The process of behavioral analysis described later is a tool for increasing mindfulness by asking you to reflect on the thoughts, feelings and behaviors involved when you act-out (page 89).

What you'll find is that mindfulness is a skill. It's not possible to be mindful 100% of the time. The key is to *try* to be mindful and, when you aren't, simply and gently try to become mindful of what you're thinking and feeling. I know this is easier said than done. Mindfulness is becoming aware of your thoughts as you move between them. When building mindfulness skills, you watch what you're thinking as you move from thought to thought. This is where the skills of discernment and the role of inquiry are important. Given that many of our thoughts are automatic, we need to slow down and ask ourselves, "What was I thinking?"

Many meditation traditions have at their core the concept of mindfulness. The purpose of the following assignment is to practice meditation to help you become aware of what you're thinking. The exercise is remarkably simple, and yet, even the most experienced meditators continue to practice. In fact, meditation is sometimes referred to as sitting; you simply sit in your experience of meditation. There is nothing else to do.

ASSIGNMENT: Mindfulness/Meditation

Start by finding a quiet, comfortable space where you won't be disturbed. Begin with a short length of time (5-7 minutes). As you gain experience, you can lengthen the time you sit. I recommend daily sitting, even for a small length of time, versus doing it once a week for a longer time. Again, make sure it's a length of time during which you won't be disturbed. Sit in a way that's supportive of your body. On a chair, sit toward the front of the chair with a straight spine; on a floor cushion, sit cross-legged with a straight spine (or use another comfortable position that allows you to keep your spine straight). I recommend you *not* lie down or lie on a bed/coach—it's too easy to fall asleep (and that isn't meditating!). Whether to keep your eyes open or closed is simply a choice. You can fold your hands inside your lap, or put them palm down or palm up on your knees. Whatever you do, do what feels comfortable. There are many different ways to meditate. The key is to meditate. As you sit, focus on your breath, breathing at a pace that seems natural to you. Simply focus on your breath.

As you meditate, continue to focus on your breath. When you recognize you're not focusing on your breath, gently come back to the breath. While the goal is to focus on your breath, you'll become aware of the thoughts that crowd much of your mind (e.g., "I can't believe my partner did that," "my boss is unfair," "my butt hurts," "I'm lonely"). You don't have to do anything with the thoughts, simply be aware of them and come back to focusing on your breath. I have two examples that might be helpful. Consider the image of a cloud in the sky. You see the cloud, and watch it come to be right over you, and slowly move on only to have another cloud take its place. Next, think of a leaf on a river. While sitting on the bank, you see the leaf come into view, pass in front of you, and to move out of your view. As you watch the cloud, the leaf, or become mindful of the thoughts in your head, come back to your breath. Simply focus on your breath. The thoughts will come and go, and you simply come back to your breath.

When you're done, discuss this experience with your support network.

Transference

Everything that irritates us about others can lead us to an understanding of ourselves. (Carl Jung)

The second strategy that's helpful in understanding our thoughts is *transference*. Transference is any reaction you have to another person, event, or circumstance. The individuals to whom you have the strongest reaction are perhaps the people who can teach you the most about yourself. Often the experience of transference occurs so quickly you neither realize it occurred nor become mindful of the content of the transference. The reality is that transference is how every individual makes sense of the world. We're constantly assessing and judging our environment based on our past experiences. It's the application of past experiences to the current situation that typifies transference. It's the way each of us knows what to do in a given situation. The problem is that no two situations are identical, so sometimes our transference might actually be getting in the way. Most of the time, we focus on negative transference, or the negative reactions we have to someone, but positive transference is also helpful to understand. In any reaction—positive or negative—you can learn what you're feeling and thinking and how it relates to your acting-out cycle. It's your reaction that tells you the most about yourself. Our goal is to be mindful of our transference.

The key is to pull back the levels of reaction to focus on the core motives/thoughts. Individuals often try to hide/avoid these thoughts. As a start, ask yourself the following questions:

- Why am I having this reaction?
- Who does this remind me of?
- What memory does this person trigger?
- Why do I like or dislike this person?

Whatever the response, you can gain insight into your internal thoughts and feelings. As highlighted, transference can occur in positive and negative ways. What you don't like about a person may be an expression of things you don't like about myself. What you do like about a person may be an expression of things you like about myself, or things you want but don't have.

Ultimately, what you like and dislike in others reflects your inner core. This is a classic psychological principle that also applies to sexuality. That to which you are drawn reflects an inner craving that you must address. That which you are rejecting also reflects an inner craving that you must address. Take the opportunity to discover what moves you in your life. Do this by being mindful of your reactions to others. Your strongest reactions reflect a deeper truth. An open, honest and fearless examination of those reactions might create profound transformation and possibility.

ASSIGNMENT: Transference

- Identify one person you like. What do you like about this person? How might this represent something that's important to you?

- Identify one moment when you experienced anger. What was at the core of the anger? How might this reveal something about you?

Taken together, mindfulness and transference are two important concepts to help you increase your awareness of your thoughts. Much of what we think occurs so automatically that we see the picture but fail to see the pieces of the puzzle. Our problematic behavior is equivalent to the picture, while the thoughts, feelings, situations, and motivations related to that behavior are the individual pieces of the puzzle. Your task through this book is to gain increased awareness by using mindfulness to become aware of your transference.

The Illusion of Fear

Another key factor in my work is helping individuals become mindful of their deepest fears. This requires us to actually examine fear. I define two types of fear—*real fear* and *existential fear*.

Real Fear

Real fear is when your existence is actually threatened in the moment. For example, "At this moment someone is pointing a gun at me and may shoot and kill me." Another example might be, "There is an out-of-control car barreling down the sidewalk toward me and I may be hit." These are examples of real fears that are actually occurring in the moment. They are few and far between.

Existential Fear

Most fears don't actually threaten your existence; they are *existential fears* versus *real fears*. Every time I say this in a workshop, participants will blurt out their fears:

- "But I might die from a heart attack!"
- "There are people who hate me in the world!"
- "A terrorist might strike!"
- "I could lose my job!"
- "She'll get mad!"

All of these things may be true, but they're not occurring in the *actual* moment or in the *actual* space you're occupying. Rather, they are thoughts about things that *might* happen. In fact, almost all of what we fear is only real in our thoughts and stories. This does not mean, however, that these fears aren't just as powerful and crippling (or more so) as *real* fears. As you've just read, thoughts and stories are powerful forces in our lives; thus, existential fear is one as well! Most of us approach life with a sense of existential fear. Examples include fear of not being liked, the need to look good or avoid looking bad, or fear of being alone. When someone knows your darkest thoughts, you may feel shame or fear they will reject you. To minimize this fear, a person will often act in unhealthy ways. Below is a paradigm that may help you recognize these behaviors.

The Paradigm of Fear

When individuals experience fear, most react in predictable ways. The theory behind the *Paradigm of Fear* suggests that people tend to fall into the primary role of *victim*, *persecutor*, or *rescuer*. When your actions are in reaction to existential fear, they exist within this paradigm. The fears usually magnify. These behaviors are generally unhealthy. Usually these behaviors trigger a never-ending cycle of more fear. Imagine a triangle, with each corner representing one of the roles listed above:

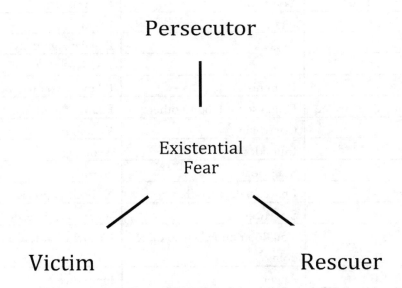

Existential Fear Roles[10]

Anytime you experience existential fear, you react in a primary role. This reaction is often unconscious and can be seen in many of your automatic responses. It's a learned behavior that has become routine. The primary role is backed up by a secondary role. You attempt to cope with the fear by using characteristics of the primary role, but then you may switch to the secondary role. In one moment you feel like a *victim,* and in the next moment you lash out, becoming a *perpetrator.* The triangle seeks balance, so when you operate from a primary (and/or secondary) role, you seek out others to balance the triangle. There's always someone or something (real or imagined) in one of the roles. Pulling this person or thing into the triangle enables you to shift roles so you can engage in all three roles of the paradigm (which makes it feel balanced).

Here's an example:

I am fearful of being alone (this is my existential fear), so I often try to fix things for people (in the role of *rescuer*—this is my *primary* role). However, others don't acknowledge how much I do for them (putting them in the role of *persecutor* and shifting me to the secondary role of *victim*). As a result, I lash out at them (shifting me into the role of *persecutor*, and the other person into the role of *victim*). The following table highlights some characteristics of each role.

Behavioral Characteristics of Existential Fear Roles

Victim	Persecutor	Rescuer
It's my fault	It's your fault	It's the persecutor's fault
I can't do anything	You fix it	I can fix it
Freeze	Fight	Flight
Passive	Aggressive	Passive-Aggressive
Depression	Anger	Anxiety
I'm hurt	I'll punish you	I'll make you feel better
Something being done to me	Doing something to others	Fixing something
Helpless	Controlling	Enabling
Shutting down	Intimidating	Avoiding
Lost child	Scapegoat	Hero
Everyone says "no"	I have to do everything	Nobody appreciates me
I'm alone	Stay away	Want to feel needed
I'll do what you say	You don't know what you're doing	I know what to do
Greed	Anger	Ignorance
Always wanting	What's wrong	Don't make waves

Transcending fear *is* possible. Below are three strategies to start with.

Remember that the existential fear isn't real. It may feel real, but it isn't. Again, very little of the fear we experience actually exists in reality. While it may hurt if someone leaves—or is angry, or doesn't like us, or we lose our job, or whatever—our actual existence is not called into question.

If you catch yourself playing the game of fear, and engaging in the three roles—stop. No matter how you try, you can't win at a game of fear. I love the line from the 1980's movie, *War Games*: "The only winning move is not to play."[11]

Start to see the fear as a challenge or opportunity to create something greater in your life. When you identify what you want more than anything else in your life, you'll do many things to move toward it. When you define what is most important in your sexual health, you'll have the outline to move toward it whenever you experience existential fear.

It's helpful to be mindful of the times you experience fear. It's essential to step outside of the fear and take responsibility for subsequent choices. I know this is easier said than done. Here's a quote I like that might help:

> *I must not fear. Fear is the mind-killer. Fear is the little death that brings total obliteration. I will face my fear. I will permit it to pass over me and through me. And when it has gone past I will turn the inner eye to see its path. Where the fear has gone there will be nothing. Only I will remain. (Dune, Herbert)*

This Litany of Fear reminds you that the fear is not real. If you can let the feeling of fear pass, you have in that moment an opportunity to make a choice that expresses you true identity. One way to do this is to identify values that express what inspires you at your core (you'll learn more on how to do this in "TEN: Spirituality, Values and Sexual Health"). When you have a bigger goal in your life, it can help you overcome your existential fears.

ASSIGNMENT: Existential Fears

<u>Identify Fears</u>

Review the diagram and table presented above. Describe 2-3 experiences in which you felt existential fear. For each experience, answer the following questions:

- What is your primary role in responding to existential fear? Which behaviors do you engage in?

- What is your secondary role? Which behaviors do you engage in?

- Who/what do you think was in the third role?

Plans for Coping

Review the primary and secondary roles you identified. Note one or two plans to start coping with situations in which you find yourself taking on these roles. Return to this list and update it as necessary.

The Stages-of-Change Model

We can never see past the choices we don't understand. (Matrix Reloaded)

The process of sexual health is a journey that leads to places you may not understand. This is scary, but it's a normal part of any meaningful change. This workbook will help you chart a path for the future, addressing things you may not necessarily understand in this moment. As you travel, it's helpful to know that this process of change has a predictable pattern. This pattern is explained in the *Stages-of-Change Model*[12] presented below. Concepts from this model are woven throughout the workbook to increase your understanding and awareness of how a person changes behavior.

What are the "Stages of Change"?

The Stages of Change Model identifies five stages between which a person moves during the process of change. They are *pre-contemplation*, *contemplation*, *preparation*, *action*, and *maintenance*.

Pre-contemplation

Pre-contemplation focuses on the lack of any change, any desire for change, and/or any perceived need for change. For many individuals, this might be the first time they've read anything about some or all of the topics covered. Phrases such as, "I didn't know it was a problem," or, "I didn't see the connection before," illustrate pre-contemplation.

Contemplation

Contemplation is when an individual recognizes or is aware of a problem, but doesn't make any changes because they are either too overwhelmed or not willing to commit to changing the behavior. Avoiding a topic and/or not wanting to talk about something are examples of this stage.

Preparation

Preparation reflects when an individual recognizes the need to make a change and also has an idea about what to do. In this stage, however, no action has been taken yet. The problem hasn't been addressed; a plan hasn't been enacted. Common statements made during this stage include: "I haven't done that yet," or "Yes, but…"

Action

Action is when an individual actually changes their behavior. This is usually when the work and struggle occur. This is also when a person can look back and see progress. Failure or giving-up can occur here as well. Understanding that the struggle—and even the failure—is simply part of the process allows an individual to re-start plans and celebrate when the plans are completed.

Maintenance

Maintenance is when new behavior becomes new habit, and it continues on its own. Sometimes continuing care plans (also called relapse prevention plans) are designed at this point to reduce the risk of relapse or failure.

Finding the Progress in Process

The process of change almost always involves struggle. Grappling with issues and overcoming obstacles demands tremendous energy, and it's difficult to continue without positive reinforcement to energize you along the way. While progress is always occurring, it's often hard to see; when progress can't be seen, it can't be learned from. The Stages of Change Model is helpful because it allows you to express where you are in the process. It allows you to reframe any action (or lack of action) within the process of growth. If you aren't willing to make a change, the model can be helpful in understanding why that's and what can be done. For example, you might ask whether you need information, uncover what the avoidance is about, figure out what else is needed, or implement plans. If you aren't willing to make a change, an underlying issue may be discovered—a barrier that must be addressed before progress can be made. As you move through the workbook, reflect on where you are in terms of your willingness to change. The topics are set up to help you clarify what you need to do to address the stage of change you are in with regard to each topic. There are no "right" or "wrong" responses, simply what you'll do next.

Processes within Processes

The Stages of Change Model is also useful because it reflects the fact that one person can experience multiple changes at once. In addition, it recognizes that any major change comes about as a result of many minor changes, each representing a process. Through this model you can identify where you are along different avenues of change. For example, you might be in the *Action* stage with regards to changing your unsafe sexual behaviors, but only just entering the *Contemplation* stage in terms of working to have your intimacy needs met. While the changes you undergo are never entirely separate from one another—each informing and affecting the others—it's helpful to track your progress in terms of the many layers of your life and self. The Stages of Change Model highlights how new discoveries occur within a natural process encompassing everything from avoidance to transformation. In addition, it allows you to see how a major change (developing and maintaining healthy sexual behaviors) can comprise many smaller changes involving specific thoughts, feelings, and actions.

Parallel Process

Picture a railroad track. When you look at one rail, it's pretty easy to guess where the second rail goes. Even if you see the railroad track disappear into the horizon, you know that if you find one of the tracks, you'll find the other track nearby. This is what I mean by the concept of parallel process. Individuals early in the discovery process often express fear and anxiety about the way things will end up. I use the concept of parallel process to help people grasp where they are going when they start the therapy process. It provides a tool to shape the direction of therapy.

For example, someone in chemical dependency recovery understands the process of recovery. A client will experience shame and guilt when they first realize they have a chemical use problem. This shame and guilt leads to isolation and increased problems. Once they start telling the stories of their chemical use, the shame and fear start to ease and the recovery process gains momentum. Connections are made to individuals with similar struggles. Eventually, recovery and a sense of hope are born, allowing a sense of being fully alive to develop. In the same way, dealing with sexual health follows a parallel process. At the beginning, feelings of shame and guilt lead to isolation. Healing occurs through sharing your story and reaching out for support. Hope is born through relationships and connections with others. Following the process of recovery in chemical dependency can give us a direction for recovery in sexual health.

As you start the healing process, certain topics may already be easy to talk about; others will become easy as you continue the process. You can take your experience from the early topics and apply them to the later topics. Such is the power of parallel process.

Gaining Insight from Current Behaviors

Anyone who doesn't take truth seriously in small matters cannot be trusted in large ones either. (Albert Einstein)

Given the stages of change, exploring current behavior assists us in changing future behavior. Even behaviors that seem irrelevant can provide insight into where you are stuck, what areas you haven't addressed sufficiently, or what struggles prevent you from maintaining movement toward your goals.

The best predictor of your future behavior is your current behavior. Individuals often claim they did something because of a past incident, but that's usually a convenient excuse to avoid responsibility. What you're doing in the current moment reflects what you'll do in the future. How you approach the small things provides insight into how you'll address the big things. In examining your behavior, you can identify your motives, desires, dreams, thinking errors, excuses, and payoffs. It's important to be open and honest about what is going on in the moment. On the one hand, if you're lying about the small things now, my guess is you'll most likely lie about the big things in the future. The things you avoid now will be the same things you avoid in the future. On the other hand, if you show courage in examining the small things now, you'll show courage in addressing the big things that will occur in the future. How you change your behavior now will tell others how you'll change your behavior in the future. As you move forward in the workbook, the way you address the assignments will give you insight into how you'll shape your recovery. Once you transcend the small barriers, you'll be able to transcend the big ones.

The Role of Relapse

Freedom is not worth having if it does not include the freedom to make mistakes. (Gandhi)

In the field of sexual compulsivity treatment, It's important to address the reality of relapse as part of the change process. It's highly probable that you'll experience some type of relapse with regard to your acting-out cycle. You'll most likely re-engage in the behaviors that brought you into treatment (those identified in the Immediate Short-Term Prevention Plan on page 5). You'll move into a realm of acting-out behaviors somewhere in your process. Why? Most likely because you're *human*! Being human means perfection isn't possible. Below are a few suggestions to help you address a sexual health relapse.

In the process of moving toward sexual health, to assume that you'll never make a mistake sets you up for a cycle of shame and guilt that's probably a big part of your cycle already. Being human isn't permission to relapse, but it does provide a starting point toward self-forgiveness. Relapse can be a learning process (guilt versus shame). By examining the relapse, you can uncover new factors associated with your acting-out cycle and set up plans to address these factors. In many cases, a relapse can help you prioritize treatment issues.

The degree and/or frequency of relapse can be a sign of progress. What often happens is that the frequency and/or intensity of acting-out decreases. Rather than hooking up with someone via a website, the behavior this time might be limited to viewing sexually explicit material. You might begin by doing this once a day, gradually decreasing to once a week or even once a month. While this behavior still needs to be addressed, it demonstrates progress.

When a small or large relapse occurs, "telling on yourself" is a reflection of the treatment progress. By using your support network, you demonstrate the skills necessary to move toward health. The amount you are able to disclose to your network is a measure of your progress. Your ability to learn from the relapse is also a measure of your progress.

The biggest thing to recognize is that it's not the relapse that's important, it's what you do with the relapse that matters. Do you take responsibility? Do you examine the response to learn why it occurred? Do you tell your therapist or someone in your support network? Do you make changes to decrease the likelihood it will happen again? A relapse can be a sign of progress, especially if you own it, examine it, tell someone about it, and make changes as a result of it.

ASSIGNMENT: Relapse Response Plan

Write out an initial plan for how you'll handle a relapse if/when it happens. Share your plan with your therapist and/or support network. Revisit and revise your Immediate Short-Term Prevention Plan as needed.

Thinking Errors

I didn't say it was your fault, I said I was blaming you. (Unknown)

All wrong-doing arises because of mind. If mind is transformed can wrong-doing remain? (Buddha)

The concept of *thinking errors* (sometimes referred to as "psychological defenses," "cognitive distortions," or even "stinkin' thinkin'") refers to a pattern of unhealthy thinking. These thinking errors are attempts to minimize pain, justify our behaviors, avoid responsibility, or otherwise help us avoid reality. As you increase your awareness of thinking errors, the variety and number of thinking errors you discover will surprise you. You'll be amazed at the presence of these thoughts and how you use them to justify almost all behavior. A great place to start recognizing a thinking error is to look at any thought that comes after the word "because." I hooked up with someone "because . . ." or "I was downloading pictures because. . .

While not universal, when we answer "because" to explain our behavior we are often using a thinking error.

In the movie Shrek, the ogre (Shrek) describes ogres as having layers, like onions. "Onions have layers. Ogres have layers. Onions have layers. You get it? We both have layers!" Like ogres, our thoughts often have deeper layers. As you delve further into recognizing your thinking patterns, it's possible to gain insight into deeper levels of meaning. Sometimes even a great reason hides a thinking error, so it's important to think outside the box and look at the layers of thought. For example, let's return to the stop sign. In asking the question, "What's one reason a person stops at a stop sign?" a number of reasons are possible. A few reasons might be, "I don't want to get a ticket," "I don't want to get hurt," or "It's what I was taught." While true, each reflects a possible deeper level of concern that needs to be uncovered. "I don't want to get in trouble" might reflect layers of guilt/shame. A possible deeper level of concern using safety as an explanation might be layers of anxiety. Some people don't stop at stop signs; rather, they sort of "roll through them." This might reflect a pattern of thinking such as, "the rules don't apply to me." As a fun exercise, the next time you're driving and come to a stop sign, ask yourself the reason you're stopping (and please, *do* stop!).

So our thoughts shape our reality and we act based on thoughts. I often hear comments such as, "I don't know what I was thinking," or, "I knew I shouldn't be doing it, so why couldn't I stop myself?" My response to these is to re-emphasize the insidious nature of the acting-out cycle; people will act on thoughts they may not fully realize are present. The speed of our thoughts is simply too fast for us to fully understand before we act on them. Some of these thoughts might be suppressed or repressed. Others may be so automatic we simply don't recognize their power. An important purpose of therapy is to help you reveal the unhealthy thinking patterns in your life.

A summary of thinking errors follows, but I must state that in no way is this list exhaustive. The mind is an amazingly creative source of never-ending thinking errors, and these examples represent just the most frequent types. One of my goals is to help you become aware of the various thinking patterns in your life.

List of Frequent Thinking Errors

Justification: Making excuses for our behaviors.

> "I deserved it."
> "It happened to me and no one cared, so why should I care?"
> "I was angry, so my behavior is understandable."
> "It's what I like, so the other person should like it too."
> "My partner isn't available, so it's alright to have sex with a different person."

"I've been working all day at the computer, so I deserve a five-minute surfing break."

Displacement/Blame: Telling ourselves someone or something else is responsible for our actions.

"He started it."

"The web page kept popping up on its own; I didn't know how to stop it."

"I was only downloading adult porn; I didn't want the child porn."

"She had a reputation, so she deserved it."

"He didn't tell me to stop."

"She started sexually chatting with me, so it was as much her fault as mine."

Minimization: Playing down the nature of the indiscretion or harm done.

"I only did it this one time."

"It was only a fantasy, I didn't actually touch her."

"The Internet is just a fantasy world, everyone does this."

"Things just got out of hand."

"It wasn't sex."

"I'll only do it one last time."

"I didn't actually connect with someone."

"It was just chatting."

"They're just pictures; no one was hurt."

Denial: Refusing to accept external reality because it's too threatening.

"I didn't know it was against the law."

"I won't get caught."

"I didn't think I would get_____." (Fill in the blank: arrested, sick, caught, hurt, etc.)

"Nobody will know I'm visiting this website."

"I didn't think my partner would care."

Catastrophizing/Exaggeration: Exaggerating the reasons for/consequences of our actions. Use of the phrases "the worst," "the best," etc.

"If I hadn't done it, something awful would have happened."

"I did what I did because I had the worst family."

"It was worth it because it was the best sexual encounter ever."

"He was the meanest guy."

Using dramatic gestures and vocalizations such as verbal sighs and/or waving hands.

Over-generalization. Use of terms such as "everybody," "never," "always," and/or "no one."

"Everybody is online doing sexual stuff."

"I'm never wrong."

"You're always wrong."

"My partner never wants to have sex."

"I know other people do it, so I figured it would be okay."

"I always get blamed."

Escape/Fantasy: Tending to retreat into fantasy in order to resolve inner and outer conflicts.

"I hoped having sex would make me feel better."

Reaction Formation: Reacting negatively to someone else because they represent something you don't like within yourself.

"I hate gays," from someone who is attracted to the same sex.

"All sex is bad," from someone who is very sexual.

Avoidance: Avoiding parts of your life by focusing on something else.

"I'll only have casual sex, so I won't get emotionally hurt."

"Having anonymous sex helps me avoid the need to come out."

The following assignment helps you to identify, reflect on, and plan to cope with the errors present in your thought processes.

ASSIGNMENT: Thinking Errors

Identify Errors

- If you have any reaction to the examples, identify the thoughts associated with the reaction.

- Start to examine patterns of thinking that appear to be present in your life. What themes appear to be present at this point?

- Review the list of thinking errors with your support network. Which errors do the people in your network identify as consistently present in your thinking?

Plans for Coping

List the top three thinking errors you identified. Note one or two plans to start coping with each of these thinking errors. Return to the list and update it as necessary. Be sure to update your Immediate Short-term Prevention Plan.

Primary Thinking Error

One often meets his destiny on the road he took to avoid it. (Jean de La Fountaine)

The term, "Achilles' Heel," has come to mean a person's principal weakness. I believe we each have a unique pattern of thinking that elicits from us the strongest reaction of fear. I call this the *primary thinking error*. I use this concept for three reasons. First, the primary thinking error is the pattern of thinking that most affects us as an individual. When experienced, it creates the most existential fear in our life. Second, the primary thinking error is the one that occurs most often. Since it's our biggest fear, we see it most often. We are constantly scanning our environment in an attempt to avoid the fear. Even though a person might engage many thinking errors over time, one constant theme is often present. It's the foundation of how the individual makes sense of the world. It's also the thought a person will use first to interpret any situation (remember *transference*?). The less information a person has about a given situation in real time, the more likely it's that he or she will fill in missing information based on the primary thinking error. Because this pattern of thinking is so ingrained in everyday life, it's very difficult to recognize. Third, the primary thinking error is often the earliest pattern of thinking present in our youngest memories.

The primary thinking error shapes our behaviors at a fundamental level. I also think the primary thinking error is a component of being human. When you look at what it means to be human, a variety of traditions (religious, mythology, psychological) recognize that we feel broken ("something isn't right in my world") and are constantly trying to fix whatever feels broken.

It's often the primary thinking error that drives your behavior. One of the applications of understanding the power of the primary thinking error is the recognition of hidden or unspoken motivations that subconsciously shape your reactions to others. Frequently, a person is saying two (or more) things at the same time. It's not surprising that, in the end, you get exactly what you mean and not what you say. Below are three examples.

First, here's a metaphor to express the power of the primary thinking error: I have two dogs. I put a lot of energy into training my dogs to walk beside me. One day, I let them go off-leash and they stayed right beside me due to their training. Even when I tried to get them to run free, they followed their training and stayed beside me. They didn't even know they were free and simply followed the training. Just as the training limited my dogs, our thoughts limit us. In fact, we're free to begin with, but often don't know we're free, so continue to act according to how our thoughts have trained us. We become the trainer that limits our behavior. The key is to recognize that you're free to start with, then discover how you limit your own freedom.

A second example: If your primary thinking error is, "I don't fit in," you might look for ways to use this thought to justify your behaviors. You might go online for a sexual chat because you avoid the risk of being rejected. You might agree to engage in casual sexual behavior because you don't want to experience the rejection that occurs after the break-up of a longer relationship. If you *do* feel rejected, you look at the rejection as further proof of how you don't fit in. As a result, you constantly worry about not fitting in, always searching for the perfect situation in which you don't have to worry about the possibility of not fitting in. It gets exhausting!

A final example: Perhaps you often say, "I want to be connected to other people." A subconscious thought you might have is, "I don't want to be hurt." As a result, the hidden thought shapes how you interact with others. You use this hidden thought in your perceptions of others' interactions. In a desire to be connected with others, you might hide information about yourself so they don't reject you. You might also assume that others have ulterior motives, and then try to protect yourself from being rejected. After a while, the fear of being hurt grows in intensity until you reach a point at which you perceive hurt in just about every encounter. In some cases, you sabotage the relationship, perpetuating the cycle of being hurt. This is an example of a *self-fulfilling prophecy*. The self-fulfilling prophecy expresses the paradox between what you say (I want to be close to people) and what you mean (don't hurt me).

In my opinion, one way to step outside of the struggle against the primary thinking error is simply not to struggle. Somewhere along the line I heard the term, *non-change*. It's similar to the way to cope with fear. You can't change the primary thinking error, but simply being mindful of the error transforms it. It's paradoxical. It's about naming and expressing what you mean and de-emphasizing what you say. Talking about the amount of fear of being hurt in the first example, and the fear of conflict in the second example, is one way to step out of the cycle. The key to transformation is awareness that the primary thinking error is often expressing what you are asking for. By focusing awareness on when we use the primary thinking error (what we mean) to shape our behavior, we can truly choose something else to shape our next action.

It's important to emphasize that you're looking for a thought and not a feeling. If you identify a feeling in the process, ask yourself "Why do I feel this? What's the thought that creates that feeling?" Too often, people will say: "I'm bad" or "I'm not good enough." My response is to ask, "Why do you feel that?"

As difficult as it's to identify the primary thinking error, the reward for identifying and recognizing it's amazing. Consider the reality that you can't break a bad habit if you don't know you are engaging in a bad habit. In golf, for example, coaches often help you unlearn bad habits you picked up along the way. So it's with the primary thinking error. It's a habitual way of thinking. New opportunities become possible when you can recognize your primary thinking error. Part of freedom is the ability to do whatever you want to do, but another part of it is being able to step out of bad patterns and choose the direction in which you want to go. As you recognize how often you use the primary thinking error, you can make a different choice toward something else that's more important.

ASSIGNMENT: Primary Thinking Error

To identify your primary thinking error, complete the following exercise by listing the thoughts that come to mind. Don't analyze too much as you go. These questions are simply tools to help you pinpoint your primary thinking error. If you can't identify it at this point, that's OK; you'll become more able to do so later on, as you start to look at incidents as they occur in real time.

- Review the list of *Frequent Thinking Errors* (see above). Which thinking errors elicit the most intense reaction from you (in contrast to the others)? The reaction may be admitting ("I think this often") or denying ("That's not me—no way!") the error. Remember the concept of transference. If any of the thinking error examples elicit a strong reaction, add it to the list of possibilities.

- Look at an incident in which you acted out. As you complete a behavioral analysis (page 91), track the thoughts backward. I use the idea of dominos as an example. Think of a thought as a domino. Each domino's fall is triggered by the fall of the domino before it, and that domino's fall was triggered by the fall of the domino that preceded it. The fall of all the dominoes can be traced back down the line to the very first domino. In the same way, a thought is triggered by a preceding thought, which is triggered by the thought preceding *it*, and so on. If you trace your thoughts about the incident back to one initial thought, you'll find your primary thinking error.

- Look back over times in your life when things did not go the way you wanted (these are often pivot points). These could be what you consider big things (such as losing a job or being called into the boss' office) or small things (such as plans with a friend falling through). What do you say to yourself in order to make sense of these situations? What might be your fear in these situations?

- When you look at your list of thoughts, restate them in a simple way. I encourage clients to rephrase each thought as a six-year-old might do. Here are some examples of primary thinking errors:
  - "It's my fault."
  - "I can't do it."
  - "It doesn't matter."
  - "Why try?"
  - "This won't work."
  - "You can't make me."
  - "I can do what I want."
  - "I don't fit in."
  - "Nobody wants me."
  - "I don't know."

Summarize what you have learned and share this with your support network.

The Acting-Out Cycle

We teach people that they upset themselves. We can't change the past, so we change how people are thinking, feeling and behaving today. (Albert Ellis)

The *acting-out cycle* is a framework used to help explain how people act out their compulsive behaviors in unhealthy ways. The entire workbook connects to this cycle. The key to changing the cycle is to first recognize the feeling triggers, high-risk settings, thinking errors, active and passive ways of acting out, and the perceived payoffs and consequences involved. I'll review each concept in greater detail further on, and the *Sexual Behavior Timeline* you generate in *Part Two: Stage 1* will help you identify the patterns of your own acting-out cycle. In the meantime, this brief introduction will help you develop an initial understanding.

Basic components of the cycle

Acting Out

Acting-out is the problematic behavior you need to stop in order to live a life you love. An *acting-out behavior* is any behavior that's problematic for you. Often, it's the same as the sexual behavior (having sex or watching porn, for example), but not always. As noted in *Other Compulsive Behaviors*, acting out doesn't just happen through sexual behavior. The key to overall health is to realize that sexual behavior is only one expression of the acting-out cycle; there are many different ways you may act out.

Setups

Set-ups are the thought triggers, feeling triggers, and situations that give the cycle momentum. The following example will help to illustrate these setups.

Let's say a person feels depressed, so s/he calls a sex phone line and winds up having a sexual encounter as a result. In this case, the feeling of depression precedes the acting-out incident— it was the trigger. In addition to this feeling trigger, a thinking error might be present. For example, "I'll only make the phone call. It isn't a big deal. I won't hook up." This represents a thought trigger. Feeling and thinking triggers aren't the only things to consider, however. The situation itself—calling the phone line in the first place (or even just being depressed at home, alone)—put the person at high risk for the problematic behavior. This high-risk situation set the person up for an acting-out incident as well.

As you move through the treatment process, you'll begin to identify additional setups. In the end, you'll be able to identify ten to fifteen setups of each type.

Payoffs/Consequences

All behavior is goal-focused, including acting out. Payoffs are the perceived or actual outcomes of a behavior. In the previous example, the perceived payoff was relief from depression. As you'll probably recognize, the payoff is usually temporary. Some of the payoffs may occur simultaneously with consequences. Sometimes the perceived payoff leads to the cycle starting all over again. It's important to think strategically regarding payoffs. Some payoffs might not be easily recognized at first. Yes, casual hook-ups might be one payoff, but another payoff might be avoiding the fear of being hurt in a relationship. Consequences are more easily recognized. Examples of consequences include: damage to relationships ("My partner is angry about my behavior"), legal ("I was arrested"), and physical ("I got drunk").

Setups
Thoughts/Thinking Errors
Feelings Triggers
High Risk Situations

Consequences/ Payoffs
Perceived or actual outcomes

Acting-out
Problematic/Unhealthy Behaviors

Acting Out Cycle

By recognizing the range of your behaviors, you can address the underlying dynamic of the cycle. This is the only way to avoid a Band-Aid approach to overall health. As you move through the process, you'll discover that the passive ways in which you act out are just as important as the active ways. For example, some people withdraw from conflict because of fear. The person then feels resentful, which results in an explosion of anger (another type of acting out).

Relationship between the Components

In the diagram above, the arrows are double pointed. This represents the fact that the cycle is dynamic—It's always shifting, moving and adapting. The cycle provides feedback to the individual, and the individual adapts as necessary to continue the cycle. I'll review this relationship throughout the workbook. An acting-out encounter may have a consequence that sets the person up to act out again. Treatment involves working through this cycle and addressing all aspects of it. Please be sure you understand the basics of the cycle at this time. As you move further into the workbook, your understanding will continue to grow.

Defining Sexual Health

The ultimate authority must always rest with the individual's own reason and critical analysis. (Dalai Lama)

Just as you can't think or talk in any productive way about "problematic sexual behavior" until you know what the term means in the context of your life, you can't very well work toward "sexual health" until you define what it is. Without a definition of sexual health that speaks to your true self—a personal definition—there is no destination towards which to travel. This book uses an adapted sexual health model to guide you through the therapy process and into living a life you love.

Toward Your Personal Definition of Sexual Health

In order to achieve the goal of developing and maintaining healthy sexual behaviors, it is necessary to define what those "healthy behaviors" are. This process of definition is not as simple as providing a list of prescribed "good" and "bad" behaviors. A specific sexual behavior may be healthy for one person, but unhealthy for another due to the fact that it conflicts with their personal values. As a result, it's necessary to recognize that the meaning of sexual health is, by definition, personal and individual. The material presented in the workbook is designed to assist you in clarifying what healthy sexual behavior is for *you*, providing the tools to help you build a *Personal Definition of Sexual Health*. Because creating sexual health is more of a process than a response to a "yes" or "no" question, various aspects of your work throughout the book will reveal a definition of sexual health that reflects your life, values and circumstances. In the final section of the book, you'll work to stabilize this definition for yourself as you move from identifying and changing unhealthy behaviors into maintaining healthy ones.

For individuals with a religious background, this approach of uncovering your personal truth is consistent with the tenants of moral theology. Within the Roman Catholic tradition, for example, the tradition teaches the primacy of individual conscience. Unfortunately, many religious traditions conclude that you'll adopt their view of the truth as *your* truth. It's both the individual's responsibility and right to come to a sense of clarity around what's right and wrong for him/herself. Yes, there may be consequences of the choices. Yes, an individual needs to be informed, educated and connected to community to hash out or discern what's right. No, it doesn't mean a person can do anything he or she wants; each of us also needs to be open to feedback. But, ultimately, each of us must follow what's right for each of us.

Sexual health requires that you choose and declare, "I choose to live my life this way; I choose to engage or not engage in these behaviors." I invite you to increase your awareness of all the ways you are told "you should" and "you shouldn't," as well as the ways you tell yourself, "I should" and "I shouldn't." In reality, anything is possible. There is significant societal pressure toward conformity in sexuality. It's your responsibility to assertively confront this pressure. What you choose is truly your choice.

Ten Elements of Sexual Health

To help you move toward sexual health, the topics in this workbook are based on an adapted theoretical model of sexual health[13] consisting of ten elements, which I briefly summarize here.

Talking About Sex. This is a cornerstone of sexual health. It includes talking about one's own sexual values, preferences, attractions, history and behaviors.

Culture, Identity and Sexual Health. In order to understand a sense of sexual self, individuals must examine the impact their particular cultural heritage has on their sexual identities, attitudes and behaviors.

Sexual Functioning—Anatomy and Beyond. One needs a basic understanding, knowledge and acceptance of sexual anatomy, sexual response and sexual functioning in order to achieve sexual health. This means freedom from sexual dysfunction and other sexual performance concerns.

Sexual Health Care and Safer-Sex Issues. There are many components to this, including knowing one's body and responding to physical changes with appropriate medical intervention. Examining one's safer-sex behaviors is critical.

Barriers to Sexual Health—Beyond Functioning. Some of the major challenges to sexual health include sexual abuse, substance abuse, mental health factors, and feelings of grief and/or anger. Other barriers can include sex work, harassment and discrimination.

Body Image. This requires challenging the notion of a single, narrow standard of beauty and encouraging self-acceptance. In order to achieve sexual health, one needs to develop a realistic and positive body image.

Masturbation, Fantasy and Sexually Explicit Material. Masturbation and fantasy can each be healthy expressions of sexuality. It's important for individuals to clarify their values on these subjects. Too often, shame is linked with masturbation and fantasy because of the historical myths associated with sin, illness and immaturity.

Positive Sexuality. All human beings need to explore their sexuality in order to develop and nurture who they are within a positive and self-affirming environment. Positive sexuality includes appropriate experimentation, sensuality, sexual boundaries and sexual competence developed through the ability to give and receive sexual pleasure.

Intimacy and Relationships. Taking many forms, intimacy is a universal need that people fill through a variety of relationships. Sexual health requires that a person know what intimacy needs are important to them, and finding appropriate ways to get these needs meet.

Spirituality, Values and Sexual Health. When there is sexual health, there is consistency between one's ethical, spiritual and moral beliefs and one's sexual behaviors. While spirituality may include identification with a formal religion, it doesn't have to.

Talking About Sex

The first component of sexual health, as noted in the adapted theoretical model above, is *Talking About Sex.* As mentioned in Sex, shame, fear, recovery, hope, and life (page 4), many people have a culturally imposed aversion to addressing sexuality and, in particular, talking about it—regardless of whether they're experiencing problems. Ironically, an aversion to talking about sex is often the source of a problem itself (as you'll note in your continued reading).

Why to talk about sex

A problem shared is a problem halved. (Proverb, unknown source)

Often in the early stages of addressing sexual health issues, the isolation a person feels is profound. With so many fears and secrets, the expectation that you'll share your sexual history with others is the first hurdle to overcome. By talking about sexuality with others, however, two important things happen: 1) you build a community of supportive people; and 2) through the process of talking with others, you gain insight into yourself and uncover layers of sexual health.

Building a community

A powerful instrument to help you move toward sexual health is the support of a community. This community is a small group of individuals selected by you to serve as support. The sharing of secrets leads to connection and community. It's in sharing secrets that you discover and break the illusion that you're alone. It's in sharing secrets that you create a connection to others. Your ability to cope with feelings of shame is increased by the support of a network.

Breaking the silence starts with one disclosure and leads to additional disclosures. Slowly, what was experienced in isolation disappears in the developing connections that occur through the sharing of secrets. As the process of disclosure continues, a community develops. Believe it or not, what was once a secret is joyfully acknowledged in community and leads to a sense of transformation. From this transformation, powerful new opportunities are created, all of which start with sharing a secret with one person.

Talking to discover who you are

The most obvious reason to develop a support network when starting this process may be to build a community. Just as crucial, however, is the fact that talking with others helps you discover who you are. It isn't until we start talking about sexuality that we understand the layers and connections of sexual health. We may not recognize negative thinking until someone says, "Wow, I really hear a lot of negative talk." Through talking with members of your support network, you may actually discover hidden barriers to your healing. You may actually talk through a solution that dispels the shame leading to a breakthrough in your sexual health.

When and with whom to talk about what

The key in this process is the application of wisdom to discern who your appropriate support people are, as well as the timing of disclosure.

Building a support network

I recommend that the person(s) with whom you disclose information be trustworthy and nonjudgmental.

ASSIGNMENT: Initial Support Network

Name four people you could start talking to about sexuality and about your sexual behaviors. Write 2-3 sentences about your current progress that you could say to each of them. This list could include your spiritual advisor, sponsor, therapist, friends, colleagues or others.

- Write one paragraph for each person that summarizes what you would like to share at this time regarding your treatment process for sexual compulsivity. Start small. Say, "I'm now in therapy. I need someone to support me, but I'm not ready to go into full detail right now."

- Examine your list and identify anyone who is already supportive in your life. Expand what you might say to these people in order to increase your self-disclosure. You might say, "I'm working with a therapist in the area of human sexuality."

- Identify a celebrity that has disclosed his or her sexual compulsivity. This can help you introduce the topic.

Initial Disclosure to Partners

As you work through this book, you'll probably experience a wide array of emotions. Your thoughts, moods, and daily behaviors may change as a result. Because of this, it may be important to share a certain amount of information with your partner sooner rather than later. However, the majority of work you do should not be shared with your partner(s) until you reach the final stages of the process. Disclosing this information to your partner is something that must be done with great care and intention, from a place of integrity and honesty. At the beginning of the treatment process, it's unlikely you'll be able to stand unwaveringly in such a place.

What I recommend you share with your partner sooner rather than later is that you are trying to understand your behavior so you can engage in different behaviors. Or, you might share some of the lessons you learn in the work. Please remember to have a conversation with your partner about respecting the privacy and security of the workbook and your journal.

It is not easy to give advice on how to move toward disclosure. You need to think about what's best for you. For some individuals, any disclosure may lead to conflict (e.g., feelings of hurt and anger, shock at disclosure). In these cases, couples therapy may be the place to start. In other cases, partners will want to be involved in the treatment progress. In this example, increasing levels of disclosure may be beneficial.

My general approach is to begin by sharing about insights and the content of the workbook. For example, "I'm reading about the acting-out cycle," or "I'm reading about types of intimacy." I see full disclosure as part of the healing process, but a later part. I recommend that at the start, the details remain undisclosed (with regard to your partner) until you reach *Full Disclosure to Partners* at the end of *Stage 2*. Disclosure is a mutual healing process that requires information from both you and your partner; this later section includes important questions for your partner to consider before full disclosure occurs. If your partner is aware of the sexual compulsivity, please share the questions for the partner located on page 200.

Finding a (Sex) Therapist

There are times when professional help is needed along the journey toward sexual health. For example, you might want support to talk about some of the issues that are raised in the work (such as abuse), or you might want additional information because you have questions about the content. Therapists can be helpful as you clarify your values. Often, my role is to simply listen as clients discern their truth. It's helpful to highlight a few strategies for finding a clinician who specializes in sexuality.

Advocate for yourself. Check out a number of websites, including *sash.net* and *aasect.org*. Call your insurance company for the names of clinicians experienced working in sexual matters.

Call. Most clinicians will take a 10-15 minute phone call to determine whether an initial interview should be set up or not. Be direct and open during the call. This is not the time to beat around the bush. Use the time efficiently. Put your issue out there: "I'm struggling with Internet porn." "I have a problem with sexual behavior." "Do you work with clients in this area?" "What's a summary of your treatment approach?" "Do you have any resources available on the web?"

Ask for referrals. If the clinician responds, "No," ask him/her for referrals. Repeat the process until you have 1-3 clinicians with whom you might want to meet.

Set-up meetings. Some clinicians will hold free 30-minute sessions, others won't. The intake interview is as much for you as it is for the clinician. In addition to answering the clinician's questions, feel free to ask questions of your own: "How busy are you?" "What's your training/experience in this area?" "How many clients have you worked with on this topic?" The more forthright you are, the more likely you are to find a clinician who can help in your recovery.

Remember, the therapist is there for you; you are not there for the therapist.

Professional confidentiality

Trust is a major component of counseling. Trust builds a sense of safety that leads to tremendous therapeutic change. Knowing that any information you share will not be told to others strengthens trust. In any therapeutic relationship, confidentiality limits what a professional can disclose to others. You are the one holding this privilege. Depending on where you live, however, there are limits to this privilege. These limits facilitate safety in the broad sense of the term, such as requiring the professional to report: suspected abuse of a child or vulnerable adult; significant and real potential harm to yourself (e.g., if you make statements such as "I'm going to kill myself"); significant and real potential harm to another person (e.g., if you make statements such as "I'm going to kill that person"); or when a court order requires the release of information.

Legal repercussions of disclosure

As you complete the assignments, it's important to be open and honest about your past and present behaviors. While it's important for disclosure to occur, it's important for disclosure to occur in a prudent manner. Be careful when making disclosures of sexual behavior. Seriously consider whether your disclosure could trigger a mandatory report as required by the state and local laws where you live. There may be a risk of legal consequences if some of your sexual behaviors include illegal behaviors. One way to protect yourself is to speak in general terms, leaving out names, exact dates, and specific locations.

Respecting the privacy of others

In addition to the potential for legal consequences, disclosures can violate the privacy of individuals within a community. One way to ensure privacy and confidentiality when disclosing information is to be specific about behaviors, but not provide any identifiable information. For example, you might want to say "sexual partner #1" instead of giving the person's full name. It's worth repeating that the goal is to be as honest with yourself and your therapist/support network as possible, while ensuring your own safety.

How to talk about sex

Comfort level talking about sex

One of the approaches in my therapy approach is to ask, "What are you not talking about?" In my opinion, this is one of the warning flags associated with a possible treatment issue. To start addressing questions of sexual compulsivity, it's important to reflect on your comfort and ability in talking about sex in general. If there is any history or current event, topic, behavior or concern that you're not talking about, it's a warning sign. I have concerns when I hear clients say, "No one can find out" or "I wouldn't want _____ to know about this." If you say these types of qualifying statements regarding a sexual behavior, you probably shouldn't be doing it. In the end, responsibility is about taking on the ownership of your behaviors and interests and sharing them with others. I'm confident that your comfort level will increase as you progress through the workbook.

ASSIGNMENT: How comfortable are you talking about sex?

Answer the following questions by placing a mark on the line:

I find many sexual matters too upsetting to talk about.

Completely Agree--Completely Disagree

I talk about my sexual feelings.

Completely Agree--Completely Disagree

I usually feel comfortable discussing my sexual values.

Completely Agree--Completely Disagree

I usually feel comfortable discussing topics of a sexual nature.

Completely Agree--Completely Disagree

Talking about sex is usually a positive experience.

Completely Agree--Completely Disagree

It bothers me to talk about sex.

Completely Agree --Completely Disagree

I usually feel comfortable discussing my sexual behavior.

Completely Agree--Completely Disagree

I feel there will be negative consequences if I talk about sex.

Completely Agree--Completely Disagree

- Reflect on the above questions and explain your responses.

- Reflect on your thoughts and feelings as you start this process. Many clients express fear, shame, guilt and hopelessness as they look at all the topics in the workbook. How present are these thoughts and feelings?

- Other clients express feelings of hope and excitement, often because they see a pathway where they had not seen one previously. How present are these thoughts and feelings?

What follows is a temporary approach to help you learn how to share information with others along the way.

ASSIGNMENT: How to talk about the healing process

Having people in your life to support you in the process of improving your sexual health is important. Developing your support network is a way to increase external accountability. Below are a few ideas on how to talk about the healing process without getting bogged down in the details of the content.

- Talk about you internal process, without necessarily disclosing the content. Share feeling statements, such as "I realize I felt sad, which is a trigger in my acting-out cycle…"

- Talk about the lessons learned. For example, "Today's topic was on intimacy, and I realize I need to develop my skills in emotional intimacy."

- Develop assertive communication skills to express needs, desires and requests. All behavior is goal-focused, including sexual compulsivity. Identifying healthy ways to get needs met reduces the future risk of acting out.

- If you can't share the topic at this time, share some of the negative thoughts or feelings that set you up to act out. You could share, "I'm really stuck on how negative my thoughts are," or, "I struggle with a lot of shame."

Assertive Communication

In moving toward sexual health, it's important to develop assertive communication skills while avoiding passive, aggressive and passive/aggressive communication patterns. Assertive communication involves expressing your needs, establishing boundaries, and setting limits. It's important to be assertive in expressing both feelings and desires. This can have a major impact on a relationship and must be done carefully. Assertive communication is an advanced skill that takes time, insight, and emotional energy to master. You'll revisit this topic in more depth once you are further into the treatment process. In the meantime, if you know you struggle with assertive communication, I encourage you to explore the topic further with your support network.

Part Two: Applying the Concepts to Your Life

As you read through the material in *Part One*, you used your journal and the assignments provided to note some connections you identified between the general concepts of sexual health and your own experiences. Moving into *Part Two*, you'll now take the time to document, explore, and address both those connections and others as you work toward living a life you love.

The work in *Part Two* is organized into three stages. In *Stage 1: Problem Identification*, you'll identify, explore and prioritize problematic behaviors in your life through a variety of assignments. In *Stage 2: Primary Treatment*, you'll learn to identify your sexual needs and values, develop the necessary skills to build the type of relationships you want, and assertively express what you want regarding type, frequency, and variety of sexual expression. In *Stage 3: Groundwork for Completing Treatment*, you'll create your future.

As you progress through each stage, you'll notice that none of the stages are self-contained. Information gathered in *Stage 1* forms the basis of the work you do in *Stage 2*, but at the same time you'll learn things during *Stage 2* that inform and reshape the information you gathered in *Stage 1*. Likewise, in *Stage 3* you'll reflect on everything you have done in *Stages 1* and *2*; as you do so, you'll find yourself in a new, more grounded place from which to revisit previous assignments in order to get even more out of them. Just as our thoughts and emotions are constantly evolving and looping back into themselves, so too the topics and assignments in this book are forever informing each other.

Stage 1: Problem Identification

Being entirely honest with oneself is a good exercise. (Sigmund Freud)

In the mental health field, the first thing that occurs in a counseling relationship is a series of interviews to gather information. This is the purpose of *Stage 1*.

During this stage, you'll have opportunities to examine your sexual behaviors. You'll complete a number of assignments to help paint a picture of your compulsive behavior. These assignments include a sex history and a sexual behavior timeline. The topics in this section will assist you in determining how out-of-control your sexual behaviors are, and understanding your acting-out cycle and its various components. Based on your findings, you'll be able to identify the major issues to address in *Stage 2* of your journey.

Writing your Sex History

As you progress through the process of addressing sexual compulsivity, it's important to describe your past sexual behavior accurately and completely. The *sex history* is the place to do this. Since the workbook is a living document, it may be helpful to return periodically to add material as you remember pieces of your history. Often, when an individual listens to another person's story, s/he remembers additional pieces of his/her own story.

At first, you may not want to put everything on paper because of what others might think. Just remember, you can't treat something that remains undisclosed. On the other hand, when you're open and honest, you have a better sense of your needs in your treatment process.

When you complete the history and timeline, please share it with your support network. I don't recommend disclosing this information (the sex history) to your primary partner at this time (that disclosure will happen near the end of *Stage 2*, page 198). For your safety, if you haven't carefully read *Caution: Risks of Disclosure* (page 5), please do so before you continue.

ASSIGNMENT: Your Sex History

Complete this as thoroughly as possible. Use additional paper or journal pages as necessary. Update it as you remember pieces of your history.

Dating and Relationship Behavior

1. At what age did you begin to date or go out with girls/boys your own age?
    a. Describe your level of self-confidence regarding dating.
    b. How comfortable did you feel?
    c. How attractive did you think you were to others?
2. If you have a same-sex attraction, when did you come out to yourself? When did you come out to others (if you have)?
3. Review the patterns of your relationships:
    a. Describe your dating behavior.
    b. How do you meet dating partners?
    c. Note the number of relationships you've had and describe the type and length of each relationship.
    d. Describe the dating/courtship that occurred in each relationship.
    e. Describe how you met and broke up with these partners, and discuss any primary concerns you have.
    f. How quickly did sexual contact occur in each relationship (if at all)?
    g. How did your self-esteem improve or decrease as you dated more frequently?

Sexual Behavior

1. How old were you when you first had sexual intercourse?
2. How old was your partner?

3. How did you feel about the experience?

4. How many sexual partners have you had? (Skip to letter (i) below if you have had too many partners to identify them all.)

   a. To the best of your ability, fill out a table (see example below) that includes each partner.

Your Age	Partner's Age	Type of Sexual Contact	Where	Length of Relationship Plus Other details
16	15	Vaginal sex, oral sex	Both parents' houses. Friend's house.	Dated for 12 months
22	21	Vaginal sex	Hotel	1 encounter

   b. Describe what behaviors occurred. Be explicit and thorough (e.g. oral sex, vaginal sex, anal sex, mutual masturbation, kissing, touching, etc.).

   c. Describe the location (home, bedroom, public space, bathhouse, bar, etc.).

   d. What was the length of the relationship (one-night stand, occasional or casual sexual encounters lasting a few months, longtime partnership, six-year marriage, etc.)?

   e. What percentage of your sexual partners have been one-night stands?

   f. Describe the circumstances in which you met your sexual partners.

   g. How many same-sex sexual partners have you had?

      i. How did you feel about it then?

      ii. How do you feel about it now?

   h. Describe the frequency and circumstances of any sexual encounters that occurred while using drugs and/or alcohol.

   i. If your number of sexual partners is too large to count, complete the assignment by examining periods of your life and estimating the number of contacts. Pick periods that make sense to you. For example:

      i. Up to age 13 (pre-adolescence), number of partners_____

      ii. Age 14–18, number of partners_____

      iii. Age 19–24, number of partners_____

      iv. First job, number of partners_____

      v. At the time of your first significant relationship, number of partners_____

      vi. After divorce and/or end of first relationship, number of partners_____

      vii. At the time you lived at a particular address or a particular city, number of partners_____

      viii. Describe any patterns you've noticed as you complete this section.

5. Describe the frequency and circumstances of any sexual contact with someone other than your primary partner (while married or in a committed relationship.)

6. Describe any circumstances in which you have intentionally avoided sexual contact with a partner or significant other. Include any underlying thoughts and feelings.

Masturbation

1. At what age did you first masturbate?
2. How did you learn about masturbation?
3. What messages did you hear about masturbation while growing up?
4. What were your beliefs and feelings about masturbation while growing up?
5. What are your beliefs and feelings about masturbating today?
6. How often do you masturbate (focus on the last 30 days)?
7. When was the last time you masturbated?
8. What thoughts and feelings did you have when you last masturbated?
9. Describe the frequency and circumstances of any masturbating you've done outside your home.
10. What objects (if any) have you used to enhance your level of sexual arousal during masturbation (e.g. items of clothing, vibrators, magazines, sexual toys, items to inflict pain)? Describe the items and circumstances of their use for sexual stimulation.

Fantasy

1. What messages and beliefs did you hear growing up about having sexual fantasies?
2. Describe your three most arousing sexual fantasies.
3. How do you feel about these fantasies?
4. Have you ever masturbated to sexual fantasies of rape? If so, describe the fantasy, including your role in the fantasy (victim/persecutor) relationship to the victim/abuser, the frequency of the fantasy, and the length of time since your last rape fantasy.

Health Concerns

1. Describe the frequency of physical problems you've experienced that affect your ability to be sexual (such as difficulty achieving or maintaining erections, difficulty reaching orgasm, difficulty with delayed ejaculation, and/or painful penetration). Describe the circumstances in which you have experienced these difficulties.
2. Describe the frequency with which you've contracted sexually transmitted infections and the circumstances under which you were infected.
3. Describe any circumstances leading to pregnancy/child-bearing (by you or your sexual partner).
4. Describe any circumstances leading to having an abortion or being the partner of someone who had an abortion.
5. Describe any circumstances when your physical safety has been in danger as a result of sexual behavior.

Abuse

1. Describe the frequency of being sexually touched or being forced to engage in sexual behavior as a child. Describe the circumstances under which these instances occurred.

2. Describe the frequency of being sexually touched or being forced to engage in sexual behavior as an adult. Describe the circumstances under which these instances occurred.

3. Describe the frequency of being the target of sexual harassment. Describe the circumstances under which these instances occurred.

4. Describe the frequency of sexual contact between you and members of your family. Describe the circumstances under which these instances occurred.

5. Generally, describe any circumstances when you abused or sexually harassed someone else (don't include specific names or identifiable information).

Internet-Related Sexual Behaviors

1. At what age did you first start using the Internet for sexual purposes? Describe the behavior and content of your first online sexual experience(s).

2. Describe how your frequency of using the Internet for sex has changed over the years. Describe any unusual patterns.

3. Describe when you have become sexually aroused while engaging in Internet sexual behaviors. What type of activity were you involved in at the time?

4. Describe what you enjoy doing most sexually online, (e.g., looking at pornography, visiting chat rooms, exposing yourself)? How has this preference changed over time?

5. Describe the frequencies and areas of sexual activity that you enjoy exploring online, (e.g., certain ethnicities, feet, animals, diapers…).

6. Have you ever done anything sexually online that might be considered illegal? Describe this in a general way (don't include identifiable data).

7. Describe the frequency and circumstances of any times you have used the Internet to arrange for an escort service or prostitute.

8. Describe the frequency of using the Internet to meet sexual partners and the circumstances under which you used the Internet to make these connections.

9. Describe the frequency and circumstances of how your offline sexuality has been affected by your online sexual behaviors?

10. Describe the frequency and circumstances of any instances when you posted (online) erotic or sexual pictures/videos of yourself or others (including via webcam or texting).

11. Describe the frequency and circumstances of any times you've masturbated with online sexual materials or activities. What type of content do you typically masturbate to?

12. Describe the frequency and circumstances of any occasions you have engaged in high-risk behaviors while online (e.g., downloading pornography at work, engaging in illegal online behaviors). What is the typical content of such materials?

13. Describe the frequency and circumstances of instances when you've had any physical problems as a result of your Internet sexual behavior (e.g., contracted an STD from a chat partner, been injured by a sex partner met online).

14. What other sexual activities have you engaged in while online that would be important to disclose?

Other Patterns of Sexual Behavior

NOTE: The following questions may involve information about illegal behaviors; don't include identifiable details.

1. Describe the frequency of paying money for sex or trading drugs for sex, and the circumstances under which you've done so.
2. Describe the frequency of engaging in prostitution and the circumstances under which you've done so.
3. Describe the frequency of having sexual touch with an animal, and the circumstances under which you've done so.
4. Describe the frequency of public sex and/or exposing your genitals to others without their consent, and the circumstances under which you've done so.
5. Describe the frequency of spying on someone for sexual gratification and the circumstances under which you've done so.
6. Describe the types of sexual magazines and movies you view for sexual stimulation.
7. Describe your frequency of using threats of violence, physical force, or any weapon to make someone perform a sexual act. Describe the circumstances (in general terms) under which you've done so.
8. Describe the frequency of participating in consensual use of restraints or consensual bondage acts, and describe the circumstances under which you've done so.
9. Describe the frequency of participating in group sex and the circumstances under which you've done so.
10. Describe the frequency of participating in alternative ("kinky") behaviors and the circumstances under which you've done so.

Children

NOTE: Please review "Legal repercussions of disclosure" (page 64) as well as "What is not Sexual Compulsivity (page 21) before completing this section.

1. Describe any sexual contact you have had with children since you entered adulthood.
2. Describe the content of any sexually explicit pictures of children you have seen or possessed.
3. Describe the frequency with which you've viewed explicit child sexual material and the circumstances under which you've done so.
4. Describe any times you've masturbated to fantasies of sex with children. Include the frequency with which you've done so.

General

1. Describe any legal consequences of your sexual behavior. Describe the frequency of legal consequences.
2. Describe any sexual behaviors or practices that are not addressed in the questions above.
3. Of the questions above, which three were the most difficult to answer?
   a. Why did you select these three questions?
   b. What made them so difficult to answer?
4. What are three things you learned about yourself by completing this assignment?
5. At this time, which three areas would you highlight as your primary areas of concern?

Sexual Behavior Timeline

The goal of this assignment is to translate the material from your sex history into a visual format. In creating your *sexual behavior timeline*, you'll concentrate on your sexual behavior, making it possible to understand how your sexual behaviors have occurred across time. The goal will be to see if there are relationships that exist between your emotions and your sexual behavior in relation to other issues. Although it may be possible to see the relationship between behaviors and other issues, it's not possible to determine cause and effect. Acting out sexually might be an attempt to cope with anxiety or depression, or conversely, it may actually be the cause of anxiety or depression.

ASSIGNMENT: Your Sexual Behavior Timeline

Complete the following exercise as thoroughly as possible. Use the information from the sex history assignment you just completed to plot events along a horizontal timeline (see example below), attempting to recall your age at the time of each event. Put as much of the history on the timeline as you can; it may be helpful to identify and plot out any major issues. Include any important pivot points (page 29). Feel free to adapt the exercise as you find helpful.

With colored pens or pencils, track relevant behaviors. This might include tracking spending behaviors, drug or alcohol behaviors, or gambling (page 21). Also, track additional life events such as depression or mood changes, stress, relationship satisfaction, job satisfaction or other important events, especially as they relate to your sexual behavior.

It might be helpful to tape a few pieces of paper together or use poster board to increase your space. Across the left-hand edge of the page, draw a vertical line. The vertical line should be numbered +5 to 0. At the center of the vertical line, draw a horizontal line that travels the length of the page. The horizontal line reflects your age across time. If you notice, the space on the timeline is not equal. Some parts of your life are less relevant, so you can save space. Other times of your life may be more expansive.

You might need to devise a code to fit everything into the timeline. Some clients have used multiple colors to chart a number of items. For some people, this might be mood, chemical use, anxiety, or whatever. If, for example, at the time of a marriage you were very happy, your mood might be charted at a +5. One client charted both the amount of chemical use and mood. Afterward, he was able to see the inverse relationship between mood and chemical use. The more he used, the lower his mood was. His lower mood may have contributed to his increased chemical use as he self-medicated in an attempt to cope with sexual behavior. Below the line are spaces in which to describe relevant events in your life. The key for the bottom part of the timeline is to examine life events and topics to see how they fit into the picture. Each timeline will be different. You're literally creating a graph of your life. What's relevant to each person varies as much the people themselves. In this example, I've included three items; your timeline might have more. Additional topics to graph include financial, relational, geographic and/or familial changes.

Example Sexual Behavior Timeline

+5					
+4		Graph the intensity of important feelings such			
+3		as grief, depression, anger, loneliness, etc.			
		+5 very intense, 0 Not present			
+2					
+1					
0					

Write out the major components of your sex history along this line

Include major life events (you made need to write small)

Age	10	12	13	18	19
Relevant Life History Info	Parents divorced	Went to JH	Felt isolated from class-mates	College	Failed out of college
Sexual Behav-ior History	Saw porn for the first time	Began getting up in the middle of the night to look at porn	Gave up soc-cer because wanted more time to look at porn	Porn use in-creased both in time and graphic, bi-zarre nature	Looking at porn and masturbating for more than 8 hours a day
Chemical His-tory Info		Began sneak-ing beer from house	Started to drink when looking at porn	Binge drink-ing	Began using pot; hooked up and used meth

ASSIGNMENT: Weekly Log of Behaviors and Fantasies

Stopping the acting-out cycle requires that you identify any sexual thoughts, feelings or behaviors on a regular basis. In your journal, write your answers to the following questions. Pay attention to the last seven days only. I recommend you do this at least once a week.

NOTE: When you first encounter these questions, you may not be sure exactly how to interpret them. Feel free to answer the questions as best you can without worrying about the exact meaning of terms. If you wish, you can use the page references provided to skip ahead for more information on specific topics.

- Describe any sexualizations and/or sexual fantasies (153).
- Describe any masturbation behaviors. Describe where, with whom, how much, your situation, thoughts, fantasies, etc. (149).
- Describe any Internet and/or phone use for sexual stimulation and/or behaviors (136).
- Describe any sexual intercourse (e.g., oral/anal/vaginal sex).
- Describe any use of sexually explicit material (160).
- Describe any other types of sexual behavior.

Behavioral Analysis

In addition to logging information about your sexual behaviors, it's critical to periodically reflect on that information in order to make connections that are meaningful. By completing a thoughtful analysis of your behaviors (or *behavioral analysis*) on a weekly basis, you can gain insight into your fantasies, thoughts, experiences and behaviors to uncover various treatment themes and intervention plans.

In your analyses, focus on identifying connections between behaviors and the possible reasons behind those behaviors. Remember to include any acting-out behavior, whether or not it's sexual. There are many connections and reasons worth noting—and many ways to analyze the information you logged in your journal. Some examples are:

Time – The relationship between behaviors in terms of chronological order. (For example, you often participate in unsafe sex *after* you get drunk.) When analyzing behaviors chronologically, it's often helpful to work backwards. (For example, after making the previous connection, you might move on to note that you often get drunk *while* you are at a club, and you often go out to a club *after* you talk to your ex on the phone.)

Mood – Connections you note between your general mood and each behavior. (For example, you are usually very *depressed* when you participate in unsafe sex.) Consider what events or behaviors seem to change your mood. (For example, you tend to feel anxious and angry after you talk to your ex, which makes you want to drink a lot.)

Place – Identifying locations that are most often linked with problematic behaviors for you. (For example, you often engage in unsafe sex when you go to a specific club.)

Every item in the analysis is a potential place to update your Immediate Intervention Plan.

ASSIGNMENT: Weekly Behavioral Analysis

On a regular basis, complete a brief behavioral analysis of the behaviors logged in your journal. Exactly how often you should complete this analysis depends largely on: 1) how often you log behaviors, and 2) how many behaviors you have to log.

Write the results of the analysis in your journal and then answer the following questions:

- What did you learn through the analysis?
- What thoughts did you have before, during and after your analysis?
- What feelings did you have before, during and after your analysis?

Discuss your analysis and responses with your support network. Review your Immediate Short-Term Prevention Plan and update your plan as necessary.

Your Acting-Out Cycle

In Part 1, I explained that the acting-out cycle is a framework used to help explain how people act out their compulsive behaviors in unhealthy ways. The key to changing the cycle is to first recognize the feeling triggers, high-risk settings, thinking errors, active and passive ways of acting out, and the perceived payoffs and consequences. Here you'll identify the patterns of your own acting-out cycle.

Thought Triggers

One of the most important aspects of the acting-out cycle is recognition of the thoughts associated with your compulsive behavior. I identified the strategies of mindfulness and transference as tools to help you identify the thoughts fundamental to your behavior patterns. Sometimes, these patterns will take a regular form related to your existential fears or primary thinking error. Ultimately, when you recognize your fear, you can start to make changes in your behavior to respond in healthy ways.

ASSIGNMENT: Relationship between thinking errors & acting-out behaviors

This assignment is designed to help you understand the relationship between thinking errors and acting-out behaviors.

- Think back to the last time you acted out. Identify two or three examples of the "because" explaining why you did what you did.

Feeling Triggers

A major factor in the acting-out cycle is the presence of *feeling triggers*. At the beginning of the healing process, it's not uncommon for a client to say, "I don't know what I'm feeling." The growth process is about learning to identify and understand the feelings. Identifying feelings is more difficult than most people realize. To that goal, this process is designed to help you increase your awareness. When you recognize you are acting out, ask yourself, "What am I feeling?" Other useful questions to ask include: "What would others be feeling?" "Am I feeling this?" and "What feeling might I guess that I'm having?" In both of these cases, end with confirming whether or not this feeling is present. It's important to remember that feelings are based on thoughts and the interpretation of the world around you. You might also ask, "What am I thinking?" and then, "How do I feel given that I'm thinking this?"

Below is a list of feelings that many people highlight as contributing to their sexual behavior. Notice that both positive and negative feelings are associated with the cycle. Keep in mind that feeling confident may lead to a feeling of entitlement, which may subsequently lead you to place yourself at risk for an acting-out encounter. Another feeling might be anger or hurt. In some circumstances, clients have reported they acted-out sexually as a way to get back at their partners (anger/revenge).

Major Feeling Triggers

Abandoned	Cheated	Envious	Jubilant	Reluctant
Accepted	Cheerful	Excited	Let down	Remorseful
Afraid	Confident	Exhilarated	Lonely	Resentful
Alone	Courageous	Fearful	Miserable	Resigned
Amazed	Cowardly	Flighty	Murderous	Sad
Ambivalent	Disappointed	Free	Nervous	Secure
Angry	Discontent	Frightened	Numb	Selfish
Annoyed	Discouraged	Frustrated	Overcome	Shocked
Anxious	Dissatisfied	Glad	Overjoyed	Stunned
Apprehensive	Distressed	Humble	Overwhelmed	Surprised
Ashamed	Drained	Humiliated	Peaceful	Thrilled
Awestruck	Eager	Hurt	Panicked	Tired
Brave	Ecstatic	Indignant	Pity	Uneasy
Calm	Embarrassed	Irritated	Regretful	Unworthy
Careful	Empty	Jealous	Rejected	Vengeful
Caring	Encouraged	Jolly	Relief	Wary
Cautious	Energized	Joyful	Relieved	Weary

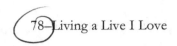

The following assignment helps you to identify, reflect on, and plan to cope with the feeling triggers in your life.

ASSIGNMENT: Feeling Triggers

Identify Triggers

- Identify 3-5 feeling triggers you experience in your life from the list above.

- Review the list of feeling triggers with your support network. Which feeling triggers do they suggest might be consistently present in your experience?

Plans for Coping

- List the top three feeling triggers you identified. Note one or two plans to start coping with each of these triggers. Remember to update your Immediate Short-term Prevention Plan as appropriate.

High-Risk Situations

The next component in the acting-out cycle is high-risk situations. This is the easiest component to identify and the easiest area in which to create prevention plans. Identifying and creating prevention plans for high-risk situations are very important, but they don't alone reduce sexual compulsivity or other forms of acting out. Underlying issues (such as thought and feeling triggers) must be addressed, or you'll be able to easily circumvent structural interventions. The structural interventions (see below) are, at best, speed bumps. They won't completely stop you from acting out, or prevent you from switching to a different type of acting-out behavior.

A *high-risk situation* is the setting in which acting-out behaviors occur. Picture yourself engaging in an acting-out behavior, as though you were pictured in a photograph. What's going on in the photograph? Ask yourself the classic questions of "Who?" "What?" "Where?" "When?" and "How?" (note that "Why" is more about thought triggers/thinking errors than high-risk situations). These questions are the tools for identifying high-risk situations:

- "What was I doing right beforehand?"
- "What was going on?"
- "Where was I?"
- "Who was I with?"
- "When did it happen?"
- "How did it happen?"

Some examples of high-risk situations are:

- "I was home alone."
- "I was taking a walk in the park."
- "I was chatting with friends at the bar."
- "I drove by the _____."
- "I had a fight with my partner."
- "I was fired."
- "I just got a raise/made a big sale/received some money."
- "I stopped at the gas station and they had magazines."
- "I saw the inserts in the newspaper."
- "I saw something on TV."
- "Someone offered me drugs."
- "I was with _____."

Developing a prevention plan for avoiding high-risk situations is simply a matter of creating a structural intervention that will get in the way of (or remove) the high-risk situation. For example, if surfing the Internet is a trigger—a high-risk situation possible structural interventions could be installing an Internet blocker or Internet tracker, having someone watch over you, or simply not having your house connected to the Internet. If the gym or another location is a trigger, avoiding that location could be a plan.

The following assignment helps you to identify, reflect on, and plan to cope with the high-risk situations in your life.

ASSIGNMENT: High-risk Situations

<u>Identify Situations</u>

- Identify 3-5 high-risk situations in your life. Use the examples above to help you come up with your own list.

- Review the list of high-risk situations with your support network. Which situations do they suggest might be consistently problematic for you?

<u>Plans for Coping</u>

- List the top three high-risk situations you identified. Note one or two plans to start coping with each of these situations. Remember to update your Immediate Short-term Prevention Plan as appropriate.

Cross-compulsivity

In the field of chemical addiction, there's a term called *cross-compulsivity*. This concept recognizes the experience of a similar underlying pattern to many different types of behaviors. I work with clients who stop their chemical use only to have their sexual behavior get out-of-control as a result. What's key when addressing different types of behaviors is to look for the underlying dynamic. These behaviors are actually symptoms of the underlying dynamic. In my experience, if you only address the surface behaviors without addressing the underlying dynamic, that dynamic will show up in different ways. In other words, once both the sexual behavior and chemical use are under control, it's not surprising to see another problematic behavior develop (such as overeating, compulsive spending, or gambling).

ASSIGNMENT: Another Look at Other Compulsive Behaviors

Chemical Dependency

A classic warning sign of the link between sexual health and chemical health concerns is the use of alcohol or drugs as "chemical courage" to overcome anxiety/shame about engaging in sexual behavior. Much of my expertise involves the link between sexual health concerns and chemical use. Hundreds (if not thousands) of research articles examine this connection. Despite this fact, sadly, very few chemical dependency treatment programs explicitly address sexuality concerns. Chemical dependency counselors are often not trained to address sexuality. Likewise, most sexual health counselors are not trained to address chemical dependency. It's rare for a program to address both concerns.

Review your sex history and timeline. Here are some questions to consider:

- What chemicals (e.g., alcohol, "poppers" or crystal methamphetamine) are linked to your sexual behavior?

- Identify the order of chemical use and sexual behavior. What came first?

- Consider whether or not sexual avoidance precedes chemical use. Might you use chemicals as a form of "courage" to overcome anxiety, shame or other feelings?

Eating Disorders

Eating disorders are closely related to issues of body image. Because of this, it's important to review how your eating behaviors are associated with your sexual behaviors. This material will also be relevant when you reach the section on *Body Image* (page 144).

Review your sex history and timeline.

- Is there any correlation between your sexual behavior and your eating behaviors or body image?

- Might an eating disorder episode precede or follow sexual behaviors?

- Do sexual behaviors trigger shame, which is transferred to eating behaviors?

Gambling

In some cases, problematic gambling behavior is a reaction to sexual behavior, sexual behavior is a reaction to gambling, or a person is caught in a cycle between the two. For this reason, it's important to assess any relationship between gambling behaviors and sexuality.

Review your sex history and timeline.

- Are you engaging in compulsive gambling behaviors?

- Does compulsive gambling precede sexual behavior, or vice versa?

- Might compulsive sexual behavior be an attempt to cope with gambling behavior, or vice versa?

- Are there any other connections you see between your gambling and sexual behaviors?

Spending

Unhealthy spending behaviors can be connected to problematic sexual behaviors. This connection may appear in a variety of ways. It's important to determine any connection that might exist for you.

Review your sex history and timeline.

- Are you engaging in compulsive spending behaviors?

- Does compulsive spending precede sexual behavior?

- Might compulsive sexual behavior be an attempt to cope with spending behavior (i.e., does spending overcome feelings of guilt or shame)?

- Are you spending money to buy love or sex?

Compulsive Working

Compulsive working can contribute to problematic sexual behaviors. Your reaction to work can trigger thinking errors you use to justify sexual behaviors. You might use sexual behavior to help escape work, or use hard work as justification for a sexual contact. In order to ensure the treatment process is thorough, it's necessary to review how work and sexual behaviors overlap. Keep the concepts of the acting-out cycle in mind as you examine the motivations behind your work behaviors.

Review your sex history and timeline.

- Are you engaging in compulsive work behaviors?

- Does compulsive working precede sexual behavior, or vice versa?

- Might you use sexual behavior to escape work, or work to justify sexual behaviors?

- Might you use work to avoid sexual contact?

• Are there any other connections you see between your work and sexual behaviors?

Consequences of the Acting-out Cycle

Sometimes there is a "final straw" that pushes a person into the treatment process. Within the acting-out cycle, I use the label *consequences*. This external event, or "straw," is often a consequence that either helps the individual realize there is a problem ("I have a problem") or causes someone else to give them an ultimatum ("Get help or else!").

The range and intensity of consequences vary, but I usually ask clients to look at the following areas:

• Physical (sexually transmitted illnesses, victim of assault)
• Relationship (break-ups, serial relationships, loss of trust)
• Legal (arrest for public sex, pornography)
• Financial (money spent on prostitutes, loss of job)
• Other (not listed above, but having an impact on your life)

The key is to recognize the consequences of your behavior within your own life and the lives of others. When you hear other people's "war stories," you're hearing examples of how bad things became as a result of their acting out. It's important not to glamorize how bad things became, but to honestly recognize the impact of your behavior.

ASSIGNMENT: Consequences of Acting Out

• Identify 3-4 consequences of your sexual acting-out. Describe any physical, relationship, health, legal, financial or other consequences of your behavior on your life.

Payoffs: What's the goal?

All behavior is goal-focused. When we act out, something within us believes that the behavior will help us reach a goal. Unfortunately, some of our goals might be in conflict with one another. Other times, we may not know what our goal is. Sometimes, the payoff is only temporary. It is my opinion that every acting-out behavior is an attempt to get some payoff, even if it's temporary. The key to long-term sexual health is to be honest about your goals and find healthy ways to achieve them. For example, alcohol is often considered "liquid courage." If the reason someone uses alcohol is to gain courage, it's necessary for the person to develop self-confidence. Sometimes, sex is about feeling connected with another person. In this case, finding healthy ways of being connected (see Intimacy, page 172) is an important task. Interrupting the acting-out cycle requires awareness of the payoffs for the sexual behavior and every other type of acting out. This essentially answers the question, "Why have (or *not*) have sex? What's my goal in doing this behavior?" While the reasons for engaging in sexual behavior may vary, it's important for you to uncover some of the reasons and payoffs that are important to you. Remember, all behavior is goal-focused. Your sexual behavior is seeking some type of payoff.

Although payoffs are always present, awareness of these payoffs varies. Some payoffs are direct ("I'm horny"). Some of these payoffs are more subtle hopes that something will happen ("If an attractive person says 'yes,' I'll be okay"). In some circumstances, the reasons for sexual behavior are clinical issues (depression, for example) or other factors you need to address (such as poor body image). This is much more difficult than you might think. To put this in perspective: A researcher identified 237 reasons, separated into 13 categories, why a person might have sex.[14]

Reasons for Having Sex

As you review your sexual behavior, consider the following reasons for having sex:

Physical

- Stress Reduction: "I am at work and this gives me a distraction."
- Pleasure: "Sex is fun." "Having an orgasm is fun."
- Physical Desirability: "I want that person." "That person wants me."
- Experience-seeking. "I'm bored and don't have anything to do."

Goal attainment

- Resources: "I'll get money/drugs."
- Social Status: "My reputation will get better."
- Revenge: "I'll make that other person mad."
- Utilitarian: "I'll get a raise/promotion."

Emotional

- Love and Commitment: "I love you." "I'm scared of my partner."
- Expression of Feelings: "I'm sorry." "I'm mad at my partner."

Insecurity

- Self-esteem Boost: "Someone wants me." "I feel better."
- Duty/Pressure: "My partner won't do what I want."
- Mate-guarding: "I'll do what you want (even though I don't want to) so you won't leave me."

Levels of Payoff

Expanding the discussion on payoffs, I think about three different levels of payoffs: primary, secondary, and indirect. I'll start with the first two types. *Primary* payoffs roughly (but not always) parallel biological needs. *Secondary* payoffs are social/interactive outcomes of the behavior. Consider the following example:

It's been a long, hard day at work. I'm stressed out and think I've earned a break. I go online and start chatting with someone who wants to hook up. I have great sex, feel great, and get even more of a sense of relief from the stress. Through this experience, I temporarily feel connected to another person; however, I also feel shameful and guilty, which reinforces the reason I needed to work so hard in the first place (to get a sense of affirmation), which leads to more stress.

Primary payoffs in this example may include:

- Great sex
- Being touched
- Stress reduction

Secondary payoffs in this example may include:

- Sense of connection/intimacy
- Finding things online that I can't find in person
- Sense of affirmation
- Addressing boredom with something to do
- Getting to be someone I'm not in real life
- Not being alone for an evening

The third type of payoffs, *indirect payoffs*, are very subtle and more difficult to identify. They may or may not be present all the time. Sometimes, a negative consequence is actually what we're seeking. Consider the following:

Some people will actually sabotage their publically stated goals out of a fear of success. These individuals usually have a high level of shame, such that their only sense of accomplishment comes from successfully getting in the way of their own progress.

Indirect payoffs in this case may include:

- Reaffirming the negative feelings I have about myself
- Being responsible for the negative feelings I have about myself (i.e., self-sabotage)

An example of an indirect payoff in the first example might be, "I can justify how much I work in order to make up for the negative feelings I have about my sexual behavior."

Notice that what a payoff is depends on the person. While some payoffs may appear similar across individuals, each person has their own unique experience of payoffs. By identifying which reasons for sexual behavior are relevant for you, you provide yourself with an opportunity to reflect on the thoughts and assumptions underlying that behavior. For example, if you identify the desire to increase self-esteem as a reason for your sexual behavior, you learn that examining the thoughts and feelings behind your low esteem will be an important task.

ASSIGNMENT: Payoffs

Identify Payoffs

- Identify the payoffs for your most recent acting-out encounter. Pay attention to all three types of payoffs: primary, secondary, and indirect. Pick another acting-out encounter and repeat.

- Analyze the sexual history and timeline for the possible payoffs listed above.

- Review this list of payoffs with your support network. Do they agree with your assessment? Disagree? Why? Which payoffs do they suggest might be particularly problematic?

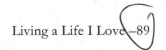

Plans for Coping

- List the top three payoffs you identified. Note one or two plans to start coping with each of these payoffs. Return to the list and update it as necessary. Review your Immediate Short-Term Prevention Plan and update your plan as necessary.

Putting It All Together—Behavioral Analysis

Sex is hardly ever just about sex. (Shirley MacLaine)

Clients often report that they don't know why they do what they do. To a large degree, I believe them. Returning to one of my favorite metaphors, I often challenge clients by asking them to list the steps necessary to drive a car. As they do, I playfully trip them up by asking questions about this or that. What they come to realize is that driving a car is a remarkably complex task; it calls for multiple thought processes requiring you to pay attention to details. As noted in *Part One* (during the initial discussion of compulsivity), the term for this is *automaticity*, meaning the ability to complete complex behaviors without active cognitive thinking (like a habit). Much of the ritual in sexual compulsivity is automatic. People fall into a trance and simply don't know why they're doing what they're doing. A helpful tool in identifying thinking errors, feeling triggers and high-risk situations is the completion of a behavioral analysis.

The *behavioral analysis* is a step-by-step examination of what happens during an acting-out experience. The goal is to help you identify additional relevant issues, so you should examine all details, no matter how small you think they are. The behavioral analysis is a way to slow down and uncover the contributing factors. In the process of completing the analysis, you'll identify a number of places to intervene and interrupt the cycle:

- Recognize and then contradict thinking errors. Challenging negative thinking by correcting thoughts or using affirmations (if you are familiar with the 12-step tradition) is a start.

- Address your feelings. Identifying ways you can connect with others in a healthy way, for example, allows you to help address feelings of loneliness. If you experience significant long-lasting sadness and depression, medications and/or therapy might be helpful.

- Recognize high-risk situations. Too much free time can make you vulnerable to a high-risk situation. Finding ways to engage in healthy fun is one way to intervene in the cycle.

In each of the behavioral analyses I conduct in my practice, I talk about an escalating pattern of behaviors that sets the stage for the next trip through the cycle. I call these trips *micro-cycles*, because a person may experience multiple trips through the cycle within a given time period. The example analysis below highlights multiple ways a person might fail to cope with setups throughout a given time period. The key is to identify ways to interrupt any and all parts of the cycle, and the behavioral analysis helps us do this.

Example Behavioral Analysis

–-START HERE-– **WHAT HAP-PENED?** Include payoffs and/or consequences	**THOUGHTS** What was I thinking? What reason did I use?	**FEELINGS** What was I feeling?	**HIGH-RISK SITUATIONS** When, where, who, what made it likely this would happen?
I spent 3 hours looking at porn and masturbating	I did it again	Shame Hopelessness	Isolation, avoided my support network, late night, no support
I went to a porn site	Just visiting one site is ok, I won't stay here long, there are only a couple of pics	Justified, entitled	No monitoring, no supervision
started surfing with no purpose	I deserve a little down time	Bored	Computer access
I was checking my email	I have to see what else needs to be done on the project	Lonely, tired, sad	Working too late, using work to give me an excuse to use the Internet
I was heading to bed	Can't talk to anyone, I'm alone, no one cares	Sad, depressed, lonely, tired.	Isolation, tired Overworked
I had a fight	I can't do anything right. My partner doesn't understand, It's my fault	Fear, sadness, shame, guilt.	Seeing someone angry, conflict, lack of assertive skills

Obviously, no one likes to relapse. It often feels like a failure. Rather than emphasizing the failure, the process of change takes a relapse and learns from it. The behavioral analysis is a tool to help you learn from any relapse. When you examine the conditions that occurred in a relapse, you might uncover an unknown issue, or you might recognize that an issue you were avoiding is more important than you previously believed. Similarly, you might recognize that you need to develop a different plan for an issue you thought you had already addressed. I find a behavioral analysis to be one of the best tools in the healing process.

ASSIGNMENT: Detailed Behavioral Analysis

Complete a behavioral analysis of a recent sexual acting-out experience using the information you learned through the assignments pertaining to the acting-out cycle. Use the example above as a model of how to format your analysis. Which thinking errors, feeling triggers, high-risk situations and payoffs/consequences can you identify? Update your current lists, as appropriate.

As noted in the "Weekly Behavioral Analysis" assignment, it may be helpful to work backwards as you complete the analysis. Start with the acting-out incident. Answer the question, "What happened?" Then ask, "What happened right before that?" and so on. While you work backwards, stay focused on what happened. It's like tracing the last domino's fall back to the first domino. Once you have a good start at what happened, complete the other columns by adding the corresponding thinking errors/thoughts, feeling triggers and high-risk settings. Try to include something in each column, but remember that if you can't think of something, you can always come back to add more later. At the end of the process, summarize the behavioral analysis. Again, every item in your analysis is a potential place to update your Immediate Short-Term Prevention Plan as needed.

Prioritization of Issues

We can never obtain peace in the outer world until we make peace with ourselves. (Dalai Lama)

Sexual behavior doesn't happen out of the blue. It occurs within a context, and it's important to understand that context. This section is designed to help you gather information from the assignments in Stage 1, including your sex history, sexual behavior timeline, acting-out cycle, weekly logs, and behavioral analyses. In reviewing these assignments, you should get an initial sense of the major issues contributing to the sexual behaviors in your life. This process of problem identification can feel overwhelming—this is a normal feeling. What happens next is the process of prioritizing the issues and setting up a plan to address the issues you identified.

This process is known as *triage*—a review and ranking of the issues, prioritization and development of treatment plans for addressing the most important issues first. In other words, first thing's first. Only you, in consultation with your support network, can prioritize the treatment topics to reflect *your* issues. It may not be wise, for example, for you to address your sexual compulsivity behaviors at this time if other issues are more critical. On the other hand, if your sexual behavior contributes directly to these other concerns, it may be very important to address them early on.

ASSIGNMENT: Prioritizing Your Issues

In this assignment, you'll simply prioritize the treatment topics covered in *Stage 2*. These topics are presented in the table below and, as you'll see, they reflect the ten components of the adapted sexual health model introduced previously. I took the liberty of grouping the material to identify workable sized assignments. As before, this is what makes sense to me. Feel free to adapt. Although the list is fairly thorough, I have no doubt you'll be able to add your own issues to the list. If something else is relevant in your life, please add it to the list. As you prioritize—and later, work through—the topics, I recommend you consider each topic, even if it doesn't seem to apply at first glance. As you review the topics, ask yourself if you can address the issue(s) on your own, or if you'll need professional help. As you read the list, score each topic area on a four-point priority scale as follows:

0 = not a concern ("I was never abused as an adult or child.")

1 = minimal concern ("I feel anxious only at certain times" or "At this time, I don't think it's connected to my behaviors.")

2 = significant concern ("My sex life is bad" or "I don't know what I want.")

3 = vital concern ("I'm so depressed I can't seem to do anything" or "My relationship is in danger of ending because of my behaviors.")

Priority (0-1-2-3)	Top 3 Rank	Topic
		ONE: TALKING ABOUT SEX 96 ASSIGNMENT: Assertive Communication 99 (Recommended for everyone)

		TWO: CULTURE, IDENTITY AND SEXUAL HEALTH 100
		Cultural Values and Assumptions 100
		    ASSIGNMENT: Your Cultural Values and Assumptions 101
		    ASSIGNMENT: Evaluating the Messages 104
		    ASSIGNMENT: Cross-Cultural Experience 105

		Feelings of Shame and Guilt 105 ASSIGNMENT: Shaming Messages 106

		Sexual Identity and Sexual Orientation 107
		  Four Components of Sexual Identity 107
		    ASSIGNMENT: Where You Fit on the Continuum 109
		  Stages of Identity Development 110
		  Men Who Have Sex with Men: Not All Gay-Sex is Gay 111
		  Bisexuality 112
		  Barriers to a Healthy Sexual Identity 112
		    ASSIGNMENT: Sexual Identity 113

Priority (0-1-2-3)	Top 3 Rank	Topic

Priority (0-1-2-3)	Top 3 Rank	Topic

Priority (0-1-2-3)	Top 3 Rank	Topic
		Four Deadly Horsemen in Relationships 185
		Relationship Satisfaction 186
		ASSIGNMENT: Relationship Satisfaction 186
		ASSIGNMENT: Identifying Relationship Strengths and Weaknesses 187
		Healing from Past Relationships 189
		ASSIGNMENT: Healing from Past Relationships 190
		ASSIGNMENT: Saying goodbye to a former relationship 191
		Forgiveness in Relationships 191
		Building the Sexual Relationship 191
		ASSIGNMENT: Healthy Sexual Interchange 193
		Types of Relationships 194
		ASSIGNMENT: Relationship Type and Jealousy 196
		Finding a Relationship Therapist 197
		Guidelines for Relationship Therapy 197
		Full Disclosure to Partners 198
		ASSIGNMENT: Preparing for Disclosure 200
		ASSIGNMENT: Full Disclosure 203
		TEN: SPIRITUALITY, VALUES AND SEXUAL HEALTH 204
		Spirituality and Religion 204
		Barriers to Spirituality 205
		Others as a reflection of your values 207
		ASSIGNMENT: Your Spirituality and Values 208
		Values to start the conversation 208
		ASSIGNMENT: Your Top Values 211
		Choose Your Life 213

To help you focus your next work, after you have scored the topics, go back and rank the top 3 areas that hold the most importance. Start with those three areas. After you finish them, identify three more, and so on. This list will serve as a tentative plan to help pinpoint the topics you should address first in your treatment process.

Stage 2: Primary Treatment

Stage 2 is where the majority of the growth will occur. The key purpose of this stage is to address the major issues you identified and prioritized in Stage 1. The material that follows is organized into sections corresponding to the ten components of the sexual health model. This will make it easier for you to build your own Personal Definition of Sexual Health in Stage 3. Complete the sections in the order that makes the most sense for your healing. Keep in mind that the workbook is designed to cover a great breadth of topics, allowing the user to see each topic within the larger context of interconnectivity. Thus, the information presented within each section is an introduction of sorts, designed to help you clarify the degree to which the topic may need additional follow-up. Work with your support network as necessary to obtain more information and support. As a reminder, the ten components of sexual health are:

Talking About Sex

Culture, Identity and Sexual Health

Sexual Functioning—Anatomy and Beyond

Sexual Health Care and Safer-Sex Issues

Barriers to Sexual Health—Beyond Functioning

Body Image

Masturbation, Fantasy and Sexually Explicit Material

Positive Sexuality

Intimacy and Relationships

Spirituality, Values and Sexual Health

ONE: Talking About Sex

As you move through this stage of the workbook, one of my goals is to help you talk about the most important issues in your life. In my opinion, the journey toward sexual health will only occur when you identify and talk about what's most important in your life. Sometimes the fear of an issue leads to silence and shame. Sometimes, a person will discover what he or she wants in conversations with others. For many individuals, we don't know how to ask to get our needs met.

Assertive Communication

Assertive communication is the process of communicating your needs, wants, desires and likes in a format that helps you get what you want. Assertive communication is clear and honest; it's respectful toward the self and others. This style of communication represents the healthy middle ground between passive and aggressive styles. An example of unhealthy communication is the response to the question, "Where do you want to eat" Passive communication will let the person always choose. Aggressive communication might be pushing your choice onto others. And passive-aggressive communication would be letting the other "guess" what you want, and getting angry if you don't get your way. While assertive communication doesn't guarantee an outcome, it's more likely to result in your getting your needs met.

Assertive communication is relevant not only to expressing thoughts and feelings, but also to expressing yourself sexually. It's important to learn the skills necessary to communicate your sexual likes and needs with your partner(s). Learning assertive communication is a challenging task, and there are many ways to do it. At first, this style of communication may feel artificial. I encourage you to view it as a template and helpful tool. The five statements below are helpful in structuring assertive communication. These statements reflect basic elements that convey the topic of concern and the request. Below each statement is an explanation.

Statement #1

I am committed to_____(write a few words on why you are doing this).

> Think about the times you've received helpful feedback. Typically, you trusted or knew that these people were on your side. Reminding your listener of your goal helps them understand that the assertive communication is focused on growth: "I'm committed to a loving relationship."

Statement #2

I think/I feel_____(state your thought or feeling).

> This is about being self-aware, about asking "What's going on inside?" It may be a thought, feeling or memory triggered by the current moment. Your ability to answer this question is improved by mindfulness exercises (page 38).

Statement #3

Because_____(explain what triggered the thought or feeling).

> This should be a simple explanation of the moment. It should be short and sweet and explicitly connected to the moment. If it takes more than one breath to say it—it's too long.

Statement #4

I need/want/would like____(express the request).

> This is a request, and the key is to be clear, specific and measurable. Again, if it takes more than one breath—it's too long. Bear in mind the distinctions between *needs*, *wants* and *likes*. Often, language confuses the importance of something. Someone says, "I need a cell phone," but in reality, they merely want or would like a cell phone. A *need* is a basic requirement for existence: "I need food," or "I need respect," or "I need you to stop touching me."

Statement #5

I commit to____(identify how you'll help the person to be successful).

> This statement declares how you'll help the other person be successful (something you'll do to support the goal). This might include such statements as, "I'll tell you when I want to be touched," or "I'll tell you what I like instead of making you guess." Helping the person to be successful reconnects you with Statement #1. This template builds the relationship.

Each statement has its own purpose for developing a stronger relationship and eventually helping you get your needs met. There are, however, a few pitfalls to avoid when communicating. First, it's important to avoid the passive approach toward communication. A classic sign of danger is use of the phrase, "Would you like to…?" instead of "I would like to." or "I expect…" Other unhelpful forms of communication are "we" statements; use "I" statements instead. Equally important is avoiding aggressive communication, including the manner of communication (e.g., yelling) or use of "you" statements, which are often more aggressive and accusatory. "You should…" is better replaced with "I want" or "I need."

Assertively expressing your requests is a significant component of sexual health. Setting boundaries and limits can have major impacts on relationships. Assertiveness is important in expressing feelings and sexual desires. I have provided only a brief introduction to the concept here. If the topic is especially relevant to you, however, or if you have significant struggles with assertive communication, please follow up with your support network.

ASSIGNMENT: Assertive Communication

Examine your sexual history and answer the following questions.

- How is the lack of assertiveness related to your behaviors?

- Identify times when you have engaged in passive, aggressive or passive/aggressive behaviors.

- How could you change these encounters into assertive communication?

- What are 2-3 barriers to assertive communication in your life?

- What are your plans to improve your assertive communication skills?

TWO: Culture, Identity and Sexual Health

All sexual values are cultural values. Given the role of culture, I recommend this topic for everyone simply to help you start thinking about how you think about sexual health. You are a product of the multiple cultures to which you belong (such as racial, ethnic, religious, or age), and these cultures are in a constant tug-of-war, shaping your thoughts, beliefs, values, behaviors, wants and desires. This includes your sexual values and behaviors. In this section, you'll look at a variety of cultures as they shape your life. I use a model of cultural identity that suggests we are each a multi-cultural identity.[15] Culture is where we learn what's right and wrong. It's also where we learn the difference between shame and guilt. Finally, our identity is defined through culture. The discussion of sexual identity touches on key questions regarding the cultural identity.

Cultural Values and Assumptions

At one point in the Broadway musical, *Wicked*, the heroine enters Oz, where the citizens wear green-colored glasses. Over time, the citizens have forgotten they are wearing green glasses and have simply concluded that everything is, in fact, green. This is why Oz appears to be an "Emerald City." In a similar way, our thinking patterns color our view of life. These patterns (or assumptions) are so pervasive that we don't always realize they're present. Sometimes the assumptions have a limited impact in our lives; other times, these thinking patterns are so unhealthy they result in painful consequences. In many ways, the cultures we belong to are the lenses through which we look at the world. Our awareness of these lenses has disappeared simply because we see through them versus seeing them. Moving toward sexual health requires moving toward understanding the cultural lenses we use to make sense of the world.

Everything we know is taught to us through our cultures. Much of what we see as sexually arousing is defined by the cultures to which we belong, such as family, race, gender, religion, sexual identity or nationality. These cultures shape sexual behaviors, values and identity. Improving your sexual health requires that you increase your awareness of your cultural values. It's important for you to understand all of the cultures to which you belong and how they influence your thoughts, beliefs and expectations.

Sometimes, the various cultures to which we belong may conflict with one another. For example, in Latino culture, *machismo* (loosely understood as hyper-masculinity) is a typical male stereotype, and it's considered wrong for a man to show any weakness or feminine characteristics. If a man who belongs to the Latino culture wants to acknowledge that he is attracted to other men, then the two cultures are in conflict. Resolving such conflicts is crucial to increasing sexual health. Some people resolve such conflicts by rejecting parts of their heritage; others work toward changing the culture they came from. The key is for you to resolve—within your overall identity and in a way that makes sense for you—the conflict between the cultures to which you belong.

ASSIGNMENT: Your Cultural Values and Assumptions

Identify two sexual beliefs you have learned from each type of culture described below.

Racial Culture. Racial Culture is often used synonymously with skin color. (This usage is limiting, but I use it here for a general discussion.) It's important to see how your thoughts are shaped by assumptions about race.

Please complete the following sentences:

I belong to the_____ racial culture. Two sexual beliefs I learned from this culture are:

Ethnic/Nationality Culture. For our purposes, I use this term to describe national origin. Are you from Poland, Indonesia, or Senegal? Some ethnic cultures cross over national boundaries and many countries have multiple ethnic groups.

Please complete the following sentences:

I belong to the_____ ethnic/nationality culture. Two sexual beliefs I learned from this culture are:

Religious Culture. This refers to shared beliefs regarding God and spirituality. In the United States, these beliefs might include (among others) Judeo-Christian, Islamic or Atheistic beliefs, but even within each religious tradition are multiple sub-cultures that shape sexual values.

Please complete the following sentences:

I belong to the_____ religious/spirituality culture. Two sexual beliefs I learned from this culture are:

<u>Age Culture</u>. The era in which we grew up and the generation to which we belong influence our sexual views. Someone who grew up in the 1930's views sexuality differently from someone who grew up in the 1970's or the 2010's. This results in different values that shape sexuality.

Please complete the following sentences:

I belong to the_____ age culture. Two sexual beliefs I learned from this culture are:

<u>Sexual Identity Culture</u>. We'll look at sexual identity in greater detail a bit further into this section; for now, let's say sexual identity includes our gender (male/female/transgender) and sexual orientation (gay/straight/bi). There are numerous values regarding sexual identity that shape our understanding of sexuality.

Please complete the following sentences:

I belong to the _____ gender culture. Two sexual beliefs I learned from this culture are:

I identify as part of the _____(gay/bi/straight) culture. Two sexual beliefs I learned from this culture are:

<u>Socioeconomic Status Culture</u>. Socioeconomic status means your level of wealth and standard of living. Your socioeconomic status shapes your view of sexuality. (For example, sharing a bed with a parent takes on a new meaning if you have a one-room house.)

Please complete the following sentences:

I belong to the_____(wealthy, middle-class, poor) socioeconomic status culture. Two sexual beliefs I learned from this culture are:

Disability Status Culture. Disability refers to mental, physical, or emotional disabilities. Some may occur at birth, others may be the result of an accident or illness. There are sexual beliefs based on disability.

Please complete the following sentences:

I belong to the _____(disabled/non-disabled) culture. Two sexual beliefs I learned from this culture are:

Geographic Status Culture. Geographic status can be national or regional. Within the United States, for example, there are differences in sexual values based on region—northern, southern, eastern, and western.

Please complete the following sentences:

I belong to the_____ geographic status culture. Two sexual beliefs I learned from this culture are:

Online/Cyber Culture. This refers to the thoughts you have about online sexual behaviors. The concept of an online culture is relatively new; even so, it has a pattern of interacting that can be discerned. Understanding the expectations you have about how you behave online is important.

Please complete the following sentences:

I belong to the_____ (describe your online/cyber identification) culture. Two sexual beliefs I learned from this culture are:

ASSIGNMENT: Evaluating the Messages

The above cultures shape your understanding of who you are as a person and, in particular, as a sexual being. Some of these messages are helpful; others may be unhelpful. You need to determine which is which. It's also important to consider the cultural messages that may be related to your sexual behavior.

- Which cultural messages are unhelpful to you?

- Which cultural messages are helpful to you?

- Each of us is a product of the many cultures to which we belong. What values from different cultures you belong to are in conflict? How do you resolve such conflicts?

Review your answers. Now think about what you've learned about yourself or others based on this assignment. How have these beliefs shaped your sexual behavior? Share this with your support network. Be sure to challenge some of the assumptions you listed.

ASSIGNMENT: Cross-Cultural Experience

From the list of cultures provided above, pick one to which you don't belong. Complete an activity where you experience that culture. For example, a straight, white male might attend a lecture during Black History Month, or participate in a Gay Pride Event. Many religious denominations offer introductory courses, providing an opportunity to learn about an alternate tradition. In learning about other cultures, you become more able to uncover the assumptions of your own.

Feelings of Shame and Guilt

By definition, culture is where we learn shame and guilt. It's important to understand the difference between these two concepts. Many people struggle with shaming messages about sexuality. As I highlight the basic differences between shame and guilt, consider how each relates to your sexual behavior.

Shame is a feeling based on the thought that as a person, you are bad, worthless, unforgiveable, and/or defective. Shame is person-focused ("I am a bad person"). The associated thought is that everyone who knows you rejects you. There's a belief that nothing can fix your shame, you'll never get better, and/or you can't find redemption. Other feelings associated with shame include despair, hopelessness, loneliness, embarrassment and humiliation. When people have feelings of shame, their behaviors often hurt both themselves and others. Shame-based behaviors can include demonstrating a lack of respect for oneself and others, justification for abuse toward oneself and others, and lack of empathy for others. Shame often exists within a cognitive framework of perfectionism ("I can't make a mistake," "It has to be perfect," or "All sexual material is bad"). People who feel shame often focus on covering-up, hiding and displaying a false front to mask their intense feelings. Because of shame, people will engage in behaviors to compensate in the hope that others will like them. People who feel shame lose a sense of boundaries in an attempt to cope. Some writers distinguish between healthy and toxic shame.[16] I believe that all shame is unhealthy, and that a person needs to distinguish between shame and guilt.

Guilt is a feeling based on the thought that your behavior is wrong, bad, awful, terrible and/or hurtful. Guilt is the recognition that you have violated your ethical values and morality. Guilt is act-focused ("I feel guilty when I have done something wrong"). When you feel guilty about something you have done, you don't have to feel shame. Because guilt is about your behavior, you can usually do something about it. You can apologize, forgive, learn, change, develop and/or grow in response to guilt. You can set boundaries, repair the damage and rebuild relationships. Guilt is normal, appropriate and even healthy. Guilt is unhealthy when you feel an inappropriate amount of it, or when you feel guilty although you haven't done anything wrong. If these feelings are present, you're probably stuck in *shame*. I encourage my clients to allow themselves to experience guilt when the feeling is appropriate. In the context of sexual health, some behaviors are wrong, and guilt is the recognition of that wrong-doing (e.g., "I lied about what I did").

Both shame and guilt are learned from the same sources, including family of origin, religion, school, friends, government, and society. Learning the concept of responsibility is also a cultural process. The goal for individuals is to learn from their mistakes. In our society, shame is taught more often than responsibility. The phrase, "Shame on you," should be changed to "Guilt on you."

It's important to examine cultural sources of shame, such as racism, sexism and heterosexism. Each of these forms of prejudice make a negative judgment on an entire group. From these cultural sources of shame, individuals learn shame directly (overt) and indirectly (covert). Individuals are taught that being different is wrong. Shame is taught overtly when children are told they are bad, they're put down as worthless, or they're made fun of and teased cruelly. People who violate the boundaries of others in emotional, psychological, physical and sexual ways teach shame. Covert shaming (such as negative comments made about gay people in news media) can be difficult to recognize. This shaming is based in poor education, poor modeling and unsupportive relationships.

ASSIGNMENT: Shaming Messages

One assignment I sometimes give clients who are stuck in shame is to list 100, or even 500, shaming messages they tell themselves. Clients will often resist, but once they start they are amazed at how easy it's to identify these messages. The second part of the assignment is to challenge the underlying thoughts that contribute to the shaming messages. (Hint: Look for the "should" in your thinking.) Ask yourself the following questions:

- List 100 shameful messages you experience(d) now or growing up.

- Who provided these messages?

- How do these messages influence you today?

- If you are part of a minority group (e.g. you're a woman, a person of color, a gay person), what shaming messages have you heard ?

- Now, repeat the same questions substituting the word "guilt" for the word "shame."

Sexual Identity and Sexual Orientation

In the realm of sexuality, identity is a place individuals use to explore, connect, and understand their fear and confusion about sexual identity. Before I get to sexual orientation, I first want to discuss *sexual identity* in the broad sense.

Identity is the statement: "This is who I am." In the process of clarifying their identity, individuals go through a process of sorting through life events and responding "like me/not like me." In simple terms, identity development is the attempt to define and understand who we are. It's an interactive process that every person goes through—often unconsciously—in order to understand his/her sexual self. Obviously, this process also occurs in the area of sexual orientation. The next section discusses the process of understanding sexual identity and sexual orientation, and the related tasks that need to be addressed. People use the two terms interchangeably, but they are actually different. All messages of sexual identity are culturally informed. It's important to review how your sexual identity relates to your sexual health.

Four Components of Sexual Identity

Sexual identity is complex. Below are four components of sexual identity.[17] Each component plays a role in your sexual identity.

<u>Natal Sex</u>. This refers to your biological makeup at birth. Often this refers to your sexual genitalia or your DNA makeup. Women have X-X chromosomes, while men have X-Y chromosomes. This often this correlates to vaginal or penile genitalia. Most of the time, identifying a person's genital or natal sex is as simple as observing the baby when it's born. ("It's a boy!" or "It's a girl!")

<u>Gender Identity</u>. Gender identity is the gender you feel you are. Most often this matches one's natal sex. "I have the genitalia of a female, and I feel female." When natal sex does not match gender identity (i.e., it isn't congruent), the situation falls under the broad term transgender. People who are transgender believe they are the opposite sex from their physical body. In such a situation, people may say they feel trapped in the wrong body. A biological male believes he is female, or a biological female believes she is male. Identifying as transgender is not a psychosis or neurosis. If you believe that you're transgender, please seek help from a trained professional following established protocols.[18] It's a complex topic beyond the scope of this workbook.

<u>Social Sex Roles</u>. Easy to understand but often misunderstood, social sex roles refer to culturally defined behaviors based on one's gender. Typically, social sex roles are divided into masculine roles and feminine roles, but these roles may change over time, hence the potential for confusion. Social sex roles reflect what a man is "supposed to be like" or what a woman is "supposed to be like." Often, social sex roles are confused with sexual identity. For example, an effeminate male labeled as gay. Common thoughts, such as "All guys do it" or "Women aren't sexual," are thinking errors related to social sex roles. These are examples of how culture shapes our social sex roles.

<u>Sexual Orientation</u>. This is most often described as a same-sex or heterosexual attraction. Although people often describe their sexual orientation in simple ways ("I'm a gay man," "I'm a lesbian woman," or "I'm a straight female"), this concept is not necessarily clear-cut. The following section explores sexual orientation in more detail.

Sexual Orientation Explored

In the pre-Internet days, if a person wanted to gain information on sexual orientation, the few places to look were typically a dictionary or an encyclopedia article. The fear of asking a librarian for help was too much for many. Now, the Internet makes such information easily available. Much research has gone into understanding the causes of sexual orientation. Generally, the conclusion is that science just doesn't know.

No single scientific theory about what determines sexual orientation has been suitably substantiated. Studies to associate sexual orientation with genetic, hormonal, and environmental factors have so far been inconclusive. According to the Sex Information and Educational

Council of the United States, "Sexual orientation is no longer considered to be one's conscious individual preference or choice, but is instead thought to be formed by a complicated network of social, cultural, biological, economic, and political factors."[19]

There are a number of myths regarding the cause of same-sex attraction. The research makes it clear that a history of sexual abuse does not cause a same-sex attraction. Same-sex orientation is not a psychopathology. In 1973, based on research showing no greater evidence of mental illness among individuals with same-sex attractions versus those with an opposite-sex attraction, the American Psychiatric Association removed *homosexuality* from its list of mental health disorders.

An individual's sexual orientation appears to be stable over time. What might change, however, is one's acceptance of, or expression of, one's sexual orientation. All major health associations in the United States, including the American Psychiatric Association, the American Medical Association and the American Psychological Association, consider it unethical to attempt to change one's sexual orientation (known as the ex-gay movement or reparative therapy).

The Kinsey Continuum

The living world is a continuum in each and every one of its aspects. (Alfred Kinsey)

In 1948, Alfred Kinsey, Wardell Pomeroy and Clyde Martin developed the Heterosexual-Homosexual Rating Scale, or the Kinsey scale,[20] "in order to account for research findings that showed people did not fit into neat and exclusive heterosexual or homosexual categories."[21] This was an early attempt to understand sexual orientation and sought to rate a person's genital sexual behaviors on a scale ranging from exclusively heterosexual to exclusively homosexual. Since then, adaptations of the continuum include fantasy content and emotional relationships. I have inserted an adapted version is below.

Adapted Kinsey Continuum

0	1	2	3	4	5	6
exclusively						*exclusively*
heterosexual						*homosexual*

ASSIGNMENT: Where You Fit on the Continuum

For each of the following, determine where you fall on the continuum above:

• <u>Genital attraction</u>. With whom do you have the most fulfilling sexual contact?

- <u>Emotional attraction</u>. Who are your closest friends? Whom do you feel closest to?

- <u>Fantasy</u>. What gender are the people in your fantasies?

- Describe how you feel about your responses and share this with your support network.

Stages of Identity Development

Many people who have a same-sex identity experience a process of moving toward a place of acceptance. This is called a *coming-out process*. Consider how your sexual behavior might be related to this process. Vivian Cass[22] presents one model of identity development that might be helpful in understanding a same-sex sexual identity. She hypothesizes six stages:

<u>1) Identity Confusion</u>. Heterosexual identity is called into question with the increasing awareness of feelings of intimate and physical attraction toward others of the same sex. The individual starts asking the question, "Could I be homosexual?" Gay and lesbian information or awareness becomes personally relevant, and the heterosexual assumption begins to be undermined. The person might actually start seeking out gay-lesbian content and contacts. At this stage, confusion is great and denial and avoidance are usually the primary coping strategies.

<u>2) Identity Comparison</u>. The individual begins accepting the possibility that homosexual feelings are a part of the self. The realization, "I might be homosexual," crosses his/her mind. Perhaps due to shame and guilt, the individual expresses a same-sex identity only online. The idea, "I may be bisexual" (which permits the potential for heterosexuality), can also be a manifestation of this stage. At this level, the belief, "This is a 'phase' I'm going through," may surface. These strategies reduce the incongruence between same-sex attractions and a view of the

self as heterosexual. The task at this stage of identity comparison, according to Cass, is to deal with social alienation as the individual becomes aware of his/her difference from larger society.

3) Identity Tolerance. This is marked by statements such as, "I only look at gay stuff online, but I don't do anything with other people." This declaration results in a sense of clarity for the individual, but also results in a sense of separation from others, because the individual recognizes s/he is different. For an individual who experiences a heightened need for peer approval and acceptance, this can be a difficult period. During this period, the individual is likely to create a well-developed facade to mask and hide this part of the self. An individual will often struggle with a constant need to hide his/her sexual orientation. Relationships are hurt, at least in the mind of the individual, because of this secret identity. Positive experiences are crucial to developing a degree of self-acceptance during this period. Contacting other gay, lesbian and/or bisexual people becomes a more pressing issue to alleviate the sense of isolation and alienation. It also provides the individual with the experience of accepting his/her whole being and not just a mask.

4) Identity Acceptance. Contact with other gay men and lesbian women increases. Finding other gay and lesbian people is important. Although this was difficult for older generations, younger generations are often easily able to find support groups. Individuals fortunate enough to have access to support groups or social events often experience a heightened sense of identity and self-acceptance. The individual moves away from hiding his/her identity to sharing it with the people in his/her life. The person can begin to address questions of "Who am I?" and "How do I fit in?"

5) Identity Pride. There is strong identification with the gay subculture and devaluation of heterosexuality culture and many of its institutions.

6) Identity Synthesis. The individual moves from a "them and us" mentality into a realization and acceptance of the similarities between the heterosexual and homosexual worlds. Exclusion gives way to less rigid, polarizing views and more inclusive and cooperative behavior.

Men Who Have Sex with Men: Not All Gay-Sex is Gay

Not all men who have sex with men will identify as being gay. In many cases, I use the phrase *men who have sex with men* to focus on the behavior versus a label. Some of these men don't identify as gay because they are in the closet and/or in denial about their sexual orientation, attempting to minimize, avoid or deny their same-sex attractions. In some cases, men who have sex with men are truly not gay. For these men, having sex with another man results in minimal guilt ("I didn't have sex with another woman") or supports the flattering notion that they can find sexual partners easily. In some situations (prison, military or religious settings), the only available sexual partner is someone of the same gender (a.k.a., situational homosexuality). For these men, if both genders were available, they would choose the opposite gender. As a final example, the behavior may have occurred under the influence of alcohol or other chemicals.

While all of these examples show men engaging in sexual behavior with people of the same sex, their behaviors don't add up to a gay identity. A great resource on this issue can be found at: www.straightguise.com. Here Dr. Joe Kort identifies twelve types of same-sex behavior that may not be the result of a gay identity. Unfortunately, there is limited similar research paralleling female same-sex behavior.

Bisexuality

In my opinion, *bisexuality* (attraction to both men and women) is a true sexual orientation.[23] What makes understanding bisexuality difficult is that it's sometimes used to describe a transitory term in the coming-out process. The multiple uses of the term leads to confusion in the larger community that can make it hard for a person to clarify a bisexual orientation. A bisexual person has to cope with stereotypes from the straight community in addition to those from the gay and lesbian communities. It's sometimes said that a bisexual has to come out twice—once in the straight community and a second time in the gay/lesbian community. As you examine your sexual identity, consider whether a bisexual orientation is related to your sexual behavior.

Often, people think bisexuality is only about sex, but there are many variables to consider. Regarding sexual orientation, there are three primary variables: genital behavior, physical attraction, and emotional attraction. For instance, think about whom you connect with emotionally. Think about whom you are attracted to intellectually or socially. You might realize, "I may be attracted to men on a physical level, but I connect better with women on an emotional level." In thinking about these variables, you get the idea that whether or not someone is bisexual will depend on how you ask the question.

Barriers to a Healthy Sexual Identity

Sometimes individuals with a same-sex identity encounter struggles that make it difficult to accept their sexual identity. Casual sexual behaviors may be attempts to cope with these struggles. Three related major barriers are homonegativity, heterosexism, and homophobia.

Homonegativity. The biggest example of a barrier is *homonegativity*. Recent research highlights how internalized negative thoughts about one's self may be the largest contributor to feelings of depression. This depression is often a contributing factor to suicidal thoughts and feelings, and increased unsafe sexual behaviors. Might avoiding negative feelings be associated with your behavior?

Heterosexism. Another major barrier to a same-sex identity is *heterosexism*, which is the bias that heterosexuality is superior to all other sexual orientations. Reparative therapy is one unethical application of heterosexism. Hate crimes are an extreme example of heterosexism, such as the infamous 1998 case of Matthew Shepard, who was attacked, brutally beaten and left to die because he had a same-sex identity. Such attacks hinder individuals' self-discovery processes, because a generalized fear leads to withdrawal and increased isolation. Other examples of barriers to a healthy sexual identity include structural barriers such as legal consequences (loss of custody of children), negative stereotypes, internalized shame and family rejection.

Homophobia. *Homophobia* is another recognized barrier to a healthy lifestyle. This is the irrational fear of homosexuality. This fear leads to avoidance of homosexuality, including the possibility of interacting with healthy role models. What has often been defined as homophobia might actually be better described as heterosexism and homonegativity.

ASSIGNMENT: Sexual Identity

- Review your sexual history. How much of your compulsive behavior was related to components of sexual identity?

- What positive, negative or shameful messages have you heard about same-sex and bisexual orientations? How have these affected your sexual health?

- What are 2-3 plans you can enact to affirm your sexual identity?

Review these questions with your support network to identify any additional issues and/or resources for affirmation of your identity.

THREE: Sexual Functioning—Anatomy and Beyond

Sexual health is not merely about the avoidance of unhealthy behaviors. It's also about the physical ability and skills—and level of comfort using these abilities and skills—necessary for sexual functioning. The goal of this section is for you to examine your level of sexual functioning; this will enable you to examine the relationship between your sexual behaviors and your sexual functioning, spot issues and develop plans for addressing those issues. Learning how to cope and function as a sexual being is an important part of sexual health.

What is Sexual Functioning

Sexual functioning is the ability to engage successfully in healthy sexual behaviors. Depending on the cause, there are three potential approaches for treating sexual functioning issues:

1) Treating physical health (i.e., getting a physical). A complete medical check-up is the starting point for intervention in cases of sexual dysfunction. Your doctor might not raise the issue, so be prepared to mention it yourself. This involves addressing any underlying physical health issues that may be present. For example, as we age, changing hormone levels can have an impact on sexual desire and functioning. This medical issue can often be addressed with medication. If there's a medical condition present, no amount of talk therapy will help, although it might be helpful in adjusting to the medical condition (or identifying alternative forms of sexual expression).

2) Treating symptoms (e.g., communication or relaxation). If the medical examination eliminates physical concerns, the source of the problem might be a mental health issue, such as anxiety or depression (page 125). Anxiety, for example, can be treated through relaxation techniques, medications and/or talk therapy.

3) Learning techniques/skills (e.g., performing Kegel exercises or sensation-focusing). Sometimes sexual functioning concerns are the result of limited information/knowledge. The intervention may simply be educational. For example, some men don't know how to stimulate the woman's clitoris to help her reach orgasm. The assignment below is one strategy on helping you let your partner know what you like.

ASSIGNMENT: Sexual Functioning

Respond to the following statements (leave blank if not applicable):

I avoid sex because of problems with sexual functioning.

Completely Agree---Completely Disagree

I don't find sex pleasurable.

Completely Agree---Completely Disagree

Most of the time, I orgasm ("come") too quickly when I'm with my partner(s).

Completely Agree--Completely Disagree

I think I might have a sexual functioning problem caused by a medical condition or prescription medication.

Completely Agree--Completely Disagree

I often have a delay or absence of orgasm when I'm with a sexual partner.

Completely Agree--Completely Disagree

I have physical pain during sexual intercourse.

Completely Agree--Completely Disagree

I'm usually able to orgasm ("come") when I'm with my partner(s).

Completely Agree--Completely Disagree

I think I might have a sexual functioning problem caused by drinking or use of illegal drugs.

Completely Agree--Completely Disagree

I have no interest in having sex.

Completely Agree--Completely Disagree

I'm generally satisfied with my sexual behavior.

Completely Agree--Completely Disagree

I feel anxious about my ability to perform sexually.

Completely Agree--Completely Disagree

I often have a delay or absence of orgasm when I masturbate.

Completely Agree--Completely Disagree

FOR MEN:

I have trouble getting or keeping an erection

Completely Agree--Completely Disagree

FOR WOMEN:

I have trouble with lubrication ("getting wet").

Completely Agree--Completely Disagree

Review and update your sexual history and timeline.

- When have you experienced sexual functioning issues? What are your plans to address these?

- Describe any changes in your sexual behavior because of functioning concerns (increased online behaviors, increased masturbation, avoidance of sex, or use of sexually explicit material because of problems with erections or painful penetration)?

Sexual Functioning Cycle

The *sexual functioning cycle* is a basic piece of information that helps individuals understand sexual functioning. It essentially describes how men and women respond in a sexual way. There are four basic stages: arousal, plateau, orgasm, and resolution. Understanding the cycle, assumptions you have about the cycle, and how your particular expression of the cycle occurs promotes healthy sexual functioning.

Below is a graph illustrating the sexual functioning cycle. In the *arousal* stage, the person recognizes someone as attractive. During this stage, the entire body (including genitalia) may enlarge and otherwise start to respond. Examples of body changes include flushed body, erection, lubrication, and so forth. Assuming the arousal stage is encouraged, the body will move toward full arousal and excitation. During the *plateau* stage, there is a heighted state of arousal. Ongoing play, foreplay, and stimulation maintain the arousal stage. If ongoing arousal isn't maintained, the body will change to a lower state of arousal. After enough stimulation, *orgasm* sometimes occurs, followed by a period during which the body needs rest. This *resolution* stage (not pictured) is a period during which the body will not start the cycle again, no matter how much stimulation occurs.

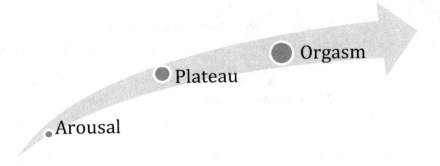

Sexual response cycle (stages 1-3)

Faulty Assumptions

Individuals will often struggle with assumptions that aren't consistent with the reality of the sexual response cycle. As we're growing up, and through our viewing of sexual explicit material and popular culture, we receive messages and learn assumptions about how a person is supposed to be able to perform. These frequently unrealistic expectations can interfere with sexual health. I encourage you to review the sexual response cycle in detail on the Internet. While each person follows this general pattern, we each have individual variations. At this point, being aware of your version of the cycle is important. The following discussion reflects typical functioning concerns.

General Types of Sexual Dysfunction

An individual's sexual response cycle may be negatively affected by a number of factors. The following descriptions of dysfunction are broad and not intended to cover the specifics necessary to address particular cases. This is a place for you to start a conversation with your support network.

Problems Achieving Orgasm

Problems achieving orgasm occur in men and women, yet women experience it more often. Treatment might be physical and may require medical review. Sometimes, a women's partner needs education to assist her in achieving an orgasm. Side effects of some medications can affect desire and interfere with orgasm. Sexual desire changes over time. Decreased sexual desire is normal in some situations (e.g., as we age). Sometimes, however, it isn't normal, such as when caused by medical issues (e.g., hormonal changes or mental health issues). *Sexual aversion* is an extreme avoidance or negative reaction to sexuality or sexual behavior. Sometimes this is a sexual functioning issue.

Female Physical Dysfunction Issues

Dyspareunia and vaginismus are issues affecting female genitalia. The primary experience is pain in the genital area, usually during penetration. The causes vary, and medical review is required for diagnosis and treatment. Although the majority of causes are medical, psychological issues (such as unresolved abuse issues) can contribute to these conditions.

Male Physical Dysfunction Issues

Male dysfunction issues are categorized as impotence problems and ejaculation problems (premature and retarded). Get a medical check-up to eliminate physical causes, and ask your physician to address any sexual functioning concerns based on biomedical causes or medications. If physical, biomedical and medication-related causes are ruled out, you should consult a trained therapist.

Sexual Functioning Barriers

Individuals view a typical sexually explicit movie and assume—unrealistically—that they need to have sex like a porn star. The performance expectations created through media have to be challenged. Real people don't perform sexually the way suggested in sexually explicit movies. In addition, many individuals struggle with so much sexual shame that they simply shut down any sexual energy. Individuals struggling with sexual anorexia/sexual avoidance may believe they lack the skills needed to engage in sex. For individuals struggling with sexual anxiety, sex evokes such anxiety that it results in unpleasant experiences, creating a cycle leading to additional anxiety. Sexually compulsive individuals sometimes focus on one type of sexual experience at the expense of all other types of sexual intimacy. Other individuals look for a particular type of sexual intimacy, but they don't know how to ask for it. Often, the individual and the partner don't feel comfortable talking about the different types of sexual intimacy. Sexual health requires development of the knowledge, comfort, and skills to engage in a variety of forms of sexual expression. Undoing the cultural emphasis on genitalia is an important part of this.

ASSIGNMENT: Identify Barriers to Sexual Functioning

Review the information above on various barriers to sexual functioning. Determine which, if any, barriers to sexual functioning apply to you. Identify a plan to address any barrier(s). Consider the following questions:

*   Has there been a time when you experienced pain while having sex?

*   Describe a situation in which you experienced a lack of sexual desire.

The next assignment focuses on learning techniques/skills as a potential approach for addressing sexual functioning issues. Sometimes, we simply need to learn the skills necessary to improve our sexual functioning.

ASSIGNMENT: Development of Sexual Intimacy Skills

As part of the process of addressing sexual functioning issues, the following exercise was designed to help clients develop comfort and a sense of sexual ability. The exercise, which walks you through a list of sexual intimacy skills presented in increasing levels of intensity, should be completed over a period of time. It's important to develop and maintain open communication with your partner throughout this process. Your partner's willingness to participate is crucial; this may require couples therapy. If you don't have a partner at this time, it may be difficult to complete this assignment at this time; you may need to develop adaptations. Beginning with the most basic skills and moving toward increasingly complex ones, be sure to consider each step. Take your time—this process of gradual progression can take months. Also, if you're struggling with intimacy issues, quickies or one-time encounters will obviously interfere with your healing.

Although they're generally presented in order of increasing intensity, the steps may not always progress from easier to harder—your experience of each will depend on your individual skills and areas of comfort. The key is to move slowly. Comfort at each level is necessary before moving on to the next step. After each experience, reflect on and talk about your experience, identifying what was easy and liked, difficult and disliked, difficult but enjoyed, and so forth. Ultimately, determine whether or not you're ready to move toward the next step. If something is too uncomfortable or anxiety producing, you may have to stay at that step for a while, or even return to an earlier step.

(Due to the on-going nature of this assignment, up-coming discussions and assignments are referenced in parentheses when relevant.)

Looking. The place to start is awareness of attraction. What kind of person do you find attractive? What characteristics do you like? Not like? Focus beyond just the physical and include aspects of how the other person talks with you and treats you. What are the other person's values regarding sexuality? Share your responses with your support system. Recognizing your attractions leads you to the next step.

Flirting. The next step is disclosure to the person to whom you are attracted. Often this is where people get stopped. This step requires addressing fears of rejection. In some cases, rather than dealing with rejection, people either shut down their attractions or settle for someone else.

Spending time together. Learning how to spend time together is the next step. This may be simply going out for coffee or dinner, or having a more formal type of date. Examine the different ways to spend time together that make the most sense for you. (See also: "Relationships and Dating Behaviors" on page 182.)

Touching. Learning healthy, safe and respectful touch is the next step. This can involve simply holding hands, perhaps dancing or even light kissing. Being able to express what you like and don't like is a part of this process. At this point in the exercise, the assumption is that you are "clothes-on." Future steps will introduce the experience of "clothes-off." The goal here is to simply be comfortable with basic touch. Focus on areas other than genitalia and breasts at this point. (See also: "Healthy Masturbation" on page 152 and "Erotic Touch" on page 180.)

Kissing and Petting. At this step, you move toward increased physical touch. Continuing with clothes on and touch focusing on areas other than genitalia and breasts, you might focus on touching parts of the face, hands, head, and so forth. As with all the steps, it's important to be aware of what you like/dislike and what feels comfortable/uncomfortable. Ongoing communication with your partner and support system is also very important.

Nurturing and Full Body Touch. Here you still have your clothes on, but the level of touch has increased to the point where multiple parts of the body are touching. You may also be sitting next to each other on a couch, or lying down next to each other. This level of touch is sometimes described as spooning or laying front-to-back. As in the previous two steps, start with touching non-genital parts of the body, moving eventually to touching the genitals/breasts over the clothes. This part of the process is deeply connected to your image of your body and genitals. (See also: "Healthy Body Image" and "What would your genitals say?" on pages 146 and 147).

Nudity. The next level is being next to each other naked. This may have to start slowly; for example, simply being in undergarments before being naked. Again, it's important to start off touching parts of the body other than breasts and genitalia. Once the touch is comfortable, move toward touching your partner's genitalia. Pay attention to thoughts you have as a result of your sexual behavior.

Masturbation and Mutual Masturbation. Continuing up the scale of intensity, the next step is masturbating yourself in front of your partner and watching your partner masturbate. Many individuals struggle with shame, guilt, and embarrassment around masturbation. The discussion on masturbation (page 149) may help you increase self-awareness on this issue. Mutual masturbation (you masturbating your partner and your partner masturbating you) is the next step. Remember to touch all parts of your partner, and don't limit yourself to the genitalia only. This step is about integrating all types of touch into a sexual encounter. At this point, orgasm isn't the goal, simply being comfortable with the level of touch and sexual intimacy is the key. Your level of arousal will ebb and flow, even within the encounter. The goals are being comfortable with your body and being with your partner without expectations. Identify which parts of your body lead to the highest level of arousal (your "hot spots") and share this information with your partner. Perhaps when you're comfortable with the touch, orgasm through masturbation can be introduced at this level. Orgasm may also be introduced in the later stages.

Fantasy. Fantasies are extremely powerful. They are far up the scale because they give others a view of the innermost part of you. It takes a lot of trust to share your fantasies with your partner. Reading the discussion on fantasy (page 153) and discussing your fantasies with your therapist/support network may be helpful before sharing your fantasy with your partner.

Penetration. The next step is developing comfort with sexual intercourse. First, focus on feeling comfortable with penetration. Understanding what you like/dislike, and what feels comfortable/uncomfortable is the key. Learning strategies and positions for penetration are necessary as well. Some people struggle with penetration due to pain, shame, or fear. As with all the steps, reflection and conversation with your support system and your partner is important. Notice how views of sexual behavior shape your assumptions about the way you're supposed to behave.

Orgasm. Clinicians disagree about whether orgasm is required as a final step or not. Many individuals do see it as the goal and they struggle with experiencing an orgasm. Too often, we assume orgasm has to be like the images we see in sexually explicit media. Obviously, orgasm feels great, but it isn't always required or needed. I have included it here because my goal is to help you develop the skills, comfort, and self-awareness necessary to experience orgasm. At this step, all of what you learned in the previous steps is used to facilitate success here. It's difficult to provide universal instructions, so working with your support system and your partner is very important.

FOUR: Sexual Health and Safer-Sex Issues

The material below reflects research into the relationship between sexual health and safer-sex concerns that underlie increased risk for HIV transmission and sexually transmitted infections (STIs). It also relates to areas of focus in your progress toward improved sexual health. The purpose of this topic is to review HIV and STIs as they relate to your sexual behavior.

This topic does not focus on prevention (www.cdc.gov/hiv/default.htm) or treatment issues (www.thebody.com). Together, these two websites cover a range of topics from prevention techniques, resources and responses to commonly asked questions about HIV/AIDS and STIs. Although prevention and treatment issues are important, the goal of this topic is to help you maintain and create sexual health by understanding your thoughts about HIV and STIs.

ASSIGNMENT: Sexual Health—HIV/STIs

Answer the following questions by placing a mark on the line (or skip if not applicable):

I fear getting HIV/AIDS or another sexually transmitted infection.

Completely Agree---Completely Disagree

It's my responsibility to use a condom with my sexual partner(s).

Completely Agree---Completely Disagree

I would use condoms if my partner asked me.

Completely Agree---Completely Disagree

My partner would use condoms if I asked him/her.

Completely Agree---Completely Disagree

Condoms are embarrassing to use.

Completely Agree---Completely Disagree

I feel I am at high risk for getting HIV/AIDS
or another STI.

Completely Agree---Completely Disagree

I worry that I might be infected with an STI.

Completely Agree---Completely Disagree

I worry that I might be infected with HIV.

Completely Agree---Completely Disagree

I want information on HIV/STIs.

Completely Agree---Completely Disagree

I feel embarrassed when seeking medical care for STIs.

Completely Agree---Completely Disagree

In the last 30 days, I have noticed physical genital changes that concern me.

Completely Agree---Completely Disagree

I have engaged in unsafe sexual behavior in the last 30 days.

Completely Agree---Completely Disagree

In the field of HIV/STI prevention, there is significant research into why people engage in unsafe sexual behavior. The research has generally suggested a number of themes relevant to sexual health including sexual compulsivity, mood (e.g., depression), alcohol and drug use, and sexual functioning concerns.

- Review your unsafe sexual behavior. Highlight 4–5 reasons for unsafe sexual behavior that are relevant to you.

- What are your personal safer-sex plans to address your unsafe sexual behaviors?

- When was the last time you talked with your doctor about HIV/STIs? When was the last time you were screened for HIV/STIs? What are your plans to address these concerns?

As you reflect on your responses, it can be helpful to see the unsafe sex behaviors as expressions of bigger issues in your life. In this context, unsafe sexual behaviors aren't the problem; rather, they are a symptom of something more. The relationship between sexual health and safer-sex behaviors can be multidirectional. For example, your mood can shape your sexual behavior and your reaction to that behavior may shape your mood, setting you up for the next round of your acting-out cycle. You might think, "I'm so ashamed of my behavior that my feelings of hopelessness and worthlessness have increased." The good part of this reality is that intervening in the process at any point is a start toward improving sexual health.

Working with clients whose self-hatred, shame, guilt, depression and/or hopelessness contribute to their unsafe sexual behaviors has been one of my saddest experiences. I started my work with one client who started his sex history by saying, "I wanted to kill myself by getting HIV." This is a classic example of why sexual health has so many components, and it highlights the difficulty many people have in moving toward sexual health. In these situations, sexual health requires addressing the underlying issues. Much of the material in this workbook applies to safer-sex issues: "If I believe I'm worthless and can get affirmation through sex, I'll do whatever my sexual partner wants in order to get him/her to stay with me—including breaking my personal guidelines for safer-sex."

While a depressed mood can contribute to high-risk behaviors, anxiety around HIV can cause some people to simply shut down their sexual expression. The anxiety leads to paralysis and fear. In some cases, the anxiety leads to sexual health concerns through ritual masturbation, sexual avoidance or use of sexually explicit material. The high level of anxiety in response to HIV can lead some people to use alcohol and drugs as a way to self-medicate and reduce the level of their anxiety. While under the influence, they might engage in unsafe sexual behavior that creates feelings of shame and guilt.

Long-term sexual health requires you to address safer-sex issues. It's important to consider the relevant issues regarding your unsafe sexual behaviors. Until you address the underlying issues, you'll remain at risk.

ASSIGNMENT: Your Safer-Sex Behaviors

Review your sexual history and timeline, noting any times you've engaged in unsafe sexual behaviors. Consider the following:

*   How is sexual compulsivity related to your unsafe sexual behavior(s)?

*   Are different feelings a possible reason for the unsafe sexual behavior(s)?

*   Describe the relationship between alcohol and/or drug use and unsafe sexual behavior(s)?

- Are sexual functioning concerns a possible reason for the behavior(s)?

- Identify any patterns and review your responses with your support network.

FIVE: Barriers to Sexual Health—Beyond Functioning

Over the next few pages I review the other major barriers to sexual health, including mental health issues and abuse. I briefly highlight additional barriers that may be present. Please consult with a trained professional if these are significant issues in your life.

Mental Health Factors

One of the largest barriers to sexual health is the presence of *mental health factors*. I highlight the three major mental health concerns most frequently associated with sexual compulsivity: Depression, Bi-Polar Disorder and Anxiety Disorders. The overlap between mood disorders (depression, bi-polar, and anxiety) and sexual health concerns is so common that the question isn't, "Is there a mood disorder present?" but rather, "Which mood disorder is present?" The connection between acting-out behaviors and mental health concerns is probably bi-directional: people use sex to cope with mental health issues and the sexual behavior contributes to increased mental health problems.

Mood disorder is the term used to describe a person's difficulty understanding, coping with, and managing a variety of feelings. Sometimes, people's feelings are out of control and they simply don't know what to do. Sexual behavior can be an attempt to cope with the feelings or, vice-versa, the sexual behavior may trigger a series of feelings that appear out of control. Understandably, some people initially avoid the diagnosis of a mood disorder because the language and cultural response are often negative and judgmental. Please be open to the possibility that you suffer from a mood disorder. Acknowledging a mood disorder can actually create hope because it gives you language to understand and strategies to treat the symptoms.

Depression

Without a doubt, a major issue related to sexual health is *depression*. In non-technical terms, statements such as "I'm sad" or "I don't have any energy" might be expressions of depression. Other behavioral indicators might be not eating or not getting out of bed. It's easy to see how sexual behavior can occur in response to feeling depressed, either through connecting sexually to in order to feel good, or shutting down sexually. Sometimes the shame of sexual behavior may reflect a bigger issue of depression. The goal here is to review depression in such a way that you might recognize how depression and sexual health concerns are related.

One difficulty in recognizing the presence of depression is that sometimes depression is part of a bigger issue. For example, the next issues I'll cover are bipolar disorder and manic episodes. In each of these issues, depression may be a symptom of the other conditions. It may take some time to generate an accurate assessment that describes all of your symptoms. I've listed a number of symptoms below that are ranked according to seriousness of the symptoms. If three or more of these symptoms are present, I strongly recommend you seek additional help.

Symptoms of depression (in descending order of severity)

- Suicide attempt
- Specific plan for committing suicide
- Recurrent suicidal ideation ("I want to die") without a specific plan
- Recurrent thoughts of death (not just fear of dying)
- Depressed mood most of the day, nearly every day
- People reporting that you look depressed
- Feelings of irritability
- Fatigue or loss of energy nearly every day
- Feelings of worthlessness or excessive/inappropriate guilt/shame
- Loss of pleasure or interest in daily activities
- Significant weight loss when not dieting (i.e., a change of more than 5% of body weight in a month)
- Decrease or increase in appetite nearly every day
- Sleeping too much (can't get out of bed)
- Sleeping too little (can't fall asleep)
- Feelings of agitation; body is restless
- No energy; body feels weary
- Difficulty making decisions
- Difficulty thinking or concentrating

> **If you are experiencing suicidal thoughts or feelings**, get immediate help at http://www.helpguide.org/mental/suicide_help.htm, call **1-800-273-TALK**, call **911** or visit your **local emergency room**. Suicidal thoughts are the most severe symptom of depression. Clinicians are trained to respond respectfully and immediately.

There are some issues that might modify a mental health diagnosis. It's important to consult with a mental health professional if three or more of these symptoms are present. The professional will work with you to identify the most appropriate diagnosis given your specific symptoms and circumstances. Again, the key is to seek the advice of a professional.

Bipolar Disorder/Manic-Depression

Another mood disorder related to sexual health concerns is *bipolar disorder*. (This disorder is sometimes labeled *manic-depression*.) As with anxiety and depression, bipolar disorder exists on a continuum of severity. Very few people experience the extreme form of the symptoms, officially labeled as *Bipolar I*. Severe forms of bipolar disorder are difficult to manage and require a multidisciplinary approach, including psychiatrists, therapists and a strong support network. There might even be a genetic component to some severe forms of bipolar disorder. The other forms of the disorder are less-severe expressions, more frequent and less recognized. Because they're less recognized, it's important to examine the descriptions and symptoms to see if one of the less-severe expressions might be present in relation to your sexual behavior. If symptoms are present, please check with a mental health professional for further assessment and treatment.

Listed below are some symptoms of manic episodes. If you experience three or more of these symptoms, please consult with a mental health professional. If all of the symptoms occur during the same time window (say, within a week), the episode may be labeled *manic*. If the number of symptoms is fewer or the duration of the symptoms is shorter, the episode may be labeled *hypomanic*. The intensity and number of symptoms often reflect the severity of the diagnosis.

Symptoms of manic episodes

- Increased energy, activity and restlessness
- Excessively high euphoric mood
- Extreme irritability
- Racing thoughts and talking very fast
- Jumping from one idea to another
- Distractibility; can't concentrate well
- Little sleep needed

- Unrealistic beliefs in one's abilities and powers
- Excessive self-esteem or grandiosity
- Spending sprees
- Increased sexual drive
- Abuse of drugs, particularly methamphetamine, cocaine, alcohol and sleeping medications
- Provocative, intrusive or aggressive behavior
- Denial that anything is wrong
- Overbearing behaviors that cross other people's boundaries
- Dramatic increase in social or work-oriented activities

Bipolar disorder usually reflects a swing from a manic to a depressive mood. Review the section on symptoms of depression. If you experience symptoms of both depression and bipolar disorder, a different treatment approach may be necessary. What makes bipolar disorder hard to assess is the difficulty recognizing a less-than-full-blown depressive episode or a less-than-full-blown manic episode. Clients will often recognize signs of depression and obtain treatment for that condition, but are so grateful for relief from the depression when a manic or hypomanic stage hits they don't see themselves as having further problems. Because of the emotional exhaustion of being in the depression stage, simply having energy is such a welcome relief for individuals with depression they don't seek further treatment. It is in the manic stage that sexual behavior might get out of control.

Anxiety

Another important mood disorder to consider and gage with regard to its role in your sexual behavior is *anxiety*. Anxiety, in the simplest sense, is a sense of fear or uneasiness. Some anxiety is helpful in that it motivates you. For instance, you might say, "I'm nervous that my boss will get upset if I don't complete the project by Friday, so I'm going to commit to completing it." In these cases, anxiety is a positive thing. In some situations, however, anxiety can be a serious problem for people. In extreme cases, anxiety disorders can be debilitating.

If anxiety becomes pronounced, it can express itself in various ways. For example, you may have trouble sleeping. You might find you dwell on a particular situation and find it difficult to concentrate on other things. Your appetite or eating behaviors might change. Alternatively, you might have a sense of vigilance or a feeling of impending disaster, as if "something bad is going to happen." In some cases, anxiety can mask other mental health issues such as depression. Below are symptoms and types of anxiety. Ask yourself, "How do these symptoms show up in my life?" If you experience two or three symptoms, please seek additional consultation.

Symptoms/types of anxiety

- Feelings of apprehension or dread
- Trouble concentrating
- Feeling tense and jumpy
- Anticipating the worst
- Irritability
- Restlessness
- Watching for signs of danger
- Feeling like your mind's gone blank
- Pounding heart
- Sweating
- Stomach upset or dizziness
- Frequent urination or diarrhea
- Shortness of breath
- Tremors and twitches
- Muscle tension
- Headaches
- Fatigue
- Insomnia

Treatment for Mental Health Issues

Treatments for mental health issues vary. I encourage you to go online and search for strategies addressing the mental health issue(s) relevant in your life. If you're working with a counselor, please ask about your counselor's level of expertise and comfort with a particular type of therapy. If you want to try something on the list below and your primary counselor can't provide the resources, it's your right to ask for a referral to a therapist who can. Here are just a few possible treatment approaches:

Medication Management

The number and type of medications are constantly changing, so please consult with a trained professional. Many individuals are not interested in this treatment approach because of fear and stigma regarding medications, but at times the use of medication is appropriate. For example, consider diabetes treatment. Some people manage their diabetes through diet and exercise, and don't require medication. For some, however, long-term insulin use is required to stay healthy. Similarly, long-term use of medications may be needed for mental health. You and your doctor can work on the best fit and plan.

Talk Therapy

Talk therapy takes a range of approaches. The number and type of interventions are simply too many to list, but some of the better known therapies include:

- Cognitive-Behavioral Therapy (CBT)
- Dialectical Behavioral Therapy (DBT) Skills
- Supportive Talk Therapy
- Eye Movement Desensitization and Reprocessing (EMDR) Therapy
- Relationship Therapy
- Alternative Therapies
- Recreational Therapy Activities such as Challenge Courses
- Eastern approaches such as Acupuncture, Yoga, and Massage

Healthy Daily Activities

One way to cope with mood disorders is to develop healthy habits that help balance the mood and create stability and balance in your life. Here are a few examples:

- Talk with someone. Ask trusted friends and acquaintances to spend time with you daily, preferably face-to-face.
- Wait until you're feeling better before attempting difficult tasks.
- Make a written schedule for yourself every day and stick to it.
- Get at least eight hours of sleep each night.
- Get out into the sun or into nature for at least 30 minutes a day.
- Make time for things that bring you joy.

Manage Your Diet

Managing your diet is another way to help with stabilizing your mood.[24]

- Stop or reduce your consumption of products that contain caffeine, such as coffee, tea, cola and chocolate.
- Stop or reduce your consumption of products that contain nicotine (a stimulant).
- Review over-the-counter medicines or herbal remedies. Many contain chemicals that can affect mood.

Exercise/Relaxation

A holistic approach to treating mood disorders can facilitate balance, including:

- Exercise daily
- Relieve muscle tension. Muscle tension is commonly experienced in the back of the neck and shoulders. One easy way to get rid of such tension is to tighten the neck and shoulders, holding for 5–10 seconds before releasing.
- Breathe. Close your eyes, take a deep breath through the nose, exhale through your mouth and repeat a few times. When breathing in, let your stomach expand as much as possible. Concentrate on breathing slowly and calmly, thinking of your slow breathing as calming your entire body.

Meditation Activities

The following activities can help you focus your thoughts, as well as express feelings regarding factors associated with a mood disorder.

- Draw
- Write in a journal
- Listen to relaxing music
- Tell yourself "I am relaxed" as you carry out breathing exercises
- Visualize a soothing image (e.g. lying on a warm beach)

ASSIGNMENT: Mental Health Symptoms

In the sexual behavior timeline, you charted your life along the horizontal axis. The +5 to 0 range helped you start thinking about your moods. Look at the symptoms of anxiety, depression and bipolar disorder. Which symptoms are present? Update your timeline by graphing these symptoms across your lifetime.

- Might your sexual behavior be attempts to reduce symptoms of a mood disorder?

- Might your sexual behaviors be a contributing factor to a mood disorder?

- Identify your plans to address any concerns raised in this topic.

Types and Impact of Abuse/Trauma

It is important to review the relationship between abuse/neglect and your sexual history and timeline. A current term for this in the treatment field is the concept of *trauma*. The many types and degrees of abuse and neglect are too complex for thorough discussion here, but a brief review is provided below. Treatment approaches vary and are not reviewed here. The major types of abuse—physical, emotional, and sexual—are categorized to help describe the abuse, but types of abuse may overlap. Please seek professional help if abuse or neglect is part of your history. More and more clinicians are willing to address trauma issues.

Physical Abuse

Physical abuse includes any behavior that causes or contributes to a physical injury to another person.

Examples of physical abuse include the following:

- Getting hit by a body part
- Getting hit with an object
- Having hair pulled
- Being burned
- Being cut
- Someone stopping you from breathing for a short period of time
- Administering a harmful substance or any substance that results in harm
- Infliction of physical injury

Sexual Abuse

Sexual abuse can include a range of behaviors. These include extreme forms of abuse such as rape, molestation, forced prostitution or incest. Other forms of sexual abuse include exploitation or use of a power relationship (teacher/student, caretaker/child, therapist/client). Less extreme forms of abuse can include manipulation of others for sexual pleasure, voyeurism and exhibitionism. Sexual abuse also includes sexual harassment and verbal degradation. Sexual contact by an adult with a person under the legal age of consent is by statute a form of sexual assault and results in automatic criminal charges if revealed. Other examples of sexual abuse include the following:

- Sexual innuendoes or provocative statements
- Engaging in sexual behavior in front of another person
- Exposing one's genitals to another person without permission
- Fondling or touching another's breast or genital area against their wishes
- An adult or older child engaging a younger child in sexual intercourse, masturbation, oral sex, or genital sex
- Adult sexual contact, such as sexual intercourse, masturbation or oral-genital sex without permission or when permission is withdrawn

Emotional Abuse

The third major type of abuse is *emotional abuse*. This involves negative statements being directed toward you. Some incidents of emotional abuse might be one-time events, but often there is a pervasive pattern of negative statements. Examples of emotional abuse include the following:

- Name-calling
- Put-downs
- Failure to affirm
- Shaming
- Judgmentalism
- Making threats
- Yelling

Overt and Covert Abuse

A lot of research and practice emphasizes addressing *overt abuse*, which is "abuse that's easily recognized." If you review the previous examples, it's easy to recognize whether something did or didn't happen. There's usually a specific person, behavior, event, time and place included in the description of the abuse. In therapy, a client might say a specific person did something and then describe in great detail what happened.

Covert abuse is equally damaging but is often hidden, covered and/or not recognized. I apply the label of covert abuse to any setting where there is an atmosphere of fear. Therefore, statements such as, "I can give you something to cry about," create an atmosphere of impending physical abuse. Another example: "Don't make me get the belt." A third example is, "Wait until your father gets home." These behaviors demonstrate covert physical abuse, which is often difficult to recognize. A client may sense something is wrong, but not be aware of a specific problem. A client may report being vigilant for no apparent reason, while the threat of abuse causes him/her to shudder at a simple look from a partner, friend, or parent. The threat and/or feelings of fear are the keys to recognizing covert abuse.

Abuse and Neglect

Abuse is typically an active behavior (I did something, or something was done to me). Just as damaging is neglect. *Neglect* is a failure to provide the necessary resources to another person. Emotional and physical neglect are often recognizable. *Emotional neglect* can be the failure to provide emotional support. *Physical neglect* can be the failure to provide appropriate nutrition, shelter or clothing. *Sexual neglect* could be the failure to provide adequate sexual education. As with covert abuse, covert neglect is very difficult to recognize. Often, only after the fact and a review of the indicators of abuse is a person able to identify covert abuse and/or neglect.

Sexual Violence

Sexual violence is any type of sexual activity you don't agree to. The amount of sexual violence in our society remains at epidemic proportions. Instances of sexual violence are notoriously underreported. Some scholars have suggested 3% of college women experience sexual assault in a given year.[25] Another article suggests 25% of girls and 16% of boys are abused before age 16.[26] Furthermore, professionals rarely recognize the concept of male-on-male rape as an issue and don't provide treatment for its victims.[27] Examples of sexual violence (sometimes referred to as sexual assault and abuse) include the following:

- Inappropriate touching (such as grabbing your breasts, butt or penis—or brushing up against you—without your consent) either intentional or ostensibly by accident.
- Vaginal, anal or oral penetration, or attempted penetration (with or without objects), without your consent.
- Being spied on (i.e., voyeurism)
- Having someone expose him/herself to you without your consent (i.e., exhibitionism)
- Sexual contact when consent is not present (see also: "Sexual Behavior and Expression" on page 167)

Sexual violence can happen to anyone at any time. A relative or person known to the victim is the most common perpetrator of this kind of violence. When a partner, wife, husband or dating partner is the perpetrator, the abuse is defined as domestic rape or date rape. The rise of date-rape drugs exacerbates the problem and provides a barrier to seeking help. Although sensationalized in the movies, stranger rape is less common, though it still occurs and is important to assess. If you're a victim of sexual violence, seek help immediately. Sometimes an individual doesn't seek immediate help for any number of reasons. It's never too late to seek help. This can include talking to a therapist, friend or religious advisor. The key is to remember that you're not alone, and that recovering from this experience is possible.

ASSIGNMENT: Another Look at Abuse

The consequences of abuse vary, and can contribute to relationship, sexual and other problems. Sometimes a person's abuse history contributes to problematic sexual behaviors and chemical use. It's important to acknowledge any experience of abuse (past or present) in the quest for sexual health. It's equally important to deal with any consequences of that abuse.

Review your sex history and timeline.

- What types of abuse might you have experienced?

- How might these experiences be related to your sexual behaviors?

History of Abuse

A common theme in sexual avoidance is a history of abuse. Due to an experience of abuse, a person may have difficulty recognizing and expressing feelings and empathizing with others. Often, people may not label the events as abuse because they don't recognize that they aren't at fault. They say they liked or respected the perpetrator or they could not believe the person would harm them. Sometimes a person thinks the abuse is a normal part of life. Victims have sometimes reported feelings of confusion because they liked the attention or they physically responded to the sexual touch.

Recovery from Abuse

If you're in immediate danger, you need a safe place to go. There are many treatment programs and/or shelters available. Look for domestic abuse or sexual violence programs in your local area. I encourage you to find help. My experience is that this can be a significant process for many clients.

Once stable, tell your story. And then tell your story again and again. Group support/therapy is helpful. The decrease in shame, fear and isolation that occurs through group therapy can be powerful. Understanding that "I'm not alone" and "Someone understands" is a powerful source of hope. I often have clients complete an "abuse history" describing the life history of abuse. For some people this is too difficult. I acknowledge healing is a long process. Sharing your story once is only the start. If you need to start slow, simply listing events is the place to start. I adapt the above assignment to be: "Describe 4 (or whatever number you can start with) events of abuse in your life." Sometimes, simply acknowledging, "I've been abused," is the first step.

Once you know your history, understand the things that trigger flashbacks and struggles in your current daily functioning. You'll need to develop plans to address the triggers. As you move forward, ask yourself what you want your life to look like. This is the hardest place to get to in therapy. The level of fear and lack of hope will need to be resolved prior to this place.

Journaling has two benefits. It's part of the therapy process, but it also helps to remind you of your progress. When you're frustrated, it's helpful to look back and recognize where you've been, what you've come through, and where you're going. Some clients beat themselves up because they can't talk to everyone at a party because they are uncomfortable. A journal can highlight the amazing progress signified by simply getting to an event. Journaling doesn't have to mean writing. With new technologies, journaling can include video recordings, art or other forms of expression.

ASSIGNMENT: Personal Victimization History

One assignment I suggest once the client is stable (i.e., not experiencing suicidal thoughts, able to function) is to work on an abuse history. Include the details such as your age, who, what, when, where and your reaction at the time. Update your timeline as appropriate. Also include your reaction today. Reflect on how the abuse affected you, and identify how it has influenced your sexual behavior. In writing your abuse history, include:

- Physical, sexual, and emotional abuse
- Overt and covert abuse
- Experiences with both abuse and neglect
- Experiences of sexual violence

- How your sexual behavior is related to abuse/trauma/sexual violence

- What your plans are to help you heal and grow

Cybersex Users - Who Are You?

Understanding the various types of online sexual users should assist you in determining if you struggle with problematic online sexual behavior. It's important to know that not everyone who uses the Internet for sexual activities does so for the same reason or to the same extent, and that not all cybersex has negative consequences. The workbook, *Cybersex Unplugged*, addresses this topic is greater detail. I briefly summarize.

Recreational Cybersex Users

Recreational cybersex users are divided into two categories: appropriate recreational users and inappropriate recreational users. The former seem to be able to explore sex on the Internet without any sign of their behavior becoming problematic. Their behavior is out in the open, not covert. Time spent in cybersex behaviors is minimal, usually totaling no more than a couple of hours a week. They don't feel embarrassed or shameful about these activities, and often they take part in them with their spouse or partner. They may, in fact, use cybersex as a way to enhance their sexual experience with one another and thus to strengthen their relationship.

Sexual Harassers

There is an in-between group of individuals who don't have a cybersex problem, but still engage in behaviors that may be a concern. Individuals may, for example, show a sex-related item or site they discovered on the Internet to others such as their work colleagues, family members, or friends who are not interested in such information or who are embarrassed by it. They do so not as a means of hurting or embarrassing others, but simply because they think such information is funny or because they like the feeling of shocking others. These individuals who use cybersex inappropriately don't try to hide their activities either. While these behaviors may be inappropriate, individuals can easily be redirected when confronted with their behavior.

Problematic Cybersex Users

People who exhibit problematic sexual behavior on the Internet tend to fall into one of the three groups:

Discovery Group

People in this group have no previous problem with online sex and no history of problematic offline sexual behavior. However, they often begin using sex on the Internet as a recreational user and become completely carried away with these online activities, spending many hours at the computer.

Pre-disposed Group

This group is made up of people who have never acted out sexually (though they have thought about it) until they discovered cybersex. They might have fantasized about exposing themselves or had the urge to see a prostitute or go to a strip club. Until they discovered the world of cybersex, however, they were able to manage their fantasies and urges. Maybe they were afraid of being recognized at a strip club or being arrested in a prostitution sting. People in this group often have clear boundaries for their urges or fantasies until they encounter the cyber world. Once that boundary is stretched or breached, little may be left to control behavior.

Lifelong Sexually Compulsive Group

People in this group have been involved in problematic sexual behavior throughout most of their lives. They might compulsively masturbate, compulsively use pornography, practice voyeurism or exhibitionism, or compulsively frequent strip clubs and prostitutes. For these people, cybersex simply provides a new option for acting-out sexually that fits within their already existing patterns of problematic behavior.

ASSIGNMENT: Cybersex

- Review the definitions of types of cybersex users, then review your sex history. How would you describe your use of the Internet?

- Share your response with your support network and obtain their feedback. How would your support network describe your computer use?

Feelings of Grief

Grief is an issue sometimes connected with sexual health concerns and, in particular, relationship history.

The Kübler-Ross Model: Process of Grief

Various theories have explained the process of grief. After all these years, I still like best the model presented by Elizabeth Kübler-Ross, who identified five stages of grief: denial, anger, bargaining, depression and acceptance.

As others have also done, I've made a few tweaks to Kübler-Ross's model to include the role of perceived losses, the role of small losses and the time focus of grief. Feelings of grief typically result from a significant loss, such as the death of a loved one, but grief from other losses can also have a powerful impact on a person's life. Take, for instance, the end of a relationship or friendship, or the loss of a job. Grief may also be due to the loss of hopes, dreams or fantasies. For example, in a gay person's coming-out process, the person may feel a loss, because recognizing a same-sex identity ends the perception of a normal life. Sometimes, the symbolic meaning of an event, location or person triggers an experience of loss. Moving from your home results in recognition of the end of a sense of security. These perceived losses could have the same impact as a tangible loss.

Some feelings of grief are anticipatory; in this situation, you might foresee the end of something. This may show up as: "This is a bad relationship and I need to get out of it, so I avoid sex, which then allows me to avoid having to deal with the bad relationship."

Critique 1

One of the critiques of Kübler-Ross's model is the perception that the process of coping with grief is linear (you simply go from one stage to the next). I think grief is cyclical; you might see the parts of a stage a number of times. You may move from acceptance back to denial, and then return to acceptance. I believe the key is to recognize that, whatever the situation, It's acceptable and healthy to be accepting of whatever thoughts and feelings you are experiencing.

Critique 2

A second critique of the Kübler-Ross model is the implication that the process occurs once and is rather quick. It's important to remember that coping with a loss takes a while. In some circumstances, the grief process can last a year or more. In addition, you can trigger grief when certain rituals, anniversaries or memories occur. Our culture often minimizes the long-term impact of grief.

Critique 3

A third critique is that these feelings are often broad and don't always reflect the immediacy of the experience. For example, I might feel sad, but flash to feelings of joy as I remember a special moment.

Stages of Grief

As you review your sexual history and timeline, pay attention to how the following stages of grief may have played out (or be playing out) in your life. A few examples describe how people might experience each stage.

Denial. The goal in this stage is to avoid dealing with the intensity of the grief. This can include actively avoiding the grief or minimizing the loss. Behaviors in this stage include not talking about the loss, glossing over it, or providing a minimal response to avoid further discussion, such as "I'm fine" or "It's no big deal."

Anger. In this stage, the energy around coping with grief goes outward. The person may feel victimized or attacked. "This isn't fair."

Bargaining. In this stage, there is recognition of grief, but the coping mechanism leads one to minimize the impact of grief. A person might begin dating before the grief is resolved (a rebound relationship). Another way this may be present is selecting a new partner with the thought, "she's better than no one" or "he isn't like the last one."

Depression. Common thoughts in this stage include "Why try?" "Nothing matters" or even "It will never get better." One of the difficulties in distinguishing between depression and grief is that depression is part of the grief process. (See the discussion of depression on page 126.)

Acceptance. By this point, the person integrates grief into his or her life, and while grief may be present, it has lost most of its intensity. This means you can acknowledge the loss, but the loss does not result in a barrier to healthy relationships or daily functioning. In some cases, the loss may actually facilitate transformation. These are signs of successful adjustment to grief.

ASSIGNMENT: Grief Analysis

Part 1: Take a piece of paper and create five columns. In the first column, list 75-100 experiences of real, perceived, major and/or minor experiences of loss. You might think that 100 experiences is a lot, but people can identify more losses than they realize. This part of the assignment can take days or weeks to complete. Complete this part of the assignment before you move on to the other columns.

In the second column, explain why this loss still holds so much power now. In the third column, identify possible thinking errors associated with the loss. The fourth column examines the relationship to your acting-out behaviors and the final column is to help you start moving forward with a plan. The examples below can be helpful.

Type of loss	Explanation	Related to behaviors	Plans and corrections	Connection to sexual health
Major loss Minor loss (plans cancelled) Real loss (relationship ended) Perceived loss (loss dream)	How does it affect me today? Why does this loss hold so much power?	How is this experience of grief related to my acting-out behaviors?	How will I address this loss? Is the loss based on a thinking error? If so, what's my correction?	How is this a sexual health issue? What are my plans?
Example 1: My partner left me.	I feel alone and hurt. I feel shame. I'll never find anyone. Nobody loves me.	My partner had an affair.	I'll talk about it with my support group and therapist. I'll read a book on dating.	I'm lonely. It's my fault.
Example 2: I didn't get the job.	I'm no good. They don't like me.	Sexual behavior fills the time and decreases feelings of boredom.	I can find another job. My job does not define me.	I'm worthless. (thinking error)
Example 3: I'm gay.	I won't be able to have children. Everybody judges me. I'll be alone. It's a sin.	No one can find out. The only place I can meet people is online.	I could adopt. There are happy gay people in, loving relationships. Not everyone believes it's a sin, some people think it's a blessing.	Gay folks can't be in a relationship. (thinking error)

Grief Analysis

Part 2:

• Describe circumstances in which you've felt feelings of grief. How has this related to your sexual health (is the grief a consequence of the behavior, or is grief a cause of the sexual behavior)? How has it impacted your relationships?

• When you find yourself feeling grief, what other feelings may be associated with the grief?

- What are your plans to improve your ability to express grief in healthy ways?

Feelings of Anger

You will not be punished for your anger; you will be punished by your anger. (Buddha)

Anger is a difficult topic to address because of its web-like relationship to many topics. It's robust, with multiple meanings and ways of being expressed. I summarize a number of issues regarding anger as they may relate to sexual health. If these are relevant, please work with your network to obtain support and additional resources. What makes anger so difficult to understand and treat is the confusion around the phrase, "I'm angry."

Sometimes, anger is a primary feeling. Feelings of anger, rage, frustration and disappointment reflect different intensities of anger. The things that trigger the feelings of anger vary. Sometimes anger is a secondary feeling—a response to another feeling that's hidden or covered. The concept of flight or fight illustrates the difficulty of analyzing anger. When people experience fear, they typically want to either run away or attack the source of the fear. In the latter case, anger is actually a response to fear. Anger may be a response to being hurt. For some people, their sexual behavior is a form of revenge to hurt another person. Anger can be a part of a process. The stages of grief discussed above show how anger is a normal part of the grieving process. If your feelings of anger are in response to another feeling, it's important to identify and address the primary feeling instead of the anger.

Strategies for Coping with Anger

Mindfulness

In the "Power of Thought" (page 37), I discussed the technique of becoming aware of your body, thoughts and feelings. This skill is also helpful in coping with and expressing anger.

Timeouts

Giving yourself a brief break from the situation can reduce unhealthy expressions of anger. I encourage clients to tell themselves, "I need 15 minutes to settle down and think about what I need to say."

Assertive communication

Review the discussion on assertive communication (page 96). It's important to learn how to communicate assertively when you feel anger.

Relaxation

Reducing overall stress and identifying ways to relax creates opportunities to focus on what's important and how you want to respond.

Meditation/journaling

The ability to reflect on an encounter during which you felt anger can improve your ability to understand the source of your reaction. Assessing your behavior can improve future responses.

Reaching out

Reaching out for support, coaching, feedback and advice when you feel anger is also helpful. A different perspective is sometimes needed.

Anger: An Issue for Follow-Up

Every once in a while I have a client who has significant problems expressing, managing and coping with feelings of anger. They may use sex as an attempt to cope with the anger, or as a way to avoid the anger. As you look at the possibility of improving your coping skills with anger, it's important to focus on healthy anger expression. In some circumstances, clients are abusive toward others. Most often, the abuse is verbal, but in some situations the client will engage in physical abuse. It's never acceptable to express anger in this way. In a similar way, attempts to avoid any and all anger are signs of a problem. If you find that you're struggling to cope with anger, or your anger continues to escalate after using the strategies above, additional support is recommended, including anger management classes or therapy.

ASSIGNMENT: Anger Analysis

- How is anger related to your sexual behavior? Is the anger a consequence of the behavior, or is anger an excuse for the behavior?

- When you find yourself angry, what other feelings may be associated with the anger?

- What are your plans to improve your ability to express anger in healthy ways?

SIX: Body Image

This next section addresses a number of components of how you see your body. It starts with body image, including genital image. Sexual health requires you to address the messages you hear about what it means to be pretty. Self-acceptance of our body is a vital part of sexual health and sexual expression. In addition, the activities in "SEVEN: Masturbation, Fantasy and Sexually Explicit Material" (see next topic) can provide insight into your self-image.

Where does body image come from?

Another component of sexual health is *body image*. Sexual health involves challenging the stereotypical and cultural images of beauty and encouraging self-acceptance. In order to do this, you have to develop a realistic and positive body image. The necessary work in moving toward sexual health suggests this is a major issue for many people. Body image is the foundation for so many parts of our perceptions, internal messages, external messages and feelings that its impact is difficult to address.

What people consider beautiful changes culturally over time. The key to addressing body image is to acknowledge the role of culture and the fact that beauty is based entirely on thought (review the "Power of Thought" on page 35). Clients who struggle with sexual compulsivity will often place unrealistic expectations on themselves and their partners. Without a doubt, mainstream American culture worships the "perfect" body and sets unrealistic expectations for both men and women. In our culture, the objectification of women has been occurring for a while. Recent developments have shown the objectification of men as well. Given the cultural emphasis on unrealistic body images, the negative messages both genders face are tremendous. The role of sexually explicit material also raises concerns because of the impact it has in shaping people's view of their bodies. The Internet's ability to churn out body-perfect images amplifies these concerns. I hear significant numbers of stories about clients struggling with accepting their own body image, as well as the body image of their partner. In a few cases, these unrealistic expectations can contribute to sexual functioning concerns. Intrinsic in the cultural messages we receive is the idea that sex is limited to youth—that older folks should not be sexual.

Researchers examining factors contributing to body image struggles suggest that a person's self-image is linked to the partner's response. Negative reactions from partners led to increased struggles with body image. As one could guess, individuals who struggle with body image issues have a better response to treatment progress when they have the support of a primary romantic partner. Individuals who receive such support have less stress and anxiety.

There are three implications that are important. First, for individuals who struggle with body image issues, the key is to gain support from the primary partner. Second, if the partner isn't supportive, it's important to address the negative impact of the partner's behavior; hearing "you're fat" isn't going to help individuals address body image. Third, partners are pummeled by the same cultural messages. Partners may need training and education as well as feedback regarding providing the necessary support.

Much of this appears to be common sense. Explicit positive and negative messages about a person's body can easily be recognized for what they are. The difficulty, however, lies is recognizing implicit, hidden, or subtle positive or negative messages.

While a lot of people struggle with obtaining the ideal body as dictated by their culture, there's a specific mental health diagnosis for people with more significant body image issues. *Body dysmorphic disorder* is characterized by constantly comparing your appearance with that of others, possibly refusing to let your picture be taken, excessive checking of a certain body part that you think is flawed (e.g., your nose or belly), feeling anxious and self-conscious around other people, calling yourself names or having plastic surgery and then feeling dissatisfaction with the results. If this is an issue, please work with a mental health professional.

ASSIGNMENT: Your Feelings About Your Body

In general, I like how my body looks.

Completely Agree---Completely Disagree

I like the look of my genitals.

Completely Agree---Completely Disagree

I feel I am too thin.

Completely Agree---Completely Disagree

I like how my breasts/chest looks.

Completely Agree---Completely Disagree

I am uncomfortable with several parts of my body.

Completely Agree---Completely Disagree

I have had cosmetic surgery to change my looks.

Completely Agree---Completely Disagree

ASSIGNMENT: Your View of Your Body

The goal of this exercise is to help you reveal the implicit messages you think about your body. Look at yourself naked in the mirror. What messages do you say about your body? How do you feel? Name three parts you like.

Healthy Body Image

The following are some guidelines that can help you work toward a positive body image:[28]

- Listen to your body. Eat when you're hungry.
- Be realistic about the size you're likely to be based on your genetic and environmental history.
- Exercise regularly in an enjoyable way, regardless of your size.
- Expect normal weekly and monthly changes in weight and shape.
- Work toward self-acceptance and self-forgiveness—be gentle with yourself.
- Ask for support and encouragement from friends and family when life is stressful.
- Decide how you wish to spend your energy—pursuing the perfect body or enjoying family, friends, school and, most importantly, life?

ASSIGNMENT: Developing a Healthy Body Image

- Examine your sexual history. How have messages regarding body image affected your sexual behavior?

- How have the messages regarding your body led to avoidant behaviors?

- What are messages you hear about your body from the cultures you belong to?

- Describe a realistic and healthy body image for you.

- Identify two plans you'll do to create a healthy body image.

What would your genitals say?

Within the concept of body image is *genital image*. The level of shame regarding genitals is significant. Our society bans their image on general TV. On the more explicit shows, you're likely to see more female genitalia than male genitalia. Sexual health includes a healthy acceptance of your genitals. When I talk about genitals, I include a broad understanding including not only the vagina/penis area (pelvic), but also the anus and buttocks, and (while not technically included but still helpful) breast/chests/nipples. People have an aversion to looking at, or otherwise being aware of, their own genitalia. Some of the most often mentioned reasons for the aversion to the genitals include the following.

- Because of abuse, some individuals struggle with being a sexual being. The topic of genitals is reduced to sex, and something to be avoided.
- Masturbation is such a taboo topic that anything associated with it becomes taboo.
- Individuals struggle with porn images. The comparison to these bodies and genital images affects our view of breasts, stomachs, chests, penises, and buttocks. The thought is usually, "I don't look like that, so I'll be rejected."

A number of exercises have been developed to increase acceptance of genitals. In the movie, *Fried Green Tomatoes*, the character played by Kathy Bates is encouraged to use a mirror to examine her vagina in order to become more accepting of her femininity. While we may laugh, the exercise has at its core the concept of self-acceptance and self-knowledge, including the genitals. To improve your genital image, get to know them better! This can include taking pictures, touching them in a self-discovery way, and identifying what parts you find pleasurable. Pay attention to more than just the pelvic area; include your buttocks, anus, and breast/chest area as well. Have a partner touch your genitals to help you discover what you like, including different types of touch.

ASSIGNMENT: Improving Genital Image

As you move forward in sexual health, especially over the next few chapters, pay attention to your beliefs and feelings about your genitals. Consider the following questions.

• What thoughts and feelings do you have about your genitals?

• What are two plans you'll implement to improve your genital image?

ASSIGNMENT: Full Body Massage

One exercise to consider is a non-sexual full body massage. Individuals who struggle with body image will often avoid being in their body. Due to shame, abuse, and assumptions regarding what a beautiful body looks like, people will often turn off the connection. A full body massage can help you (re-)discover your body. Schedule a full body appointment with a massage therapist—most will recommend a 60- to 90-minute session. They are often licensed or certified. After you complete the massage, talk about the experience with your support network. Consider the following questions:

• What did you like?

• What didn't you like?

- What was comfortable?

- What was arousing?

- Would you do this exercise again? Why or why not?

SEVEN: Masturbation, Fantasy and Sexually Explicit Material

As noted in Part One, masturbation and fantasy can each be healthy expressions of sexuality. It's important for you to clarify your values on these subjects. Too often, shame is linked with masturbation and fantasy due to historical myths and cultural assumptions.

Masturbation

The purpose of this section is to examine the role of *masturbation* in your sexual life. An article that presents the basics and history of masturbation is available at Wikipedia (www.wikipedia.org/wiki/Masturbation). I appreciate the review of history including many of the cultural myths. The article also includes descriptions of some of the benefits of masturbation. It's important to examine your thoughts and the historical messages you have received about masturbation, as well as how these have helped or hindered your sexual health. For example, many religious traditions teach that masturbation is a sin. Another example is the belief, "If my partner masturbates by him/herself, it means s/he isn't interested in me.

Often, in the struggle with sexual compulsivity, individuals have to unlearn unhealthy patterns of masturbation (often associated with shame and guilt, and frequently linked to problematic behaviors). For some people, masturbation is a form of harm reduction. By masturbating, they know they will reduce the risk of other sexual health problems. Moving toward integrating masturbation into healthy sexuality means moving away from the typical form of masturbation. It also means moving from shame to self-exploration and discovery.

The questions below are a good place to start in assessing your views about masturbation.

ASSIGNMENT: Your Feelings About Masturbation

Respond to the following statements:

I enjoy masturbating.

Completely Agree---Completely Disagree

I believe masturbation is sinful.

Completely Agree---Completely Disagree

Masturbation is a healthy way to have sex when I'm horny.

Completely Agree---Completely Disagree

Masturbation with my sexual partner(s) is a healthy expression
of being close to each another.

Completely Agree---Completely Disagree

Masturbation is a healthy way to learn about my sexual desires.

Completely Agree---Completely Disagree

Masturbation is a positive source of comfort and pleasure.

Completely Agree---Completely Disagree

Masturbation is a form of healthy sexual expression.

Completely Agree---Completely Disagree

Masturbation can be helpful in overcoming sexual dysfunction.

Completely Agree---Completely Disagree

I masturbate to explore my body.

Completely Agree---Completely Disagree

I masturbate too much.

Completely Agree---Completely Disagree

I feel guilty when I masturbate.

Completely Agree---Completely Disagree

Masturbation is a good way to reduce stress.

Completely Agree---Completely Disagree

Masturbation is a good form of birth control.

Completely Agree--Completely Disagree

Now review each question again, paying attention to your reaction. Review your sex history and the questions about masturbation. As you review your responses, pay attention to your past and current thoughts and feelings about masturbation.

The following questions will help you further clarify your opinions, beliefs and values about masturbation. Think about the role masturbation will play in your Personal Definition of Sexual Health.

ASSIGNMENT: Messages About Masturbation

• Review the discussion on culture (page 100). Identify two messages about masturbation from each culture to which you belong.

• What are your current values toward masturbation?

• Under what circumstances is masturbation healthy for you?

• Under what circumstances is masturbation unhealthy for you?

- What are your guidelines for disclosing your masturbation behaviors to your partner?

- What's your partner's reaction to these guidelines?

The following exercise will help expand your experience of masturbation from a quick and dirty activity (lasting 3-5 minutes, on average) to a sensual self-affirming opportunity. This applies to both men and women.

ASSIGNMENT: Healthy Masturbation

Make sure you have the time for the following exercise. What follows is one example, but you can adapt it to your personal interests. For this example, I'll assume you're in your bed (but experiment with other locations/positions). Start by making sure you're comfortable, including music, candles, aromatherapy, oils, bath, or any activity that can help you relax. The fun is in the experimenting.

First, start by being aware of your breath. Breathe in and out, slowly and steadily. As you move through the experience, it's important to maintain your breathing. Sometimes as a person becomes aroused, s/he may forget to breathe. When you sense that you're holding your breath, gently remind yourself to keep breathing.

Next, continue by touching your body with your hands (without lubricants). At this point, don't focus on your genitalia. Touch your face and ears; massage your neck, arms, and fingers. Feel your chest, moving to your stomach. Massage your thighs and include your legs and feet (and toes!). The slower you move through *all* of your body parts, the better. Vary the intensity and type of touch. You can use your thumbs, palms, fingernails, back of the hand, tips of the fingers, back of the fingers, and so forth. Repeat the touch and be mindful of what you enjoy. Perhaps gently tug at your hair, or pinch your skin. Each of us has erogenous zones that vary in sensitivity. Find the zones and types of touch that are most sensitive for you.

As you continue touching your body in different ways, include touching your genitalia, nipples, and buttocks. Continue varying the touch. Move back and forth between all your body parts. You may find that your genitalia will change in the level of arousal throughout the experience.

Optional activities might include using other pieces of clothing or items. Various items might be different fabrics, cold/hot items (not too hot!), feathers, or sticks (such as a dowel). The key here is to experience a range of touch.

As you go through the experience, vary the type of touch of your genitalia (for example, the grip of the penis, the massage of the clitoris, the surface of the anus). Each type of touch will lead to different experiences. Experiment and enjoy. If you don't like something, or it feels unpleasant, do something else.

Remember to breathe.

After you've felt your body, repeat the full body touch, but this time consider using oils, waters, water- or silicon-based lubricants. Each will create different experience. Some might be sticky, slick, sensual, and so on.

Continue to breathe.

Your body will increase in excitement simply due to the stimulation. Depending on how long you want to prolong the experience, you'll notice that if you're very genitally stimulated, moving the touch to other body parts will extend and slightly decrease the overall stimulation, thereby prolonging the experience.

Continue to breathe.

At some point in the experience, particularly if you're focusing your touch on the genitalia, you may get to the point where you experience an orgasm. Remember, however, that orgasm isn't necessarily the goal. Understanding what you like and providing self-pleasure is the goal.

Practice and repeat.

After your experience, review how you felt and what you liked, and talk about the experience with your support network.

Fantasy

In moving toward sexual health, it's important to clarify misperceptions that exist about *fantasies*. Having fantasies does not mean you are oversexed, even if you fantasize or think about sex often. Sexual fantasies have many negative societal biases and messages that need to be confronted. Generally speaking, fantasies are normal aspects of our sexuality. Just as a note, *all* Internet behavior is based on fantasy! Seriously, I can't stress enough that all of your online behavior is related to fantasy. Given the conduit, all of the chat, pictures, and experiences exist in a realm where the mind has to fill in the blanks to make the experience feel real.

Everybody has fantasies and daydreams. Some clients don't like the word "fantasy," but I believe everyone has them. If the word doesn't work for you, use one of the following: daydreams, future hopes, wants, or desires. Substitute whatever word works for you as you complete the following assignment assessing your views about _____ (fill in the blank).

ASSIGNMENT: Your Feelings About Fantasy

Respond to the following statements:

If I fantasize about sex, I'll become obsessed about sexual thoughts.

Completely Agree---Completely Disagree

It's difficult for me to share my sexual fantasies with my sexual partner(s).

Completely Agree---Completely Disagree

Sharing a sexual fantasy with my sexual partner(s) enriches my sex life.

Completely Agree---Completely Disagree

Sexual fantasy helps me learn about what I like and don't like sexually.

Completely Agree---Completely Disagree

Sharing a sexual fantasy is a good way to get to know what a sexual partner likes.

Completely Agree---Completely Disagree

I enjoy fantasizing about sex.

Completely Agree---Completely Disagree

I feel guilty when I fantasize about sex.

Completely Agree---Completely Disagree

I enjoy hearing about my sexual partner's sexual fantasies.

Completely Agree---Completely Disagree

Sexual fantasy helps me express my sexual desires.

Completely Agree---Completely Disagree

Sexual fantasy is a safe outlet for sexual behaviors I choose not to act on.

Completely Agree---Completely Disagree

The following questions will help you further clarify your opinions, beliefs and values about fantasy. Think about the role fantasy will play in your Personal Definition of Sexual Health.

ASSIGNMENT: Messages About Fantasy

- Review the discussion on culture (page 101). Identify two messages about fantasy from each culture you belong to, then answer the following questions:

- What are your current values regarding fantasy?

- Under what circumstances is fantasy healthy for you?

- Under what circumstances is fantasy unhealthy for you?

- What are your guidelines about disclosing your fantasies to your partner?

- If applicable, what's your partner's reaction to these guidelines?

Sexual Fantasy vs. Sexualization

I distinguish between a *sexualization* and a sexual fantasy by using a three-second rule. The three-second rule refers to the amount of time you think about a person. What transforms a sexualization into a sexual fantasy is the thought or fixation on a particular person, image or object. If the thought is less than three seconds, It's a sexualization. If it's longer than three seconds, it's a fantasy. I came up with the three-second rule in response to clients asking for a helpful guideline on when the process switches from a sexualization to a fantasy. I base this rule on clinical experience and not necessarily on any hard and fast research. Nor does it have to be three seconds: it could be two or four seconds.

Sexualizations are normal; they happen outside our realm of control and they're part of our sexual drive. Sexualizations simply happen. Throughout the day, many sexualizations occur. A sexualization is recognition that someone is attractive to you. Often sexualizations can occur outside one's primary sexual partner template. A straight man can recognize a handsome guy, just as a gay man can recognize a beautiful woman. In these situations, there is simply recognition of the sexuality and sensuality of another person. It's our response to the sexualization that raises issues for further treatment.

Sexual fantasies are thoughts and feelings about sexual behaviors and ideas we find sexually arousing. Sexual fantasies may represent what turns us on. Sexual fantasies are also a form of self-stimulation. Simply having a fantasy does not mean we have to act on that fantasy. Fantasies exist only in thoughts; they are not in themselves real. This also means that a fantasy about a negative traumatic event is also not real.

Fantasies are Neutral

Fantasies themselves are neutral. They are normal and healthy. At the same time, it's important to emphasize that some fantasies are risky or unhealthy. The content, frequency, intensity and focus of the fantasy may raise issues you need to address. Fantasies can be helpful in understanding your sexuality. By examining your fantasies you can get a sense of what you find arousing. You can understand your needs and share them with your partner and support network. Sometimes a person can channel his or her energy into sexual fantasies to allow a healthy release. Sharing fantasies is difficult for some people, yet the process of sharing your fantasies can create positive intimacy with your partner.

Fantasy as Avoidance

If a person uses sexual fantasies to avoid or escape from reality, or the fantasies are one's only form of sexual expression, then I have some concern. Some clients have used fantasies as a form of escape from unpleasant thoughts and feelings. The key is for you to figure out which fantasies are healthy and which are unhealthy.

Unhealthy Fantasies

Occasionally, thoughts of inappropriate or unhealthy behaviors may occur as themes in your fantasies. This is an important issue for individuals with a pattern of sexually offending behavior. It's also true for people in chemical dependency recovery when sexual fantasies include drug use. How you respond to the unhealthy fantasies is a key step toward sexual health. You can redirect and change the fantasy through changing the plot of the fantasy. If you find that you can't do this, it's important that you stop the fantasy and avoid actively encouraging the unhealthy fantasy. Changing your environment and talking with your network can help you avoid these unhealthy fantasies. It's important that you not masturbate to these fantasies, because you might make them stronger or more frequent. If you recognize that unhealthy fantasies are increasing in frequency, intensity or content, you could be in a high-risk situation.

Learning from Fantasy

Dreams are often most profound when they seem the most crazy. (Sigmund Freud)

It takes a lot of courage to show your dreams to someone else. (Erma Bombeck)

The goal of this section is to emphasize not only the importance of acknowledging fantasies, but also the importance of studying them in order to gain insight into our underlying patterns of thinking and move toward sexual health. Consider the following possibilities: Fantasies may be a form of harm-reduction. Fantasies may be a form of alternative sexual expression. Fantasies may be a form of avoidance. You need to clarify the role of fantasy in your life. Letting your support network know you're having unhealthy or risky fantasies can be a part of your prevention plan.

I believe fantasies are amazingly powerful in helping an individual uncover/reveal part of his/her deepest core. In our fantasies, we can create and clarify our values regarding sexuality and our relationship with others. Jack Morin identifies the concept of *core erotic thought*, which he uses to demonstrate how our thoughts shape our sexual fantasies. Examining our most powerful fantasies gives us insight into how we see our basic selves. In his book, *Erotic Mind*, Morin discusses how fantasies changed in light of the therapeutic process. Specifically, he describes how negative and damaging fantasies slowly decrease as clients address underlying issues. As the clients move toward health, Morin suggests that the fantasies changed as a result of the therapeutic work.

The following exercise will help expand your understanding of fantasy and the role it plays in your life.

ASSIGNMENT: Interpreting a Fantasy

The following is a helpful tool to use in examining the core of a person's fantasies.

The first step is to have a solid fantasy to work with. This occurs when an individual writes his/her fantasy. I ask clients to write the fantasy as if a reader could enact the fantasy based simply on what's written. For some people this might be the equivalent to a screenplay or script. I'm not expecting material that's word for word, but enough detail to have a pretty good sense of the actions and motivations of the individuals. The content of the fantasy can be anything, including relationship, dating, wants, joys, fears, the search, hunt, and so forth. I do encourage the individual to include sexual contact as well.

Second, I remind the individual this is a process of inquiry. The client is the one who makes the determination if something fits. I (or a group) may provide suggestions, but ultimately the client says, "This fits the best." There isn't a right answer, simply today's better answer. Future reflection might nuance what's uncovered. Within inquiry, it's important to brainstorm different thoughts about the underlying motivations. It might be helpful to review the section on inquiry (page 30).

Third, remember that many conflicting answers can be applicable at the same time. This reflects the tension within the individual. The concept of layers within the individual is important.

Fourth, when possible, look for an expression of the primary thinking error (page 52). Often in the fantasy, the primary thinking error loses its power or is somehow addressed/resolved.

Fifth, the following process is helpful to my work with clients. Feel free to adapt it. In my process, I have the client read through the entire fantasy without interruption. The goal is to understand the fantasy in context, length, and direction. Then, I have the client reread the fantasy. In the second time through, I'll stop at places (usually a clause, or each sentence) and complete analysis on that piece (page 89). With some clients, I'll revisit the fantasy one week, or one month later.

Sixth, use open-ended questions for each section. After you ask each question, engage in basic reflection of content/feeling, and ask, "What else?" Here are some basic questions that I start with. Feel free to adapt/add things as you find useful.

1. Describe the motivation that's going on in that moment.

2. Describe anything from your history reflected in that moment.

    a. Describe the historical event.

    b. Describe how you felt.

    c. Describe what you thought.

    d. How is this important to you today?

3. What would happen if it were to come true?

4. Describe your fears if this was to happen.

5. Describe your hopes if this was to happen.

6. How would you feel if this was to happen?

7. What would you think if this was to happen?

Review the experience with your support network.

Sexually Explicit Material

One of the more controversial issues in the field of sexual health is the role and use of sexually explicit material. Notice the language: I use the phrase *sexual explicit material* to describe any content used in a sexual manner instead of using the problematic term *pornography*. (Pornography is often assumed to be limited to nude magazines or nude videos.) I use this approach for two reasons. One reason for the change in language is to step beyond the controversy of the language. Another is to highlight the need to assess adequately the use of *any* material a person sees as sexually explicit or might use in a sexually stimulating way.

Sexually explicit material includes sex images (DVDs, Internet, magazines), but it also includes benign advertisements such as images from catalogs, storefronts or billboards. The number of clients who report they looked at bra ads while growing up demonstrates how material can be sexually explicit without being pornographic. Some find the models in Victoria's Secret, Abercrombie & Fitch, Men's Health and/or the Sports Illustrated Swimsuit Issue sexually explicit. Although these images are not nude, people do use them for sexual purposes, including masturbation and fantasy.

Experts have differing opinions on the use of sexually explicit material. Some clinicians believe any and all sexually explicit material is unhealthy because it exploits others and can be misused. Some religious traditions believe that looking at sexually explicit material is tantamount to infidelity and therefore is a sin (equivalent to coveting your neighbor's wife). Other clinicians have a neutral reaction to the use of sexually explicit material and focus on the surrounding context. Still other clinicians use sexually explicit material to educate couples and to help them address sexual functioning issues and facilitate the sharing of sexual thoughts with a partner.

Regardless of professionals' opinions on sexually explicit material, it's important to understand how the material shapes your view of sexuality. The impact can create healthy or distorted images of sexuality. What's in the media isn't always reality. The role of sexually explicit material in your life plays a part in your sexual health. My approach is to help you identify your current use of sexually explicit material, review your values regarding the material, and focus on the role of the material in your sexual health. Taking on the values that (you think) others hold—or what you think they want you to hold—only sets you up for failure. Frequently, I work with clients who present as having a problem because their partner objects to sexually explicit material.

ASSIGNMENT: Sexually Explicit Material

Review your sex history and timeline. Identify the type and amount of sexually explicit material you've used. As you increase your awareness of the type and amount of material, also focus on what you find arousing or attractive. As mentioned, the content can range from pictures, videos, online materials, and stories to advertising material and even art. As a starting point in your personal assessment, begin with an extremely conservative definition of sexually explicit material. Note any medium with content you sexualize. Focus on how much material you explicitly seek out versus material simply present in your environment. The key is to become aware of the degree to which sexual content is present in your life.

- What sexually explicit material have you used? Describe how you have used this material.

- How do images in sexually explicit media shape your image of your body?

- How do images from sexually explicit media shape how you see your partner's body?

- What sexually explicit material do you think is acceptable to use? Why?

- What explicit material do you think is not acceptable to use? Why?

- What are your guidelines about disclosing your use of sexually explicit material to your partner?

- Have you reviewed these guidelines with your partner? Does your partner agree with these values? If there is disagreement, what's your plan to address the disagreement?

- Review your responses and obtain feedback from your support network.

EIGHT: Positive Sexuality

In previous sections, I focused on factors associated with acting-out behaviors; here I reshape the conversation to help you think about what you want. Here I want you to focus on what's right versus what's wrong. As I have said, all behavior is goal-focused. How do you get your sexual needs met in a healthy way? Such questions are the focus of this section.

What is Positive Sexuality?

To understand *positive sexuality*, we must first understand sexuality in a brand new way—as a normal, vital, and positive aspect of your life. Too many people suffer pain when they think about sexuality. Give yourself permission to be a sexual being. Rather than repressed, hidden or shamed, positive sexuality celebrates your sexual energy and being. Yes, this includes sexual behavior, but it includes much more as well.

The key to this section is discovery. Earlier in the book I used the metaphor of a child in a playground. It might be helpful to revisit that here: If you watch a child in a playground, you see her meandering through all of the play areas. She might stop at the swings, or the merry-go-round. Next, she might check out the slide. Then, perhaps she might build something in the sand. When she likes something, the child stays in the area. So, too, is the role of discovery in the realm of sexuality. Sex is adult play, so check out what you like or don't like. Enjoy the positive experiences and let go of the unpleasant experiences. Pay attention to what energizes you, makes you feel alive, leaves you light-hearted, reflects integrity in your life, and can be shared with your support network.

Your task in this section is to challenge most, if not all, of the messages you have heard about sexuality. This doesn't mean you have to discard your beliefs. Instead, understand both the letter and spirit of the messages. Sexual health is a journey. Today's thoughts are for today. What you like today is for today. What you want is for today. You have the privilege of addressing tomorrow's likes and wants tomorrow.

Balance is important in the journey. You can change your mind on this journey. I place good/bad sexual experiences on a different continuum than healthy/unhealthy ones. You can have a sexual encounter that feels good but is unhealthy (think meth/sex), and a bad experience that's healthy (think too tired to function, but emotional intimacy). My hope is that you have great experiences along the way. Sometimes, the only way we know what's sweet is to compare it with what's sour. Enjoy your journey in sexual health!

Sexual Expression

Sex and Ice Cream

Sometimes it's easier to explore sexual health issues through the use of a metaphor. A metaphor I like regarding sexual expression is ice cream (and the inspiration for the cover).

Who doesn't like ice cream, one of god's primary gifts to humanity! Imagine if you will, sitting down with a serving of vanilla ice cream. Think of the creamy feeling, and the taste of vanilla as you eat the first spoonful. Even the frozen vanilla Yogurts are good. The soft-serve ice creams are great when you want something in a hurry. Some of the premium brands have done a great job making vanilla ice cream almost a spiritual experience! The extra cream makes the texture extra smooth. Using real vanilla, perhaps with pieces of vanilla bean, creates an amazing experience.

Because vanilla ice cream is so good, and so many people like it, I have decided to impose a new rule. Vanilla ice cream in all its variation is the *only* form of ice cream that's good/holy/sacred. Only vanilla ice cream can be created, served, and sold. I have declared this, and so it is. Absurd, isn't it? But that's what we've done with sexual expression. Individuals in power decide a particular form of sexual expression is good/holy/sacred, then they impose this value on everyone else. Absurd, isn't it?

Sexual health requires you to make a choice about what's good/holy/sacred in your life. Yes, you might like vanilla, but vanilla is far from the only flavor of sexual expression. What do you like? Choose.

Historical Sexual Behavior and Expression

Throughout history, there have been attempts to define sexually appropriate behavior. Within the Judeo-Christian tradition, for example, the Holiness Code of the early Israelites was an attempt to define healthy sexual behavior reflecting their values, knowledge and community goals. For a small nomadic people, sexually healthy behavior emphasized procreation. The society's patriarchal system viewed women as property, so most of the holiness code focused on male sexuality. For a society with limited information on biology, the Holiness Code attempted to identify sexually healthy behaviors as a function of blood and energy: loss of blood equaled loss of energy and reflected a threat to survival. As a consequence, women were to be avoided during their menstrual periods, and masturbation was condemned since it resulted in the loss of energy.

Fast-forward two thousand years to a Europe dominated by the Romans with a new religion (i.e., Christianity) gradually extinguishing paganism. Hence, it was important to reject anything that reflected paganism, including the sexual component of the pagan traditions. Fast-forward another two thousand years to today and we have a society unlike any previous society, one that understands biology, genetics and multicultural reality. This reality leads to corresponding attempts at defining sexual behavior and a diversity of sexually healthy behaviors.

Many of the historical attempts to define sexually healthy behaviors have emphasized actual sexual acts and condemned the behavior within the context of a religious statement ("This act is unhealthy; it's a sin"). As a result, these definitions are bound by culture and time. Too often clients are stuck in the trap of asking the expert to define what he or she should do. Too often, based on their worldview, clinicians are ready to proclaim what's healthy and what's not.

In the last thirty-five years, experts in the field of human sexuality have attempted to define sexual health. While not reviewed here, the process of defining sexual health has experienced multiple revisions, discussions and bumps along the way. At one point, scholars argued that a universal definition was not possible given the diversity of people, sexualities, cultures, and circumstances. More recent attempts have attempted to facilitate an interaction between the individual and culture by incorporating a dynamic feedback process in clarifying sexually healthy behaviors. The goal is to help you start thinking about the values that shape your life. As you begin to identify these values, your responsibility is to assess the consistency between these values and your sexual behaviors. This is not a do-it-yourself, go-it-alone, I-can-do-anything-I-want task. You need your support network. It reflects the community that's there to provide support, encouragement and accountability.

Unhealthy Sexual Behaviors

The consensus among experts in a variety of fields (medicine, mental health, child welfare and clergy) is that only one behavior has consistently been defined as unhealthy: sexual behavior that's exploitive or done without consent. For example, exploitation of children is one of the few universally consistent behaviors condemned across time and across cultures. Yet, even this example has gray areas. In modern America, the definition of a child who can give legal consent for sexual contact ranges from age 14 to age 18. Centuries ago, it was not uncommon for a 12-year-old girl who had just completed puberty (i.e., had a period) to be considered an adult. Today, our collective culture would define this as abuse. Another gray area is exploitation. Activists working against the pornography industry argue that the material exploits women. If so, how does one explain gay pornography? These gray areas highlight the danger and difficulty of universal declarations.

An example sure to raise hackles is the assertion (by a significant group of people) suggesting that sexual behavior focused on procreation within marriage is the only form of healthy sex, and that any sex act that isn't open to procreation, even within a marriage, is a sin. This approach denounces as sin any form of masturbation or use of sexually explicit material because it doesn't lead to procreation. Some people have modified this approach to emphasize that any sex within marriage is healthy. Still others further modify this approach, believing that any consensual sex within marriage is healthy, recognizing that some traditions emphasize the wife's religious duty to submit to her husband.

Recently, there has been a push within the Lesbian, Gay, Bisexual and Transgender (LGBT) community to emphasize monogamy as the only form of healthy sexual expression and the need for marriage rights as a validation of these healthy behaviors. Sadly, where to draw the line of healthy versus unhealthy sexual behavior seems to depend on what side of the line you fall on. If you are outside the line, you redraw the line to include your sexual behaviors.

Healthy Sexual Behaviors

The approach taken in this workbook emphasizes a dynamic process between the community (i.e., your support network) and the individual. Your values determine what behaviors are healthy for you and define what's a healthy. However, this is not a free-for-all. Part of the process includes disclosure and community conversations within your support network to review your continuing care plan. As part of Stage 3, you'll identify values and sexual behaviors that are congruent and that reflect your Personal Definition of Sexual Health.

Four Values Helpful in Defining Healthy Sexual Behaviors

What follows are suggested values that I use in my work with clients to help them consider if an encounter is healthy or not. They are meant to be a starting place during the process. You will build on these values when you move to Stage 3.

Life Giving

The sexual behavior is a positive aspect in your life. The experience makes you feel alive and energized. Your personal identity (and your partner's) is affirmed, created and even expanded. You can walk away from the experience with your head held high. There is a sense of fulfillment and even pride in the experience. This does not necessarily mean the experience is limited to "great sex"; rather, there is an enhancement of identity and personhood for those involved. Sexual behavior is sometimes referred to as adult play, suggesting a sense of fun, playfulness, and timelessness.

Open and Honest

Healthy sexual behavior is above board, open, and honest. Not being open and honest is an immediate red flag. While you may not talk about the incident with everyone because of discretion, you could disclose the activity to your support network. In disclosing to your support network, the members would respond that the behavior is consistent with your values and continuing care plan.

Consent

Full consent and awareness are present in the encounters. Consent implies that all partners are actively giving permission to engage in the behavior. Consent requires appropriate disclosures and considerations. This value assumes that if the behavior occurs in the real world, full disclosure has occurred with your partner, including the risks of STI's and/or pregnancy, relationship status/availability, or any other statuses your partner should be aware of. There is a decided lack of manipulation in the experience. (An example of manipulation is saying, "If you love me, you would have sex with me.")

In some circumstances, consent is not possible. Children are not able to give consent. Relationships with power differences (for example, student/teacher, boss/employee, and therapist/client) are by definition non-consensual. Other circumstances exist where the ability to give consent is questionable because of mental health issues, chemical use or financial status (e.g., survival sex, where one trades sex for shelter). Another notion embodied within consent is that all parties need to be aware of the experience, which is why exhibitionism and voyeurism are unhealthy and illegal.

Finally, within the concept of consent is the concept of respect for a partner's boundaries and limits. If consent is removed (i.e., one partner saying "Stop," "No," "I don't want to"), the behavior must stop. Any person can remove consent at any time, with or without a reason.

Responsibility

As a value, responsibility requires that, ultimately, you fully assert your sexual needs, likes and dislikes. How are you protecting your values? Are the limits you're agreeing to truly yours? Or are they limits you think are necessary because someone else wants you to have them? It's up to you—not the other person—to affirm, communicate and protect your values. Not to choose is still choosing

Your Sexual Expression

This assignment focuses on helping you discern what sexual behaviors are healthy in your life. The questions reflect basic areas for you to consider at this time.

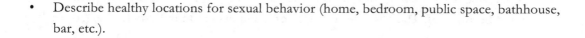

ASSIGNMENT: Sexual Expression

<u>Sexual Behavior</u>

- Review your sex history. Identify and describe what behaviors you like? Be explicit and thorough (e.g., oral sex, vaginal sex, anal sex, mutual masturbation, kissing, touching, etc.).

- Describe healthy locations for sexual behavior (home, bedroom, public space, bathhouse, bar, etc.).

- Describe who a healthy sexual partner is for you.

- Describe the ideal frequency of sexual behavior.

- Describe the types of sexually explicit materials (i.e., magazines, movies, and websites) that are healthy for you.

- Describe any interest in alternative ("kinky") behaviors and the circumstances in which these are healthy for you.

Boundaries

Boundaries refer to the limits we choose in life. It's the process of defining what's acceptable. Boundaries vary between individuals. You define your own boundaries.

Typically, we think of boundaries as being healthy, rigid or blurred. Healthy boundaries are well defined, clearly communicated and respectful to yourself and others. Healthy boundaries are an expression of your identity and although they can change, they are generally stable across time and situations. Changes in boundaries can occur in response to unique circumstances, the environment and people. Our personal experience can lead to a healthy expansion or restriction of a boundary. For example, if you are tired and lonely, a boundary may be that you'll not have sex. But once you're in a relationship, given the same circumstances, you may choose to have sex with your partner because of the adult play aspect. While boundaries can change, you should view any rapid changes in your boundaries and limits as a warning sign.

Two types of unhealthy boundaries are blurred and rigid boundaries. They represent the opposite extremes of the spectrum (with healthy boundaries in the middle). *Blurred boundaries* are too flexible and too changeable. With blurred boundaries, we tend to let the outside environment or other people dictate our beliefs, values and limits. In this situation, we may feel used, violated, exposed and hurt. Our identity is lost. I've experienced many clients who think they have a problem because their partner thinks they have a problem.

At the other extreme are rigid boundaries. *Rigid boundaries* often appear to be extreme stances. In substance-abuse treatment, we talk about an "all-or-nothing" way of thinking or a "take-no-prisoners" mentality. The consequences of rigid boundaries are often isolation, loneliness and judgmentalism.

Types of Boundaries

Three types of boundaries are worth focusing on: physical, emotional and sexual.

Physical

Physical boundaries involve the space around us. When working with children, I use the idea of a "bubble space" surrounding us that intuitively helps children understand how close they can get to another person. The concept of a bubble space supports the idea that boundaries are flexible. Depending on the circumstances, the size of the bubble space changes. For example, we are more comfortable if someone sits next to us in a room full of people, as contrasted with the discomfort we feel when only two people are in the room. Depending on the person and the culture, there are different rules on how close you can stand to someone. With friends and family members, our bubble space is smaller; with strangers, it's larger.

Emotional/Intellectual

Emotional/intellectual boundaries reflect your right to your feelings and thoughts. As individuals, we have the right to our feelings and beliefs based on values, spirituality, education or cultural affiliation. Our emotional and intellectual boundaries define our personality and identity, and they are a major component in our sexual health. The key is to examine how your boundaries shape your sexual behaviors.

Sexual

Sexual boundaries reflect your right to your feelings, thoughts and behaviors in the realm of sexuality specifically. As in category above, we have the right to our feelings and beliefs about sexuality. These boundaries are a major component in our sexual health. You began to define these in the "Sexual Expression" assignment above.

Boundary Violation

A boundary violation occurs when someone deliberately or accidentally infringes on the limits of what you are comfortable with. A physical boundary is violated when you are touched when you don't want to be touched. An emotional boundary is violated when you are subjected to constant criticism, when someone reads your mail or email without permission, or tells you what you should feel or think. The list of potential boundary violations is infinite. For some clients, unhealthy boundaries are a major issue in the recovery process. Below is a list of warning symptoms of unhealthy boundaries for you to review as a starting place.

Warning Signs of Unhealthy Boundaries

- When you don't want sexual contact, but go along with it anyway so the person will like you.
- Telling someone you like a behavior when you don't.
- Saying you want to get together with someone when you don't.
- Using drugs in a sexual setting when you don't want to.
- Not expressing your sexual desires or preferences with a partner and simply going along with what they want.
- "Falling in love" with anyone who reaches out to you.
- Acting on a first sexual impulse even when you say you'll wait until you know the person first.
- Using sex to express anger or loneliness.

- Being sexual for your partner, not yourself.
- Going against personal values to please others.
- Not noticing when someone else shows poor boundaries.
- Touching a person without asking.
- Letting others tell you what you should or should not do.
- Letting others tell you what's and is not healthy sexual behavior.
- Expecting others to automatically know what you want.
- Engaging in unsafe sex when you say you'll not.

Healthy Boundaries

Developing healthy boundaries is easier said than done. Learning boundaries is often through trial and error. There is no magic way to develop and express your boundaries. Identifying what you like and dislike is essential. Healthy boundaries are a function of assertive communication where you express your likes and dislikes. It's important that if you don't like something, it's something to communicate and place outside what's acceptable. If you like something, include it within your boundaries. It's your responsibility to express your boundaries to others. As a reminder, this discussion serves as a complement to the Sexual Expression and Assertive Communication sections above. Please review those topics again in light of this discussion of boundaries.

ASSIGNMENT: Boundary Issues

- Review your sexual history and timeline. Using the list above, ask yourself whether any warning symptoms of unhealthy boundaries are present. Pay attention to thoughts, feelings, experiences or behaviors that might indicate a possible boundary violation.

- If any warming symptoms are present, see if you might be able to trace the symptoms back to a possible boundary violation. Share these concerns with your support network and identify plans to address them.

- Review your sexual history and timeline again. Which of other people's boundaries might you have crossed?

NINE: Intimacy and Relationships

This is often the most popular section of the workbook. Often, individuals who struggle with sexual compulsivity limit the meaning of intimacy to sexual behavior. In fact, there are many forms of connections that we have with others all the time. The recognition that there are many ways to connect is new for many individuals. This section will address the topics of intimacy, relationships and dating behaviors, and full disclosure to a partner, as well as how they fit together in your Personal Definition of Sexual Health.

Be mindful of what you think when you hear someone say, "We were intimate." From a societal level, we often link intimacy to sex. Undoing that link is a key value of this section. In fact, there are many ways to be intimate with others, beyond even our primary relationship. Nevertheless, most of us will find we get our intimacy needs met through our primary relationship. One key to sexual health is addressing and building a strong relationship. This requires us to know who we are, assess our current relationship, and assertively ask for what we want. The last topic of this section addresses the importance of disclosure in relationships as an opportunity for additional intimacy, healing and setting the stage for long-term sexual health.

Intimacy

The majority of most people's life energy is focused on developing connections. This is true regarding sexual behavior. One of the major goals of sexual behavior is the belief that it will produce a sense of intimacy, yet, ironically, one of the major consequences is the destruction of intimacy. In this section, the goal is to help you become aware of the types of intimacy that are important to you, strategize on getting these intimacy needs met, and eventually develop the type of relationships that you want.

ASSIGNMENT: Intimacy and Sexual Behavior

- As you review your sexual history and your timeline, describe how intimacy (or the lack of intimacy) and sexual behavior relate in your experience.

Intimacy Needs

I see you. (Avatar, The Movie)

I love that line from the movie *Avatar*. The phrase has two meanings. First, it's an expression of the sensation of sight. When I look at someone, I see them. This is the standard meaning we use when we run into someone on the street. The second meaning is amazingly profound. It reflects the intense connection that occurs in the experience of intimacy. In the movie, they highlight how it means, "I see into you." It's saying, "I see you, I know you, I am one with you, I connect with you," and even, "I love you." Such a powerful statement in three simple words! It's what all of us seek.

One of the best definitions of intimacy is the feeling of connection with another person. Intimacy is the soul-to-soul connection between two people. Intimacy is a connection with openness and honesty. The need or desire to connect with others is healthy and normal. Most of the memorable moments in our lives are about the experience of intimacy. Similarly, most of the painful memories are about the loss of intimacy. If we look at the present moment, there are many types of intimate connections occurring all the time. Each moment of life is a possible connection to another person, if we only see the other person. Each moment of life is an experience of intimacy. If we limit our ability to see these intimate connections, then we limit our ability to experience intimacy. The question to consider is, "How am I connected to the person next to me at this time?"

Types of Intimacy

To expand our understanding of intimacy, it's helpful to review different types of intimacy. Below, I examine different types of intimacy.[29] After you review the various types of intimacy, next think about how to build intimacy in your life. Under each type of intimacy are suggestions for enhancing your intimacy skills in that area, but they are not the only ways or necessarily the correct ways. Use what works for you or develop other ideas. While you review this section, consider how your acting-out behavior may have been unhealthy ways to meet these intimacy needs.

Emotional Intimacy

Emotional intimacy is the sharing of significant experiences and feelings. Emotional intimacy is the foundation of all other forms of intimacy. It's the ability to talk without fear. Anything you are afraid to talk about is a possible moment of transformation of fear into intimacy. When fear is present, talking about it can facilitate a stronger and closer relationship. Emotional intimacy includes the ability to share one's hopes and dreams.

- Examine life events that have hindered your ability to be emotionally intimate. These issues might be grief, abuse and/or fear. Share these examples with your support network. Identify plans to address any concerns.

- Read a self-help book. This type of book will help you start to identify and cope with feelings and emotions. Visit a local bookstore and examine titles that speak to you.
- Appropriately share your inner thoughts, feelings, desires and needs with other people in your life.
- Find a support group. Pick a group, such as AA or another program that addresses an important issue in your life. A wide range of topics exist that may fit your concerns. You'll get a lot of experience sharing your feelings, thoughts, dreams and struggles.

Sexual Intimacy

Sexual intimacy is more than just the physical act of sex. Talking about your deepest and darkest sexual secrets is a form of sexual intimacy. For many of my clients, I am the first individual they talk to about sexuality.

- Attend a workshop on sexuality.
- Share your fantasies with your partner.
- Strategize with your partner about how to make part (or all) of a fantasy come true (within the rules of your relationship).
- Read a book on sexuality and share with your partner what you liked and disliked.
- Share your work from this workbook with others (as appropriate).

Intellectual Intimacy

Intellectual intimacy is the closeness resulting from sharing ideas. There is a genuine respect for each person's opinion. Agreement on a topic is not required for intellectual intimacy. The process of sharing, reflecting and discussing highlights the aspects of intellectual intimacy.

- Take a class. Check out community colleges, local art groups and area newspapers for classes that may interest you.
- Teach a course.
- Start a book club.
- Join a listserv on a topic of your choice.
- Check out the Internet blogs on a topic of your choice.

Artistic Intimacy

Artistic intimacy relates to experiences of beauty. This can include expressions of art such as music, plays and movies, but also natural beauty such as sunrises, listening to a thunderstorm, and taking a day hike.

- Beauty is definitely in the eye of the beholder, so what do you find beautiful? After you have figured it out, seek it out.
- If you like art, visit a museum, an art space, a play or a movie.
- Love nature? Check out local hiking or outdoor groups to join.

- Missed your shot at American Idol? How about joining a local chorus?
- Traditional art not your thing? Walk through your city and photograph graffiti you find interesting. Seek out information regarding body art (tattoos).
- Peruse non-X or R rated Internet sites such as Flickr.

Creative Intimacy

Creative intimacy is the intimacy of shared discovery. The key component is the process of co-creating with another person. Both you and the other person can grow in deeper ways through the experience.

- Bring a friend with you to any activity you enjoy and would like to share.
- Join an art class.
- Read a book on "possibility," such as the *Power of Now* by Eckhart Tolle, or *Power of Intention* by William Dwyer.

- Begin a blog.

Recreational Intimacy

Recreational intimacy refers to the experience of play, stepping beyond the struggles of life and simply spending time together. The types of play include sports, outdoor activities and indoor activities. Sometimes other types of intimacies are incorporated into recreational activities, such as going to a movie (aesthetic) and then talking about it afterward (intellectual).

- Go to the gym, walk or engage in other physical activities.
- Find a club or group to join. For example, most cities have hobby or recreation groups such as bowling or volleyball. Do what you enjoy regardless of what others think. You might be surprised how many people share your interests.

Work Intimacy

Work intimacy occurs in the sharing of tasks. It can include projects, events or the process of long-term commitment regarding work or family. These tasks vary in type, intensity and duration and could include completing a project at work or cleaning up the house. The feeling of satisfaction when completing a task with another person is an example of work intimacy.

- Volunteer for work events or tasks. Join a committee at work.
- Talk with your co-workers about what's going on. As appropriate, perhaps ask them what they did last night or over the weekend.
- Volunteer for organizations or events that are close to your heart. These could be community activities such as a festival or a political campaign.

Crisis Intimacy

Crisis intimacy occurs because of major and minor tragedies. Personal crises may be illness or accidents. Larger forms of crisis intimacy can be community experiences of a natural disaster. In these situations, people step outside of their limits and connect. Strangers will go beyond typical behaviors. The long-term response of the gay community to HIV is a great example of this type of intimacy. The community response to breast cancer is another example.

- Volunteer for a cause that you think is important. This could include rescue missions, food drives and cleanup duty.
- Learn from the crisis and develop long-term safety plans.

Commitment Intimacy

Commitment intimacy is the experience of hope and possibility in response to addressing an issue, cause or event bigger than one individual. This can range from a short-term task (completing a social service project) to a never-ending task such as social justice. It's the process of transforming the world.

- Identify a cause or value that means something to you. Volunteer your time, talent or treasure.
- Within the 12-step tradition, service work is about commitment intimacy.

Spiritual Intimacy

Spiritual intimacy develops through sharing the most important areas of concern including values, the meaning of life and the core of our being. It's an experience of possibility and transcendence beyond the daily experience of who we are. It can include religious traditions and practices, but ultimately it's about how we connect with personal meaning (or, "God," in whatever way you understand Him/Her/It).

- Talk to the spiritual advisor of a group different from the one in which you grew up.
- Join a church.
- Join a 12-step group. This could be AA but it might also be a 12-step group for partners of AA, sexual compulsivity, debtors, eating and even Emotions Anonymous.
- Join a group that discusses life values.

Communication Intimacy

Communication intimacy is the process of full disclosure with another person. It's the process of being open, honest and truthful. This includes giving and getting difficult and constructive feedback, even when it's not easy to do so.

- Simply say what you mean, and mean what you say. (Too often, people say what they think other people want to hear.)

- Learn how to be present and listen to other people by attending a listening training program.
- Continue to share insights into your progress with your support network.

Conflict Intimacy

Conflict intimacy is the process of connecting and respectful fighting, as well as facing differences with others and struggling to understand one another. There is a sense of closeness that transcends conflict and ultimately leads to a closer relationship. The power of "make-up sex" highlights how conflict intimacy is so powerful.

- Recognize that healthy fighting is a normal part of a relationship.
- Learn how to fight in healthy ways by reading a book on conflict management/resolution.
- Attend an anger-management course.

Touch/Physical Intimacy

Touch/physical intimacy is the process of affirming and being affirmed by another through physical contact. Classic social psychology research has suggested that the failure to receive touch can have a severe negative health, social and emotional impact on a person. Due to the nature of our subject here, this type of intimacy requires a closer look and is explored in more depth below (see "Touch Needs").

- As a friend for a hug.
- Get a massage.
- Snuggle with someone you define as appropriate.

These types of intimacy are simply a place to start. They are not exclusive, or exhaustive. Instead, they are designed to help you start thinking of what you want in your life and how to start getting your needs met in healthy ways.

ASSIGNMENT: Top Intimacy Needs

Review the types of intimacy above.

- Identify the top three types of intimacy most important to you.

- How would you know if these intimacy needs are satisfied in your life?

- Identify 3–5 people who can help you meet those intimacy needs.

- If you are not satisfied with your levels of intimacy, identify a plan to increase your level of satisfaction.

- Review your sexual behavior timeline in light of the need for intimacy. How have you coped with, damaged, or otherwise tried to get these needs met? Where might acting-out behaviors be related to this?

Now that you have reviewed the types of intimacy, the key is to identify what types of intimacy are most important for you and begin moving toward those types. Think about what *you* want versus what you think others want you to want.

ASSIGNMENT: Practicing Intimacy

Pick one of your top three types of intimacy. Identify and complete a plan to experience that type of intimacy. Review the experience with your support network.

Touch Needs

Touch/physical intimacy (or *touch needs*) is a form of intimacy requiring special focus. The overlap between sexual intimacy and touch intimacy leads to significant confusion. Because types of touch exist on a continuum, it's sometimes difficult to pinpoint exactly when a touch moves from physical/non-sexual to physical/sexual. Such a difference is often in the eye of the beholder. This makes a clear distinction difficult. The key is to know where your boundaries lie. For example, when is a hug a sign of affirmation versus the start of a sexual encounter? Below are a number of concepts to consider in reviewing the type of touch that you want in your life followed by exercises on erotic and sensual touch.

Nurturing touch is a healthy and normal part of being human. Touching people is one way of reaching out/affirming them—and being affirmed yourself. Unhealthy touch is the opposite. Unhealthy or *exploitive touch* is manipulative, forced or unwanted. It can be a way someone expresses hurt, anger or fear. Some touch is confusing; it occurs in the middle or grey area of the touch continuum. In this confusing center are experiences of touch that appear healthy but leave a person unsure about the intent. Examples may be a hug that includes a brush against breasts, buttocks or genitalia, or a kiss that goes on too long. In moving toward sexual health, it's important to recognize healthy and unhealthy touch and to identify ways to get your touch needs met. You may also want to review the topic on abuse (page 131).

In modern American culture, there is a significant barrier to touch. Many of the messages about touch actually sexualize it. As a result, we may misinterpret the messages of another person. In America, two guys holding hands are seen as a gay couple rather than two friends together, different from the way these two would be viewed in many Middle Eastern cultures. There are also gender differences. Touch is culturally encouraged for many women, but not for men. The typical woman has a better understanding of touch needs than the typical man. The misunderstanding of touch raises significant problems regarding sexual harassment claims. In sexualizing touch, our culture has deprived us of ways to get healthy needs met in appropriate ways. This misunderstanding can lead to miscommunication, conflicts and resentments in sexual, social and emotional relationships.

ASSIGNMENT: Touch Needs

- Describe 2-3 examples where your touch needs have not been met. Identify possible barriers and plans to address these.

- What are the messages you have heard about touch from your family, culture, religious tradition or community? How well can you ask others to help with meeting your touch intimacy needs?

- In developing ways to get your touch needs meet, it's also important to be clear about your motivations. In reviewing your sexual behavior, how many times have you engaged in the behavior when what you were looking for was simply affirmation through touch?

ASSIGNMENT: Sensual Touch

It is time for another massage! In addition to re-connecting you with your body, a non-sexual full body massage provides a chance for you to experience touch over all parts of your body (excluding genitalia). Revisit the masseuse you worked with for the previous "Full Body Massage," or try out a new one. Afterwards, review the experience with your support network.

ASSIGNMENT: Erotic Touch

Review the exercise on masturbation (page 149). This exercise increases the level of interaction with your partner. In this exercise, you link sensual massage with the masturbation exercise you did previously, touching all parts of your partner's body in different ways. Working with a safe partner, you'll touch your partner starting with focusing on many parts of the body other than the genitalia, and moving toward including genitalia. The goal isn't orgasm, but simply the experience of being touched in erotic ways. For some individuals, this exercise may need to occur in sequence with other assignments (see "FIVE: Barriers to Sexual Health—Beyond Functioning" on page 125). Now exchange roles, and repeat. The goal is to extend the duration for 60 minutes or more. Practice assertive communication skills highlighting which types of touch you like, and where you like to be touched. Afterwards, review the experience with your support network.

Barriers to Intimacy

Barriers to intimacy can be internal or external. *Internal barriers* reflect issues in our life and our interaction with others. They may be historical (history of abuse) or current (shame or depression). These barriers can be unhealthy thoughts we have about ourselves or about others. The level of self-doubt, or negative statements, you have about yourself is a classic internal barrier to intimacy. Overcoming, correcting and changing these thoughts are necessary. One example of a person with an intimacy barrier is someone who identifies as a gay man but who believes he is sinful. Another example is an individual who has been abused. These individuals must address the internal story before healthy intimacy is possible. In both cases, casual sexual behaviors might be easier due to the reduced fear of getting hurt. Long-term growth will need to address the fear.

External barriers are outside of us. Examples of these barriers may be isolation or a lack of resources to connect with others. Some of the "-isms" (such as sexism, racism, and heterosexism) are external barriers. With these situations, setting up plans to help you address how the external barriers affect your life can be a helpful approach. Other times the barrier may be a lack of skills that negatively influences a person's ability to communicate with others. In these cases, therapy and coaching may be helpful. You'll not find intimacy when you shut down and isolate yourself out of fear. Resorting to the Internet, instead of direct, human contact, is one way people have figuratively "shut down." Intimacy is learned through trial and error. Intimacy sometimes requires the pain of rejection, failure or betrayal. It's not possible to avoid these risks and have intimacy. Your reaction to life's hurts and fears can lead to opportunities for intimacy. The reality is that the other person is probably just as fearful as you are. The question is: Which person will be the first to transcend that fear?

Consider your acting-out behaviors. Often, the acting out is an attempt to address intimacy needs. Clients have often talked about how they were bored and went online. Or, you may be lonely but don't know how to get communication/emotional intimacy needs met except through sexual behavior. Think about the intimacy payoffs you were trying to get met through your acting-out behavior. Until you develop healthy intimacy skills, you risk returning to unhealthy behaviors.

ASSIGNMENT: Barriers to Intimacy

- As you review your sexual history and timeline, describe 2-3 barriers to intimacy (or the lack of intimacy). Identify plans to address these barriers.

- Review your timeline for sexual behaviors and/or other forms of acting out. Identify 2-3 unhealthy behaviors that were attempts to meet your intimacy needs. Identify plans to address these unhealthy behaviors.

Relationships and Dating Behaviors

Culturally, one of the major influences in a person's overall happiness is the presence of a partner. When I ask clients, "What would an amazing life look like?" there is an almost universal desire to have someone to share life with. "To be loved" is a key desire for many individuals. For some individuals, how to meet and date a partner is a major barrier toward relationship health. The material below is to designed to provide basic information to help you determine what you want in this regard and how to go about getting it.

Dating and Courtship

As you journey toward relationship health, it's important to reflect on what you want, whether or not what you have is healthy, and how to move toward what you want/consider healthy. For individuals in an existing relationship damaged by sexual behavior, it might be helpful to date (symbolically) your current partner. Using these ideas may help re-kindle and heal your current relationship. For some individuals, this information may help in developing a relationship. Even the best relationships can move toward closer connections. For this last group, the topics below may enrich an already rich relationship.

As people start addressing their sexual health issues, eventually they start meeting others, including dating and eventually courtship. Often, dating triggers new awareness of unknown issues, or recognition that you need to spend more time on issues you addressed previously (such as shame/guilt, cultural issues, or healing from abuse). Below are eight ideas designed to help frame the desire to date as a process. Perfection isn't required (or possible), but addressing these areas will increase your chances for positive experiences.

1) Readiness

Clarify whether or not you're ready to date. Dating requires that you have a sense of self, and that you are comfortable in your overall progress. Dating requires assertive communication. It requires that you've defined your basic boundaries including level of disclosure, when disclosure will occur, and a multitude of desires and wants. Examining past dating experiences and addressing triggers is important. One part of this process consists of asking yourself how much you are willing to share about your sexual behaviors. Talking with your support network and addressing their feedback is important.

2) Boundaries

Clarify your boundaries about which sexual behaviors would be acceptable. Set up explicit boundaries about the type of sexual behavior that can or can't occur. This needs to be clarified before you start dating.

3) Goals

Identify your goals. Be honest with yourself and your support network about what you are looking for in your desire to start dating. Are you looking for friendship? Sex? Relationship? Children? None of these goals is better than any of the others, but be honest. Develop the skills to effectively communicate these goals with your potential partners. Communicate and get feedback from your support network.

4) Planning

Clarify the type of date you want. Sometimes starting small is the best plan. You might go on a coffee date on a Saturday morning. You might do a lunch date. Instead of calling it a date, describe it as a "social chat" or "meet-and-greet." Taking the word *date* off the table and focusing on the social interaction can reduce stress and anxiety. Scheduling it during the day, or in the morning (versus Friday evening) can create clarity regarding your goals.

5) Activities

Identify activities that you want to do. You can use this to start a conversation about what your potential dating partner likes to do. Think outside the box. Review the suggestions on intimacy to consider alternatives to the classic date. You might go to church, go to a museum, or go to lecture.

6) Safety Plan(s)

Create safety plans. These safety plans include many types. Physical safety is obviously important, but emotional safety is as well. Ensure your safety by scheduling an "escape plan" or an "out." If you're going for a coffee date at 11:00 a.m., set up a meeting with a person from your support network for 1:00 p.m. to talk about the experience. If the encounter goes well, you can always have a second encounter. This plan creates physical safety in that the support network person will be expecting you; it creates emotional safety in that it provides a time limit, which can be especially useful if the experience is unpleasant. In addition, these plans can address possible high-risk concerns (e.g., ensuring you don't have sex on the first date).

7) Maintain Perspective

Remember dating for what dating is. It's a chance to meet and interact with others. You're not making a lifetime commitment to the person on a single date. By addressing the expectations and assumptions you bring to the conversation, you can maintain your focus.

8) Known Concerns

Address known concerns beforehand. For example, if you're an introvert develop topics you feel comfortable sharing and asking about. Make sure you are asking questions versus letting the other person set the agenda. If you're the classic extrovert, make sure you listen as well.

ASSIGNMENT: Your Dating Process

- Reflect on the stages above, what's the stage you need to practice most?

- Pick one of the stages you would like to implement. What are two things you could do to implement the stage?

The Language of Relationships

Much of couples therapy focuses on communication skills. Using the helpful metaphor of language, undoing the assumption that we all speak the same language is often the first place of intervention. Consider the following:

English is the predominant language in the United States and the assumption is that we all speak English; however, even within the United States, different words are used to describe the same concept. For example, New Yorkers enjoying a Coke might be drinking *soda*, but Midwesterners enjoying the same drink would be drinking *pop*. Different words are used in other English speaking countries, like England. Americans on a road trip store their luggage in the *trunk* of their car, but the British store it in the *boot*. When the Americans arrive at their destination, they might take the *elevator* up to their desired floor rather than the British *lift*. Likewise, there are significant differences between Spanish in Latin America and Spanish in Spain. Even Arabic has multiple dialects, and these differences are barriers to communication. So even though people may speak one common language, it's crucial to be aware of differences present in that one common language. These differences are referred to as *dialects*.

In working toward sexual health, it's important to learn how to understand and translate the different dialects of sexual behavior and intimacy. In relationships, we all have different dialects of communication. These dialects are informed and shaped by the multiple cultures we belong to, our family of origin, and our life history. Often, there is enough commonality to be able to communicate with a partner. Most relationship problems stem from communication problems that show up in the guise of unmet expectations and assumptions, hidden wants and needs, past hurts and pains, and unspoken hoped-for joys and goals.

A classic example is fighting. In some families, conflict is forbidden. A partner learns that anger can't be expressed. Another partner may come from a family where conflict is resolved quickly and respectfully. When two partners come together, the dialect of conflict is an obstacle to be resolved. The resolution is often as simple as teaching each other their respective dialects. The same idea can be applied to mundane things, like the level of cleanliness in the house, or difficult areas, such as sexual expression, needs and values.

The difficulty in this process is that much of our dialect regarding relationships is automatic and habitual. We assume everyone has the same language, mannerisms, assumptions, and expectations in a relationship. That assumption is often the source of the relationship problems. Teaching each other your individual dialects and learning to translate your partner's dialect is a necessary skill for building powerful and strong relationships.

Four Deadly Horsemen in Relationships

John Gottman researches couples therapy. He is well known and respected for his work at pinpointing factors that contribute to long-term relationships as well as behaviors that facilitate the demise of relationships. One of the metaphors he identifies is that of the "Four Deadly Horsemen" in relationships—those behaviors that bring about an end of a relationship (playing on the four deadly horsemen of the Apocalypse, or the end of the world.)[30] Here are the "horsemen" he identifies:

Criticism

Criticism is focusing or otherwise only seeing the negative components of a partner. We all understand the basic negative impact of negative criticism. The non-verbal forms of negative criticism are sometimes equally (or more) difficult to address. Ever get that "look" from your partner? Assertive communication is the path out of criticism. The difference appears small, but the implication is significant.

Defensiveness

Defensiveness focuses everything on your partner's mistakes. The defensiveness creates a barrier to admitting your own part of the conflict or struggle. This approach reflects the saying, "The best defense is a strong offense." By avoiding your role in conflict, you project onto the partner all of the problems. Owning your behaviors and taking responsibility for your part of the conversation is one helpful strategy.

Stonewalling

Stonewalling refers to the avoidance of the partner, or passive-aggressive behaviors. This is where your words don't match your attitudes and behaviors. Again, assertiveness is a helpful strategy here. It may also be helpful to focus on the value of integrity, or "saying what you mean and meaning what you say." Uncovering or otherwise revealing your hidden/secret thoughts and feelings is necessary.

Contempt

Contempt is the judgment that occurs in a relationship. Much of Gottman's research has focused on the subtleties of how contempt shows up. It usually serves to demean the individual. Finding healthy ways to address the underlying issues is important. Taking responsibility for your thoughts/feelings, as well as developing assertive ways to communicate them is necessary. Being mindful of your judgment is necessary.

If you notice any of these behaviors in your relationship, seek help. Often one of these patterns is linked with the others, leading to a flood of issues to be addressed. As the saying goes, "the four deadly horsemen don't travel alone."

Relationship Satisfaction

I had a great many sex and love cases where people were absolutely devastated when somebody with whom they were compulsively in love didn't love them back. They were killing themselves with anxiety and depression. (Albert Ellis)

Relationship satisfaction is a major component of sexual health. It's important to examine how your sexual behavior is related to relationship satisfaction. As in other topics, acting-out behavior can be both a cause and a consequence of relationship satisfaction concerns. In this topic you are encouraged to focus on your level of satisfaction in your current (or most recent) relationship. Long-term personal happiness, health and wellness are correlated with healthy relationships. One of the more difficult tasks in any relationship is being able to talk with your partner(s) comfortably about sex. The issues can range from simply how often to have sex and or what to do during sex, to whether the relationship should be open, monogamous or some variation thereof.

The following questions will help you assess your thoughts and feelings surrounding your current relationship situation.

ASSIGNMENT: Relationship Satisfaction

Respond to the following statements:

Talking about sex with my sexual partner(s) is a satisfying experience.

Completely Agree---Completely Disagree

Overall, I feel satisfied about my current sexual relationship(s).

Completely Agree---Completely Disagree

I have difficulty finding a sexual partner.

Completely Agree---Completely Disagree

I feel my sexual partner avoids talking about sexuality with me.

Completely Agree---Completely Disagree

When I have sex with my partner, I feel emotionally close to him or her.

Completely Agree---Completely Disagree

Overall, I feel close with my sexual partner(s).

Completely Agree---Completely Disagree

I have difficulty keeping a sexual partner.

Completely Agree---Completely Disagree

I feel I can express what I like and don't like sexually.

Completely Agree---Completely Disagree

I feel my sexual partner is sensitive to my needs and desires.

Completely Agree---Completely Disagree

Some sexual matters are too upsetting to discuss with my partner(s).

Completely Agree---Completely Disagree

- Review your responses. Summarize what you learned.

If you are like most readers, you'll find yourself dissatisfied with some aspect(s) of your current relationship situation. The assignment below helps you identify strengths and weaknesses in your relationship by graphing topics onto a target.

ASSIGNMENT: Identifying Relationship Strengths and Weaknesses

On a large piece of paper, start by drawing a target with three circles. You are essentially drawing a target that you might use for archery. The outer circle should take up the entire paper. Within that circle, center a mid-sized circle, and within the middle circle, draw another smaller circle.

What follows are topics that you'll graph into one of the circles. There are three color categories you'll use to chart the topics—red, yellow and green (see below). Chart any/all of the following as appropriate. If not a concern or issue, simply cross it out and leave it off the graph. Focus on how you perceive the topic, not on how you think you should perceive it. This is your list, not your partner's list. (Your partner can do his/her own list, and you can share with one another.)

The outer circle is where you'll write the *red topics*. They represent the concerns furthest from the bull's eye. These are the topics that are most out of balance, and represent your biggest concerns in the relationship.

The middle circle represents the *yellow topics*. They are the ones you might modify with "It depends." The yellow topics could also represent what's getting better (a red moving toward green) or getting worse (green moving toward the red). The yellow circle might represent issues you'll address later, or issues that you never thought about before, but you recognize as important.

The inner circle represents the *green topics*. These are the topics that you have a lot of satisfaction with in your life. They are topics that reflect the joys, hopes and desires that are in agreement with your values and what you want.

Start with your personal frame of reference, "How do you see your issues?"

RED: *Unhappy, problem, concern*
YELLOW: *Depends, sometimes, getting better/worse, don't know but should*
GREEN: *Strengths, likes, happy about*

- Your comfort in talking about sex
- Disclosing your sex history
- Your cultural values regarding relationships
- Your feelings of shame
- Your feelings of guilt
- Your sexual identity/sexual orientation
- Your sexual functioning
- Your sexual skills
- The types of sexual contact you have with your partner
- The frequency of sexual contact
- Your safer-sex behaviors (risk for pregnancy/HIV/STI)
- Your sexual compulsivity behaviors
- Your sexual avoidance behaviors
- Your alcohol use
- Your other chemical use

- Your eating behaviors
- Your spending behaviors
- Your mental health diagnosis(es)
- Your experience of sexual, physical or emotional abuse
- Your level of Internet/technology use
- Your level of online sexual behavior
- Your types of online sexual behavior.
- Your body image
- Your partner's view of your body
- Your frequency of masturbation
- Your ability to engage in assertive communication
- Your personal boundaries
- Your desire for intimacy
- Your most important types of intimacy
- The type of touch/physical intimacy

- The frequency of touch/physical intimacy
- Your ability to talk to your partner

- Your spiritual values
- Your religious beliefs

Next, address your partner's frame of reference: "How do you see your partner?"

- Your partner's comfort in talking about sex
- Disclosure of your partner's sex history
- Your partner's cultural values regarding relationships
- Your partner's feelings of shame
- Your partner's feelings of guilt
- Your partner's sexual identity/sexual orientation
- Your partner's sexual functioning
- Your partner's sexual skills
- Your partner's desired types of sexual contact
- Your partner's desired frequency of sexual contact with you
- Your partner's safer-sex behaviors (risk for pregnancy/HIV/STI)
- Your partner's sexual compulsivity behaviors
- Your partner's sexual avoidance behaviors
- Your partner's alcohol use
- Your partner's other chemical use
- Your partner's eating behaviors
- Your partner's spending behaviors

- Your partner's mental health diagnosis(es)
- Your partner's experience of sexual, physical or emotional abuse
- Your partner's level of Internet/technology use
- Your partner's level of online sexual behavior
- Your partner's types of online sexual behavior
- Your partner's body image
- Your partner's view of your body
- Your partner's frequency of masturbation
- Your partner's ability to engage in assertive communication
- Your partner's personal boundaries
- Your partner's desire for intimacy
- Your partner's most important types of intimacy
- Your partner's type of touch/physical intimacy
- Your partner's frequency of touch/physical intimacy
- Your partner's ability to talk to you
- Your partner's spiritual values
- Your partner's religious beliefs

Despite its length, this list is far from exhaustive. Are there any topics that you're happy about that are not on the list? If there are other topics you're worried about, or are a major concern, add them to your chart.

You can use this list to highlight treatment issues. After you complete this assignment, you might review the placement of these issues on the target with your partner and vice-versa. You can learn a lot about each other by recognizing similarities and differences in the perception of the topics. By the way, where you are in agreement with positive aspects—congrats and enjoy!

Healing from Past Relationships

When a dog bites a child, there is a high probability that the child will have a negative reaction to dogs in the future. This is an example of transference (page 38). Any reaction you have to a person may be built on your history of experiences. When you have a reaction to a current partner, this reaction is built on your past experiences. When positive, this is helpful. When negative, this can create a barrier that may possibly doom the new relationship.

The amount of hurt arising from past relationships is a major barrier to future relationships. The amount of hurt caused by sexual behavior affirms the need for healing as well. Before you can begin again, you need to clear away the garbage of hurt and anger arising from past relationships. Many people will say they are over their ex, or over the partner's sexual behavior, but my experience suggests otherwise.

ASSIGNMENT: Healing from Past Relationships

It is important to have a clear understanding about the connection between your life history and your sexual behavior. Review your sexual history and timeline. Consider the following questions:

- How have your past relationships affected your sexual behavior and vice-versa?

- How has your sexual behavior affected your relationships?

- Was your sexual behavior a response to something your partner did? If so, describe the details.

- Was your partner's behavior in response to something you did? If so, describe the details.

ASSIGNMENT: Saying goodbye to a former relationship

Here are a number of strategies I have found that are helpful in healing from past relationships. They are designed to help create forgiveness in your life.

- Write a goodbye letter. Share it with your support network. Set the letter aside and repeat writing a letter and share it again. Repeat again. Keep and review each version. After you've done this ten times, sit down and review each letter. You will be able to identify a number of themes. Hopefully, you will be able to see your progress in the healing process. Once you have done this about ten times, review with your support network. If you choose, send the eleventh version of the letter.

- Get Support. Reach out to friends, family and professionals.

- Complete an inventory. Honestly assess your role in the relationship conflict. Step out of the victim role. Recognize that "it takes two to tango." Move forward.

- Establish a boundary. Despite what your ex might say, your ex's behavior is about your ex, not you. This is important. Remind yourself of it.

It's important to seek help if there are other issues connected to a past relationship. Sometimes the feelings of grief and hurt are so strong that some type of grief therapy might be important. Many of the issues covered previously are possible barriers to future relationships, including depression, types and impact of abuse, stages of identity development, and feelings of shame and guilt. Until these are addressed, you may be stuck on an escalator trying to go the wrong way.

Forgiveness in Relationships

Life is an adventure in forgiveness. (Norman Cousins)

Forgiveness is not about forgetting. Forgiveness is not about letting the other person off the hook. Forgiveness is about your healing. It includes helping you heal from negative thoughts and, at the same, helping you let go of painful feelings. It's also an extreme act of compassion when you can forgive the person who hurt you. In some religious traditions, raising forgiveness to a radical expression is offering compassion to the one who offended you. This brings about your radical transformation.

Building the Sexual Relationship

The main goal in any couple's relationship is open and honest communication between partners about what they want, what they don't want and what makes them happy. When your behaviors match your values, it's a sign of sexual health. It's your responsibility to communicate your values to your partner. The degree to which any behavior is consistent with your values is a decision that ultimately rests with you. Regarding sexual expression with your partner, four general tasks are important:

Basic Tasks for Communicating About Sex

Tell your partner

Have you told your partner what you like and don't like? Too many times, I have run into couples that say to one another, "I didn't know that." For any number of reasons (shame, low self-esteem, fear of being judged, not wanting to upset their partner), clients will not talk about their likes and dislikes. In many cases, acting-out behaviors may be a result of not knowing how to talk to your partner about what you like or don't like.

Ask your partner

Once you know what you like, you should concentrate on what your partner likes and dislikes. It's important not only to know your partner's likes and dislikes, but why he or she has these interests. For example, a couple didn't engage in penetration because it physically hurt. It turned out the pain was due to warts, and once that condition was addressed the problem went away.

Learn

Don't be shy if you don't know how to do something. You might need to learn the basics regarding foreplay, stimulating the clitoris, the sexual response cycle, stretching the vaginal and/or sphincter muscle, proper cleanup and so on. You may need to educate your partner.

Get help

If after going through the first three steps you find you are still having problems, you may want to seek some outside help. This does not necessarily mean therapy or counseling, although professional help is a good option for more challenging problems. Try having a frank out-of-the-box conversation in which you look at creative outlets and avenues to get your sexual needs met. These could include talking to your spiritual adviser, attending a sexuality workshop, or reading various "how-to" books. You might go online together to review possible interventions to address the problems. Each of these interventions might be helpful in breaking the logjam in your relationship.

Additional Considerations

If you and your partner have completed each of the four basic tasks above and are still having problems, you may need to consider the following. The three topics below require honest and often difficult discussions between you and your partner, but they are important to address.

Prioritizing

Some relationships don't focus on sex because they are rich in other ways, such as shared values or emotional connections (see the section on *Intimacy*, page 173). Consider the importance of your sexual request. Are you willing to live without it? In looking at the whole picture, you might have to agree not to engage in the behavior. This is often the case in alternative (i.e., kinkier) types of sexual behavior. If you absolutely are unwilling to live without the type of sexual behavior, consider the next two ideas.

Substituting

If your need or desire is important enough that you choose not to live without it, you and your partner need to negotiate an alternative way to get your sexual needs met. This can be difficult, eliciting significant fear, jealousy and raise other issues. It may require changing the type of your relationship (see below).

Transitioning

In my experience, ongoing and significant problems regarding sex can be symptoms of underlying problems within the relationship. While no one likes to hear it, the failure to arrive at a solution might suggest the relationship may not be a healthy one. An example of behavior in an unhealthy relationship might include saying things like, "Yes, I'll do it," when you don't intend to follow through. Constantly trying to persuade your partner to engage in a behavior is manipulation and not a healthy sign A hard and honest look at your relationship may reveal that it's not healthy and that it may need to end. If you are both stuck in this area and don't see a solution, seeking outside professional help may be the best, and possibly the last option for you.

ASSIGNMENT: Healthy Sexual Interchange

This assignment builds on four preceding ones: "Development of Sexual Intimacy Skills" (page 119), "Full Body Massage" (page 148), "Healthy Masturbation" (page 152), and "Erotic Touch" (page 180). You're encouraged to apply your experience from these assignments here. The goal is to start applying the development of sexual intimacy skills with your partner, and of course, have fun along the way.

Working with a safe partner, touch your partner as first outlined in the sexual intimacy skills assignment (page 119). In reviewing that exercise, what types of touch are comfortable and enjoyable for you. Starting with the these skills, add the experience from the full body massage. What areas do you want touched, either because they are sensitive, or will help you relax and enjoy the experience? Continue building on the types of skills, and include the concepts for the masturbation exercise by touching your partner on places other than the genitalia, eventually moving toward including genitalia. Pay attention to other senses besides touch: sight, sound (music, or type of talk), taste (yes, taste!) and smell (e.g. candles, partner's scent). In this exercise, the goal is to integrate all of the senses. Practice assertive communication skills highlighting what you like and what you want. Afterwards, review the experience with your partner and your support network.

Depending on your progress, you and your partner may have to practice this many times (practice makes perfect). For some people, this exercise creates too much stress, so it may take time to proceed through the various practice sessions.

Types of Relationships

As we've discussed, culture is very powerful in shaping our view of what's a healthy relationship. Our current culture emphasizes that sexual behavior should occur within a monogamous relationship, and that only monogamous relationships are healthy. How much do you agree with this expectation? In fact, there are a multitude of different types of relationships. Sexual health requires that you clarify the type of relationship you want. This is a controversial area and clinicians legitimately differ in their opinions. The primary approach taken in this book is that you have the responsibility to choose the type of life you want to live regarding sexual expression and relationships. I mention three types of sexual relationships:

Celibacy and Singledom

Celibacy is often confused with remaining single (singledom), but it's different. Definitions vary, but I define celibacy as a choice not to engage in any sexual contact with anyone. There are opinions saying that any sexual expression including masturbation, fantasy and use of sexually explicit material go against the idea of celibacy. Some religious traditions impose celibacy as the only acceptable path for groups of people (usually LGBT individuals or non-married individuals). Also, some religious traditions impose celibacy as a discipline in order for a person to qualify to be a minister in that tradition.

Rightfully understood, however, celibacy is less about telling yourself "you can't do that" than it's about emphasizing something greater in a person's life. Celibacy allows a greater commitment to the major focus in a person's life. In this approach, celibacy is believed to facilitate other types of intimate relationships (page 173). In my opinion, a healthy expression of celibacy is possible. It does take work and self-understanding, and celibacy doesn't turn off the sexual energy within a person. If you choose this, you must find healthy ways to channel your sexual energy. It's very important to choose celibacy for the right reason. I've run into many individuals who choose celibacy out of fear, a history of abuse, or low self-esteem. If these are the motivating factors for choosing celibacy, it's only a matter of time until a commitment or vow of celibacy will be broken (and/or cause significant negative consequences).

Singledom is the choice to remain single and not be in a primary relationship. Often, people don't consider singledom as a choice, given the assumption from the primary culture that everyone should be in a relationship. The pressure toward coupling is both profound and subtle. Watch what happens with your couple-friends when you break up a relationship. Think about Grandma's first comment when you go home for the holidays: "Have you found someone yet?" It's an expression of concern for your happiness, but it does demonstrate the social pressure toward coupling, and it implies that something is wrong with remaining single. Singledom is simply an option on how to live out your life. It may, or may not, include celibacy. It may be short- or long- term. It is simply a choice. As in all other choices, the reason that you are choosing to be single is the key question for you. Understanding your motivations (including perhaps some of the unspoken reasons) is a key to sexual health.

Monogamy

Most of this book is built on an assumption of monogamy (I chose to do this simply because this is what most people are seeking.). *Monogamy* is typically defined as sexual contact exclusively between two individuals within some type of committed relationship. Even this definition has different interpretations, resulting in confusion and conflict. For some people, monogamy is expanded to prevent any emotional relationships with anyone but the primary partner. Some interpretations of monogamy also view use of sexually explicit material as a violation of monogamy. So, for some couples, online sexual behavior would be a violation of the commitment to monogamy, but in other couples, this would be okay. The key is for you and your partner to clarify your opinions.

Healthy monogamy is about trust and commitment. It means working with your partner to put the other first. Paradoxically, in putting the other first, your needs are met, in part because your partner is putting you first. Monogamy isn't passive; it requires tremendous amounts of work. This book is designed to start the necessary conversations regarding healthy monogamy, to make it possible for you to choose monogamy for the right reasons. When monogamy is chosen out of fear, it's less an expression of love than an expression of control over your partner. There is a decided lack of trust. (The same concerns exist in choosing celibacy or singledom. Celibacy or singledom chosen out of fear is probably not a healthy choice.)

Open Relationships

Open relationships are typically defined as relationships where there exists a primary sexual and emotional partner followed by a secondary partner or partners. (Given the focus of the book, there isn't the space to fully address *poly relationships* and *alternative relationships*. For more information on these, read *Ethical Slut* by Easton and Litsz, or check out www.xeromag.com). Within the concept of open relationships, there are a variety of definitions and expressions. If you choose an open relationship, it's important for you and your primary partner to clarify ground rules and expectations. *When? Where? With whom?* and *How often?* are all questions you should address. Others include: What are your plans for communicating and coping with fear, jealousy and insecurity? What are your safer-sex rules?

If you want an open relationship, examine what unmet needs (if any) exist within your primary relationship. Significant reflection should occur within your support network to clarify the reasons you want an open relationship. In particular, be careful that you are not simply trying to get out of the primary relationship. If the primary relationship is not healthy, it's important to address the issues first. If it should end, do this with integrity instead of forcing a rift that ends the relationship. One guideline is that all partners be open and honest in the conversation. Both partners must agree with a sense of internal integrity with any decision. It might be better to end a relationship than agree to a type of relationship that's inconsistent with your values.

ASSIGNMENT: Relationship Type and Jealousy

Dating and Relationship Behavior

- Describe what would be considered a healthy date?

- Where is a healthy place to meet partners?

- When you meet someone for the first time, what do you consider?

Relationship Patterns

- Describe your dating behavior.

- How do you meet dating partners?

- Describe the dating/courtship that occurred in your relationship.

- How quickly did sexual contact occur in the relationship?

- Clarify what type of relationship you want in your life. Explain this to your support network. Review this with your partner.

- Jealousy can occur in any type of relationship. What's your plan to address feelings of jealousy when you experience them?

Finding a Relationship Therapist

As in the case of individual growth, there are times when professional help is needed for a couple to journey toward sexual health. See "Finding a (Sex) Therapist" (page 62) for suggestions on how to go about finding a therapist. Remember to ask specifically about working with couples. Complete an Internet search on "marriage" or "couples" therapists.

Guidelines for Relationship Therapy

Clarify goals. Before you start, to the best of your ability, clarify your goal(s). While it might be hard to acknowledge, if you know that you don't want to stay in the relationship, be honest up front for the sanity of everyone. This includes your sanity, your partner's sanity and the clinician's sanity.

<u>Time commitment.</u> Many times the individuals in the relationship will start therapy during a rocky period. If either one of the individuals is unsure about the future of the relationship, your therapist may ask for a time commitment from both of you to discern your intentions and to work on the relationship.

<u>Relationship as client.</u> Remember that the relationship is the client, not the individuals. Most individual therapists will not do relationship therapy when working with one member of the relationship. There are appropriate exceptions, so this is not an absolute rule. Check with the therapist.

<u>Share everything.</u> During the intake session, put everything on the table, whether it's sexual issues, insecurity, jealousy, communication, respect, or whatever. Often, the second and third sessions are individual meetings to provide each individual an opportunity to put additional issues on the table that may be too difficult in the first session. Sharing everything is important. For example, if you engage in alternative sexual behaviors, or if you had a sexual contact outside the relationship, say so. It's better to put it on the table sooner than later.

<u>Juggling expectations.</u> A juggling metaphor in relationship therapy helps to demonstrate the challenge of relationship therapy. At the start of relationship therapy, there are three balls to juggle: Person A, Person B, and the Relationship. The three balls of relationship therapy make creating change in the relationship more difficult than individual therapy. It's important for both individuals to have realistic expectations about the timing of disclosure in light of overall progress.

Full Disclosure to Partners

When individuals address their sexually compulsive behavior, it affects their partners as well. Cleaning up the impact of the behavior in the relationship is vitally important, and often the source of some of the biggest fear for the client. In this section, there are two assignments, one for each member of the relationship to consider regarding the possibility of full disclosure. For the partner, a variety of issues must be addressed, including emotional, physical and sexual issues. It may be helpful if the partner obtain his/her therapy/support as well. I recommend that both partners clarify their respective commitments to the future of the relationship before disclosing sexually compulsive behavior. One partner's disclosure of sexually compulsive behavior triggers a parallel coping process for the other partner. Treatment includes getting information, including understanding the language of people in the field. Therapists and those involved in the 12-step movement often use a jargon for shorthand communication. Learning the meaning of these terms is important. As you move away from crisis and shock, stay focused on your emotional and physical health. Incidentally, if the computer is shared, family members may have access to sexually explicit material. It's nearly impossible to fully remove all inappropriate files, so it's important to address basic safety issues and to set boundaries to maintain other people's safety.

As a person copes with a partner's compulsive behavior, it's important for the person to triage priorities. The person must identify what has to be done today, in the next month, the next three months and the next year. Partners typically have feelings of despair, hopelessness, confusion, and anger. Shock, depression and grief may also occur. Sometimes individuals blame themselves, either due to ignoring signs or simply not knowing. Part of the healing process is to gain support from professionals, peer networks (groups) and family or spiritual community members.

If the behavior led to an actual encounter, the partner may be at increased risk for HIV/STIs. I recommend that you meet with your health care provider. Be completely open and honest about the purpose of the visit. Some providers will assume that individuals in a relationship are not at risk for HIV/STI. The partner will need to be explicit and say, "I found out my partner has multiple sex partners and I'm worried about being infected with a STI." The relationship will need to determine safer-sex guidelines in light of any risky behaviors.

After both individuals have addressed their respective issues, couples therapy can facilitate the healing of the relationship. Relationship issues can address blaming statements by the partner. Often there is a sense of powerlessness that comes with not knowing what to do and how to get your partner to stop the behaviors. Treatment for the individual and the partner includes clarifying what you both need and want in a relationship and assessing honestly where the current relationship is going. This is a chance for you to clarify your boundaries and develop the skills to protect those boundaries. Some partners may feel pressured by their support network to leave the relationship. Unfortunately, no guidelines are available for the decisions you and your partner might need to make. Some relationships can continue; others should end. If you know you are not going to stay in the relationship, disclosure of your sexually history or timeline is not necessary (although any potential exposure to STIs must be acknowledged). If you know you want to stay in the relationship, such disclosure can occur. I'll not work with couples that use the process of disclosure as ammunition against each other. In this approach, disclosure is about repairing, reconciling and taking full responsibility in order to foster an ongoing relationship.

What do you share?

After discovering that his partner was engaging in sexual behavior that violated their relationship rules, a client commented that coping with identity theft was easier than coping with the loss of his image of the relationship. He reported that he felt like a part of his identity was ripped away.

In the context of this book, *disclosure* is the process of sharing parts of your treatment history, sexual history, sexual behaviors and timeline. Disclosure may include all of these aspects, or only parts of material. Not everyone agrees, but my bias is toward full disclosure or at least giving the partner the right to set the level of disclosure. This is something you and your partner will need to address. Your treatment process, as set forth in this section, is designed to help you respond to your partner's needs.

One issue rarely addressed is the disclosure of your history to any future partners. The timing and level of detail of your future disclosures are important to consider. You wouldn't necessarily avoid disclosure of a chemical addiction or health issue, and I see the issue of sexual history as similar.

ASSIGNMENT: Preparing for Disclosure

This assignment is twofold. The first section contains instructions and questions for your partner to answer before you start any disclosure process.

<u>Questions for Your Partner:</u>

Instructions: Please answer the following questions. When you are finished, share your responses with your partner (the reader/user of the workbook). Once you have done so, your partner will prepare a response to your request.

• Who is your primary support network? What's your plan to reach out for support when your partner completes his or her disclosure?

• What therapy or personal growth work have you done to address treatment issues triggered by your partner's sexual behavior?

• What are your feelings and thoughts about disclosure?

- Are you committed to staying in the relationship? If not, I don't recommend disclosure. If you are ambivalent, why do you want disclosure at this time? What work do you need to complete in order to strengthen your commitment to the relationship before disclosure?

- What's your goal for disclosure?

How much detail do you want to receive? Consider the following:
- Your partner completed a sex history. The sex history is very detailed and includes questions addressing frequency, intensity, consequences, duration, location, types of behaviors, number of partners, and online behaviors. Which of these questions would you like answered?

- Your partner completed a sexual behavior timeline. Would you like to see this timeline? At what time in your partner's history do you want him to start? Since dating? Last disclosure? Lifetime?

- If there are additional (non-sexual) problematic behaviors, would you like to know about these compulsive/addictive behaviors?

- Is there any information you don't want disclosed to you?

- Your partner will complete a continuing care plan addressing the major high-risk situations, thinking errors, and feeling triggers in his/her life. Would you like your partner to share this plan?

- What do you need to make this a healing encounter for you?

- Are you prepared to respond to your partner with your own disclosures (if appropriate)? Why or why not?

Questions for You (the reader):

- Review your partner's responses to the questions above. If you are unable to respond to your partner's entire request, what are your plans to address your partner's request for the type and amount of disclosure?

- What feelings and thoughts do you anticipate in preparing for disclosure?

- What do you need to make this a healing experience for you?

- What are the barriers toward full disclosure? What are your plans to address these barriers?

The assignments above are the foundation tasks for full disclosure. Knowing what your partner wants disclosed is key. Knowing what you might struggle with in disclosing the requested information is vital. In my opinion, these two pieces are required before full disclosure.

ASSIGNMENT: Full Disclosure

This exercise is a helpful template to facilitate full disclosure. Use/adapt it as you both find necessary.

<u>Confirm your willingness.</u> After both you and your partner have completed the above questions, first confirm that you are both willing to go through the process. This starts with a confirmation by each of you to use the information to strengthen the relationship (and not as a reason to end the relationship, or as ammunition to hurt one another). If you can't confirm this commitment, please postpone disclosure and address the underlying issues.

<u>Decide when and where.</u> Clarify and negotiate a neutral setting for the disclosure to occur. Please make sure you schedule enough time. Pick a date that's not already emotionally charged (in other words, don't do this on your way to holiday dinner with the in-laws!). Consider if you need someone else there during disclosure; sometimes this may need to occur in a couple's therapy session. Consider if you want a support person nearby or on standby.

Begin. Start by reviewing the receiving partner's response to the questions on page 200. Use these questions to structure the discussion. Start by answering each of the questions, allowing the partner to ask clarifying questions. Remember to respond openly and honestly; a lie of omission is as damaging as a lie of commission. Take a break when necessary. Either of you can call a timeout and/or suspend the disclosure if necessary. Identify a plan to resume the disclosure process if you call a timeout or suspend the disclosure.

Debrief. After disclosure, debrief the experience. This includes asking each of you, "What are you thinking? What are you feeling? What are you present to? What do you need?" End with a ritual to celebrate the relationship and the reaffirmed connection that occurs in disclosure. (Yes, conflict is a form of intimacy, page 177). This ritual could be dinner, a walk, a date, meditation, or burning the papers created to answer the questions.

TEN: Spirituality, Values and Sexual Health

This section addresses spirituality, values and sexual health. There are some positive sexual health values taught by many religious traditions. Too often in the area of sexuality, however, religious messages may actually be a barrier to sexual health. A distinction between religion and spirituality is offered. A journey toward sexual health may require alternatives to a religious tradition. For many, the concept of a *higher power* is helpful. Nevertheless, a common theme in both religious and spiritual traditions is recognition of the importance of core values that shape your life. As I have stated, it's both your right and responsibility to define what's healthy in your life. This means you choose how to live your life. Remember, though, that this is not a free-for-all. Sexual health expresses the values by which you want to live your life. There should be consistency between your values and your behavior. I end this section by identifying strategies that you can use to help identify the core values that you will use to assess your Personal Definition of Sexual Health.

Spirituality and Religion

It's important to start the conversation about spirituality by introducing a distinction between spirituality and religion. The distinction reflects the difference between the individual and the community. *Spirituality* reflects the individual's faith, values, and experiences of the holy. Spirituality is "my story." It's the individual's experiences of something greater in his or her life. Spirituality reflects the most important values in a person's life. It's these values that often shape our actions. As a parallel process, *religion* reflects the community's faith, values and experiences of the holy. It's the integration of the individual's experiences into a community. The two are different but related.

It's through one's experience of spirituality that one connects with a community. In the workbook, it's the role of the support network to represent the community in your life. The support network helps you clarify when a behavior is consistent with your values. This is the counterbalance to your right and responsibility in choosing your behavior.

To develop your spirituality, it may be helpful to review your understanding of scripture and tradition to create a positive approach to life. Scripture and tradition are not always an enemy to spirituality. Within a tradition, a sense of wholeness and acceptance is possible. Tradition expresses a community's experience of "God" or "The Holy." This is true whether it's a long-term tradition (such as Jewish, Christian, Muslim, Catholic, Buddhist traditions) or a newer tradition (such as fellowship after a 12-step group).

Barriers to Spirituality

Whether or not you use your religious tradition of origin in the formation of your spirituality is up to you. For some individuals, the faith they grew up in can be helpful. For others, it's a barrier that can't be overcome (review the discussion of cultures on page 100). Three barriers to spirituality are religiosity, fundamentalism and lack of education. Consider how these barriers may be present in your life.

Religiosity

Religiosity is based on the performance of religious duties or rituals without the integration of spiritual values. It's focused on appearance. Early on, I discussed the need for integrity (page 33). Many individuals profess a faith but fail to live by that faith. Their behavior is focused on appearances, on looking good, and using religion as a means of looking good. The number of public sex scandals by those who profess a religious tradition illustrates this point. In emphasizing a healthy life, many religious traditions actually suppress sexuality versus finding healthy outlets. Religiosity is one means of suppressing sexuality.

Fundamentalism

Fundamentalism occurs in two primary ways: scriptural fundamentalism and dogmatic fundamentalism. Essentially, fundamentalism sets up a thinking error that one view of scripture or belief is the only right view. This creates a series of judgments about who qualifies as a person of faith. Fundamentalism dictates only a narrow manner in which faith can be expressed. In an attempt to help people, the fundamentalist approach usually results in excluding many people. When you start to see a diversity of cultures, it's easier to see a variety of options for sexual health.

Lack of Education

Lack of education is a third barrier. Many people simply have too little education in their faith tradition to begin the process of uncovering the richness of that tradition. Not many individuals can explain the dogmas and doctrines that can provide a rich resource for future growth.

As you move toward increased spiritual health, it might be helpful to address any struggles you have had with religiosity, fundamentalism or with feeling judged and rejected by your religious tradition. It may also be helpful to increase your education within your tradition. Addressing your struggles and increasing your education might help affirm your sexual health and clarify your values.

Theology of Story

The process of developing spirituality is to recognize the importance of story, similar to the power of story in our own identity (page 36). Spirituality starts and ends with a theology of story. A theology of story is based on the following. This is a process where we identify experiences of God. (For convenience, I use the term, *God*, but use whichever term works for you. Alternatives include: *Higher Power, Goddess, Spirit, Wisdom, The Absolute, The All*, and so forth.) When we have an experience of God, we often share this experience with others. As you experience God and share the story, you will probably hear others' stories of experiences of God. When you bring these stories together, you create a community that will often share a collection of stories. A theology of story helps us recognize that scripture is a collection of stories of people's experiences of God. Typically, these oral stories were written down, collected and made official across time. In other words, a person had an experience of God, and then shared the experience with another person who was also so inspired that he or she shared it with others. People wrote down and collected these stories. This collection eventually became what we see as scripture.

The application of a theology of story to our daily life is important. A theology of story asks, "What experiences of God have I encountered in my life?" It's in recognizing these experiences that we begin the process of seeing how God is present in our life. The difficulty is that we have lost the ability to share new stories. Many people don't see their experiences of the holy simply because they don't think this way. More often, we are looking for the grand miracle and so fail to see the holy in our current moment. Furthermore, because of fundamentalism, scriptures have unfortunately become a basis to condemn people instead of being a collection of people's experience of God. The use of scriptures as a weapon has led to a difficulty of sharing our personal stories.

Part of the process of developing your spirituality is to understand how you experience God in various ways by discussing three approaches to developing spirituality: *positive spirituality, generativity* and *creative mythology*. Each can give you insight into your own story of God experiences.

Positive spirituality emphasizes a process of uncovering the values by which you choose to live your life. It's future-oriented. A person will make decisions about what's healthy and express values as a reflection of his or her experience of God. Positive spirituality focuses on goals or values such as wholeness, integrity, fidelity and growth that a person seeks to express. For those with a religious tradition, the values you choose to live by can come from your religious experience. Many values identified in the scriptures and traditions are positive. Examples include love, integrity, forgiveness and responsibility. Other labels for these values are virtues. These values shape our life. A typical example of this is the WWJD ("What Would Jesus Do?") bumper sticker. A person with a WWJD sticker has declared "As a Christian, who believes in Jesus, I use His life to shape my behavior as an expression of my beliefs." For those who have negative experiences with religious traditions, the values you choose to live by can come from any personally powerful experience.

As opposed to positive spirituality, which is future-focused, *generativity* focuses on the now. Generativity asks the question, "How am I being made whole in the now?" In other words, in this experience (or with this thought) "Am I brought to a sense of wholeness, or am I left distracted and broken. In the realm of sexual health, does this behavior help or hinder my well-being?"

The concept of *creative mythology* is based on research by Joseph Campbell.[31] It focuses on how people express meaning in their lives. Campbell says creative mythology is "present when an individual has an experience of order, horror, beauty, exhilaration, which seeks to be communicated through signs, images, and words." Campbell's research suggests that a focus on the experience of something amazing, either good or bad, shifts an individual's understanding of reality, and that in these experiences a person connects to God. Creative mythology is an attempt to identify and express meaning of something greater in a person's life by noticing these important experiences. Mythology is a way one person's heart speaks to another person's heart. Notice the similarity between creative mythology and the concept of intimacy (page 172).

Others as a reflection of your values

Happiness is when what you think, what you say, and what you do are in harmony. (Gandhi)

The task is to define the values by which you want to live your life. It's done in community/connection with others. The process of clarifying your values, and the behaviors consistent with those values, is the experience of discovering your truth. My experience suggests a client is much more successful when their life reflects their truth. For some individuals, discovering or naming their internal truth is asking a blind man to describe a color. Due to shame, guilt, fear, failure, or any number of reasons, many individuals can't name the most important values in their life that truly represent their core.

Paradoxically, others can be the source of the primary values in your life. What we like and dislike in others reflects our inner core. This is an application of the discussions on transference (page 38) and transcending fear (page 42). Briefly, that to which we are drawn reflects an inner craving that we must address. That which we reject reflects an inner craving that we must address. Transference is a tool where you can recognize what's most important in your life. You can recognize these values by identifying various pivot points in your life (page 29). It's in these pivot points that you get a sense of something more in your life. In the pivot points you experience awe, amazement, horror, and beauty, all of which can be used to connect with others. The experience is rewarding, but isn't always easy. Sometimes these are values that we have and want to express more; other times, they may be values we don't have and want to obtain.

ASSIGNMENT: Your Spirituality and Values

To begin this process, I give my clients a number of assignments to identify pivot points that can be useful in identifying the values in your life. This assignment will help you to start thinking about something greater in your life.

Identify three people who inspire you. These people may be real or fictional, living or dead, someone you know, or simply someone you've read about. For each person, identify why this person is an inspiration to you. Identify two or three values this person has expressed through their life. As you think about each person, you may start to identify themes that are important to you.

Name three times when you experienced a sense of timelessness. Some authors describe this as "being in the flow." In this context, *timelessness* is the experience of time passing without your awareness. Think of a young child playing outside all day. You say to the child "Come in for bed." To the child, the day passed with a sense of timelessness. They simply were completely in the moment. Describe the settings in which you experienced timelessness, focusing on who, what, when, and where. What words do you use to summarize how these experiences inspire you?

As you examine the individuals and experiences in your life that are important, make note of common themes, values and experiences. These themes are expressions of your experience of something greater in your daily life. These themes are often the values that are most important in your life.

Values to start the conversation

In identifying the values that are most significant, you can give voice and express to what's most important in your life. Asking, "What value is important to me?" is, in fact, clarifying what matters to you. I hear the question, "What values should I use?" Obviously, the response is, "What you choose." The question also belies the struggle of, "Where do I begin." These values in table 6 below are a number of values to consider. Find the values that inspire you. If you find one that you like, continue to research the term. Ask yourself, "What does a life of _____ look like?" These words are simply a place to start shaping your behaviors.

List of Values/Virtues[32]

Value/Virtue	Brief Description
Accountability	The quality or state of being accountable; especially: an obligation or willingness to accept responsibility or to account for one's actions. To give care. A concern for.
Charity	Generosity and helpfulness especially toward the needy or suffering. Aid given to those in need.
Chastity	Purity in conduct and intention.
Commitment	The firm carrying out of purpose.
Compassion	Awareness of others' distress together with a desire to alleviate it.
Confidence	A feeling of reliance on one's circumstances. Faith in oneself.
Contentment	The quality of feeling satisfied with one's possessions, status, or situation.
Courage	A quality of spirit that enables you to face danger or pain without showing fear.
Creativity	The ability to create. A quality involving the generation of new ideas or concepts, or new associations of the creative mind between existing ideas or concepts.
Curiosity	A desire to find out and know things.
Diligence	Conscientiousness in paying proper attention to a task; giving the degree of care required in a given situation. Persevering to perform a task.
Empathy	Identification with and understanding of another's situation, feelings, and motives.
Enthusiasm	A feeling of excitement. Flowing with eager enjoyment or approval.
Excellence	The quality of excelling; possessing good qualities in high degree.
Faithfulness	Steadfast in affection or allegiance; loyal.
Flexibility	Adaptable, able to be changed to suit circumstances.
Forgiveness	To cease to feel angry or bitter towards a person or about an offense.
Generosity	Giving or ready to give freely, free from meanness or prejudice.
Gentleness	Moderate; mild, quite; not rough or severe.
Gratitude	Being thankful.
Honesty	Truthful; sincere; not lying or cheating
Hope	The general feeling that some desire will be fulfilled
Humility	A disposition to be humble; a lack of false pride.
Integrity	Moral soundness; Integrity is consistency of values and actions. Unbroken completeness with nothing lacking.
Joyfulness	The emotion of great happiness
Justice	Fair, impartial, giving a deserved response.
Love	A deep, tender, ineffable feeling of affection and solicitude toward a person, such as that arising from kinship, recognition of attractive qualities, or a sense of underlying oneness.
Loyalty	Steadfast in allegiance to one's homeland, government, or sovereign. Faithful to a person, ideal, custom, cause, or duty.
Mercy	Clemency: leniency and compassion shown toward offenders by a

Value/Virtue	Brief Description
	person or agency charged with administering justice.
Moderation	The avoidance of extremes in one's actions or opinions
Openness	Ready and willing to talk candidly. Not secretive.
Patience	The ability to endure delay, trouble, pain or hardship.
Peace	Freedom from mental agitation; serenity.
Perseverance	Being persistent, refusing to stop despite failures, delays and difficulties.
Prudence	Wise or careful in conduct. Shrewd or thrifty in planning ahead
Resourceful	The ability to act effectively or imaginatively, especially in regard to difficult situations and unusual problems.
Respect	Admiration for others. Treating people with due dignity.
Responsibility	Having control over and accountability for appropriate events.
Selflessness	The quality of unselfish concern for the welfare of others.
Service	Work done by one person or group that benefits another.
Simplicity	Straightforward; not complex or complicated. Unpretentious.
Steadfastness	Firm, resolute; determinedly unwavering.
Tranquility	Serenely quiet and peaceful; undisturbed.
Trust	Having confidence in others; lacking suspicion
Truthfulness	Accurately depicting what's real.
Unity	Freedom from division. Oneness.
Vitality	Exuberant physical strength or mental vigor, energy.
Wisdom	The trait of utilizing knowledge and experience with common sense and insight
Wonder	The feeling aroused by something strange and surprising.
Zeal	Ardor. A feeling of strong eagerness. Tireless devotion.

As I stated, this table is simply a place to start. Whatever you choose is what you choose; the key is to expand the values to a helpful tool that you can use to shape your behaviors in your life. To do so, you need a deeper understanding than what's listed in the table. What follows is an expanded conversation of a few values to model what I want you to do in your journey. A good place to start is the Internet, and Wikipedia.

Justice

Justice is often reduced to holding people accountable, sort of like a punishment. This is a start, but justice is also about restoring a sense of harmony and connection. Justice is about caring. Justice is more than just fairness; it's also about the common good. Peace and justice are often linked, with justice being a pre-requisite for peace. Within justice are social justice and positive social change. There are a variety of types of justice that can be explored.

Generosity

Generosity is often seen as giving to others on a monetary level. Generosity can also include giving of talent and time. Included are the concepts of focusing on others and working toward the common good. In interpersonal relationships, generosity is giving someone the benefit of the doubt by interpreting comments and statements from a view toward growth instead of failure. In recovery, generosity may reflect sharing your inner thoughts when you would otherwise desire to hide. Generosity is the antidote to greed and narcissism. It involves giving without the expectation of reward. In relationships, it's going beyond assumptions of fairness. Some consider generosity to be "love in action." It includes going beyond what's easy when things are tough. One concept of generosity is "paying it forward."

Wisdom

Wisdom is more than intelligence; it's the application of experience with knowledge. Within the concept is a sense of integrity and being grounded. Applying wisdom creates justice. Wisdom can also include leading by experience. Wisdom can represent the unspoken voice of silence from within. Wisdom embraces paradoxes, and sees the whole within the one, and the one within the whole. Wisdom involves the ability to avoid being distracted by the clutter of life and staying focused on what's important. Knowing when to act and when to wait reflects wisdom. Wisdom is self-knowledge and knowing what actions are consistent with your values.

Courage

Courage includes the concept of bravery. It's not just about acting without fear; it's also about acting through fear. Without a doubt, you will experience fear moving forward; courage is about continuing to move forward. Sometimes courage is staying true to your values even when you face opposition or experience hopelessness. Sharing everything with your support network is an example of courage. Opportunities for courage primarily occur when you face a struggle or challenge. Different religious traditions include concepts of fortitude, and linking courage to love. Courage implies standing up for justice when faced with injustice.

Integrity

Integrity requires a level of self-awareness and commitment to live according to the inner truth. As noted previously, integrity is "saying what you mean, and meaning what you say." Honoring your word is a major part of integrity. Integrity occurs when your behaviors and values are consistent with one another. (You may also want to review the discussion of integrity and authenticity on page 33.)

ASSIGNMENT: Your Top Values

Think big about your future. What would a life you love look like? You need to step forward to identify and claim the values that you find important, the values that you will use to shape your life. What works for some people will not necessarily work for you. We may learn from each other, but your path is uniquely your own. Your task is to identify values that are important to you. Ask yourself how your values shape your behaviors, your limits, your response to fears and your boundaries. Does a particular behavior move you closer or further away from your values? Alternatively, what would a person who lives by the value _____(fill in the blank) do in this situation? My experience suggests that when you live a life based on your values, you are living a life you love. The five values that are most important to you are:

1.

2.

3.

4.

5.

Choose Your Life

I took the one less traveled by. And that has made all the difference. (Robert Frost)

The ending line of Robert Frost's *Road Not Taken* emphasizes the power and responsibility of choice. There are two primary interpretations to the poem, both of which are valid in applying values to sexual health. The primary interpretation of the poem reflects that your life is your life, and we each choose how we are going to live our life. The second interpretation is that the power of choice often makes the act of choosing worthwhile. It has meaning since we were the one to choose.

The challenge is to ask, "How willing am I to do whatever it takes to express my values in living?" Your inspirations are often people who, despite their fear, choose actions that express their values. Think of people such as Martin Luther King Jr., Gandhi and Mother Theresa. They expressed their values in their daily lives to the degree that the world recognized them as inspiring.

The values that inspire you are remarkably stable, yet they can sometimes change. More often It's our awareness, language and skill in understanding and expressing our values that change, more than our values themselves. Forgiveness, for example, has many layers of meaning. Value clarification is a continuing process. It's a process, not a product. When you succeed, life will be amazing. And yes you will fail, and life will be amazing. Perfection is not required, but integrity and authenticity to your values and truth is how a person lives a life they love. Each moment is an opportunity.

And then... Repeat

It is unwise to be too sure of one's own wisdom. It is healthy to be reminded that the strongest might weaken and the wisest might err. Gandhi

Now that you have finished Stage 2, use the values from "TEN: Spirituality, Values and Sexual Health" and review your responses throughout the workbook with this new lens. Are your values expressed in your responses? If so great; if not, great. What is left is to start again. In the process, you can gain a deeper awareness of what you need to express a life you love. My experience is that individuals have new levels of understanding when they review past assignments. Ongoing analyses of these assignments may provide insight into creating a new breakthrough. Repeating assignments may allow new understanding of previously forgotten materials or new understanding of your relationships. A decrease in feelings of shame may allow you to deal with a deeper secret not previously shared.

Stage 3: Groundwork for Completing Therapy

Early in the book, I identified two primary goals: 1) eliminate unhealthy sexual behaviors, and 2) replace those with healthy sexual behaviors. These two goals reflect the necessary steps toward living a life you love. They complement each other. In Stage3 you will review what you did and learned in the first two stages. The continuing care plan reflects the goal of eliminating unhealthy behaviors while the Personal Definition of Sexual Health reflects the goal of identifying healthy sexual behaviors (this is what helps you live a life you love). I start with the continuing care plan.

You use your values to shape your continuing-care plan in a profound way. The key questions involved are: What are the thoughts, feelings or high-risk situations that are the biggest concern for me in living a life based on my values? Will this behavior violate my values? How do my values shape the next step for me? For example, in each moment you face fear, you can either succumb to the fear (falling into the triangular roles of persecutor, victimizer, or rescuer that move you into the acting-out cycle), or choose to engage in behaviors that express your values. (For a review of these concepts, see "The Power of Thought," "The Illusion of Fear," and "The Acting-Out Cycle" in Part 1.)

I believe that personal growth never really ends. In my work with clients, I learn about myself based on their stories. Every time I update this workbook, I learn more about sexuality. While growth is always ongoing, I do believe that the need for formal intervention can end. As I wrote in the early pages, I believe my job is to work myself out of a job. In preparation for the completion of the formal work, this stage is about consolidating the lessons learned in Stages 1 and 2 by summarizing remaining issues and current plans. The primary focus of the workbook has been helping you move toward the Personal Definition of Sexual Health.

Continuing Care Plan

The *Continuing Care Plan* (CCP) simultaneously addresses elimination of unhealthy behaviors while helping create a short-term life plan. In other words, these are the things you know will get you into trouble. How do you know what goes into your continuing care plan? You know because the plan is based on your responses to the assignments and exercises from the previous two sections. It may include material from your Immediate Short-Term Prevention Plan as well. The continuing care plan brings together all of the pieces so you can see the "big picture" of the puzzle for prevention and safety. In the business world, the concept of *risk management* refers to identifying potential risk factors and developing plans to address them. By having and implementing plans, you can reduce both the risk of something happening and the extent of harm done if something does happen. By knowing your "early warning signs" (i.e., feeling triggers, thinking errors and high-risks situations), you can follow through with plans.

It's possible to identify the factors that have the highest risk of failure relevant to your life. These plans simply reflect knowing the major concerns.

The CPP is both a short-term plan (what gets me in trouble now) and long-term (what gets in my way of living a life I love). You have already done the hard work of gathering information and addressing issues, now you can use that material to generate a CCP that will help you maintain the positive change you have enacted. The CCP focuses on preventing the acting-out cycle by identifying plans for the most important factors in your acting-out cycle. Your weekly log may be useful as you do this. By reviewing your sex history and sexual behavior timeline, and studying behavior analyses that you completed throughout Stage 2, you will build a plan specific to your needs.

Living in Minnesota, for example, I know I need to make plans to address the weather. If I forget something, I may have a problem. Experts here talk about winter survival kits for our cars; I put winter tires on versus the general tires. I stock up my house on food and water in the event of power failure. These plans reflect known concerns.

Even the best-laid plans can run into difficulties. Planning can involve more than one option. The more options there are, the greater the possibility for a better outcome. Instead of simply stocking up the house, there are specific types of foods that are suggested because they provide high energy when there is a possibility of it getting cold.

S.M.A.R.T. Plans

SMART plans reflect a way to create specific plans with options to help you be successful. These plans take a little work to create, but once created they become helpful in addressing barriers to overall health. This is important. When stuck in the depth of the trigger, a pre-established SMART plan is a recipe for getting out of the bad situation.

The term is an acronym based on the following characteristics:

- Specific: The plans are detailed and explicit.
- Measurable: You can determine if the plan has been followed. I usually have a number associated with this (1 person, 1 phone call, 1 date, 1 time, 1 hour, etc.).
- Attainable: It's something you can complete in the established time.
- Relevant: The plan is connected to the triggers, feeling or high-risk situation.
- Timely: You will have the goal completed within a set time frame.

An example is depression as a feeling trigger. Using the SMART framework, you can develop plans to cope. Three smart plans include:

- Daily take my medications as prescribed.

- Continue to meet once every two weeks with my therapist.

- Talk to one member of my support network daily.

Each of the tasks identified for depression is a SMART plan reflecting the definition of SMART. As a support person, someone would be able to ask, "Did you call?" "Did you take your meds?" and so forth.

ASSIGNMENT: Your Continuing Care Plan

Review the work you did involving your acting-out cycle. First, list five of each of the following: high-risk situations, thinking errors, and feeling triggers. Next, identify two plans for how you will address each.

High-Risk Situations

1. _____

Plans for coping:

2. _____

Plans for coping:

3. _____

Plans for coping:

4. _____

Plans for coping:

5. _____

Plans for coping:

Thinking Errors

1. _____

Plans for coping:

2. _____

Plans for coping:

3. _____

Plans for coping:

4. _____

Plans for coping:

5. _____

Plans for coping:

Feeling Triggers

1. _____

Plans for coping:

2. _____

Plans for coping:

3. _____

Plans for coping:

4. _____

Plans for coping:

5. _____

Plans for coping:

Toward a Personal Definition of Sexual Health

The shoe that fits one person pinches another; there is no recipe for living that suits all cases. (Carl Jung)

The underlying sexual health model used in this book highlights ten components for addressing sexual health. Too often clients want me to tell them what behaviors are healthy, as if a universal definition exists. This is where you actually create a *Personal Definition of Sexual Health* that reflects your life, values and circumstances. It's important to complete this section using the five primary values you identified (see "Your Top Values" on page 211) as a lens to examine your Personal Definition of Sexual Health. Much of this topic is about gathering together the work you've previously completed.

ASSIGNMENT: Your Personal Definition of Sexual Health

Complete the following sections based on the information and insight you have gained up to this point.

ONE: Talking About Sex

Talking about sexual health remains an important part of your ongoing journal of sexual health. Early in the book you were asked to start the process of naming a support system. By now, I hope you have a solid network of support.

The 3-5 individuals you use as your primary support are:

Name   Phone

Review all of your work in the workbook, including the sex history and sexual behavior time-line. Is there anything you haven't shared with your support network? Anything you are not talking about with these individuals is a treatment issue that you still need to address. If there is something you haven't shared, describe your plan to initiate appropriate disclosure.

TWO: Culture, Identity and Sexual Health

All cultural values are sexual values. As you complete the workbook, review all the different cultures to which you belong.

Which culture has the largest impact on your sexual values?

- Are the cultures that you belong to currently in harmony regarding sexuality. Yes/No. If no, describe your plan to resolve this conflict?

- Describe any shaming messages you currently experience. Describe your plan to address these shaming messages.

- Moving toward a personal definition requires knowing who you are. One area to consider is how you define your sexual identity (page 107 for definitions).

- What natal sex apples to you?

- What gender describes how you see yourself?

- On the Adapted Kinsey Continuum of attraction, identify the number that best describes how you think of yourself.

0	1	2	3	4	5	6
exclusively						*exclusively*
heterosexual						*homosexual*

- Sexual attraction: _____

- Physical attraction_____

- Emotional Attraction_____

Describe how you feel about your responses.

THREE: Sexual Functioning—Anatomy and Beyond

- What issues or factors affect your sexual functioning, or ability to orgasm? What is your plan to address these factors?

FOUR: Sexual Health Care and Safer-Sex Issues

- Who is your primary physician? Have you talked with him/her regarding your sexual behaviors and questions regarding health issues? If no, your plans are?

- When was the last time you talked with your doctor about HIV/STIs? When was the last time you were screened for HIV/STIs? If it has been more than six months since the last screen, identify a plan to talk with your doctor.

- Your personal safer-sex plans to address your unsafe sexual behavior are:

FIVE: Barriers to Sexual Health—Beyond Functioning

The workbook reviews a number of barriers to sexuality including the following. A current issue is defined as impacting your sexual health in the last 30 days.

Identify any of the following that may be a current issue for you:

Name	Lifetime Concern	Current Concern
Abuse experienced as a child	Yes No	Yes No
Abuse experienced as an adult	Yes No	Yes No
Mental health concerns		
Depression	Yes No	Yes No
Bi-polar	Yes No	Yes No
Anxiety	Yes No	Yes No
Grief	Yes No	Yes No
Anger	Yes No	Yes No
Internet sexual compulsivity	Yes No	Yes No

If you identify any current concerns, update your Continuing Care Plan to include them.

SIX: Body Image

- Review the topic on body image. List three messages you have about your body?

- Describe your image of your genitals (page 147).

- List your plans to create a healthy body image and a healthy genital image.

SEVEN: Masturbation, Fantasy, and Sexually Explicit Material

Review the topics on masturbation and fantasy. If you haven't already completed a fantasy analysis, please do so. I can't stress enough the value of this exercise.

- What are the healthy fantasies you want to foster?

- What are your unhealthy fantasies, or fantasies you want to avoid?

- What are your guidelines about disclosing your fantasies to your partner?

- What are your current appropriate masturbation behaviors? (Where, when, how often?)

- What are your guidelines about disclosing your masturbation behaviors to your partner?

- What sexually explicit material is acceptable to use? Why?

- What sexually explicit material is not acceptable to use? Why?

- What are your guidelines about disclosing your use of sexually explicit material to your partner?

- Have you reviewed these guidelines with your partner? Does s/he agree with these values? If there is disagreement, what's your plan to address the disagreement?

EIGHT: Positive Sexuality

Sexuality is a major focus of energy in life. The following questions reflect that sexual energy is healthy and, when channeled in healthy ways, can bring new life and strengthen relationships with your partner and others in your life. The following questions are integrative. Your responses should be harmonious with your values. Review the discussion on sexual behavior and expression (pages 164-168) and the "Your Top Values" assignment (page 211). Evaluate whether or not your responses are consistent with the values you identified.

- Who is an appropriate sexual partner for you (age, sex, relationship, etc.)?

- What types of sexual behaviors are healthy for you?

- What types of sexual behavior do you choose to avoid?

- When is it appropriate to be sexually active?

- Where is it appropriate to be sexually active?

- What are healthy reasons to engage in sexual behavior?

- What are unhealthy reasons to engage in sexual behavior?

- What is your preferred amount of physical touch?

- What kind of touch is acceptable?

- What is your plan to communicate these responses to your partner?

- What do you need to learn about your partner to help him or her experience sexual health?

NINE: Intimacy and Relationships

- Review your relationship history. Describe any current concerns regarding any of your past relationships. Include your plans to address these concerns.

- Review the topic on intimacy (page 172). The top three types of intimacy that are the most important for you are?

- How satisfied are you with the level of intimacy in these three areas? Summarize your plans to increase your level of satisfaction are?

- Review the material on disclosure on page 198. What are your plans for disclosure of your sex history to current or future partners?

- Review the topic on relationship satisfaction (page 186). Identify two or three behaviors you will do to improve your relationship(s).

- The type of relationship (review page 194) you want is?

TEN: *Spirituality, Values and Sexual Health*

- Create a bumper sticker statement integrating the most important values in your life. For example, my bumper sticker is: "Committed to Courage, Healing and Freedom."

- Review the topic on spirituality and values (page 208). Does anything listed in the 10 components conflict with your spirituality or personal values? If so, reexamine and resolve this conflict.

- Ask yourself, "Am I living a life I love?" Why or why not?

A New Beginning: Continuing the Conversation

Namaste

Within many cultures and traditions, there is a practice of bowing. This bowing is to recognize and show respect for the other. As you finish your first journey through this book, I bow to you: The student and teacher within me honor the student and teacher within you. Sexual health is a journey and I am happy to share the journey with you through this book. Often the most profound moments in my life occur in the area of sexuality. I've come to see this experience as an opportunity of ministry.

Additional Resources:

Life Coaching and Sexual Health

Now that you've moved through the workbook once—keep moving forward in your journey! In my experience, the more enjoyable conversations occur when a person is experiencing a transformation regarding sexuality. Often when people learn that I am a therapist, they tell me about their life. They are eager—hungry even—to share who they are with me. I've heard stories everywhere—the gym, the coffee shop, walking the dogs, at parties, and in meetings. People have a real need to discover, understand, embrace and express their personal stories, perhaps as a way of gaining support. In our society, however, the only acceptable venue for seeking support is often through the medical model of a "problem." We assume people seek professional help because bad things are happening; thus, we don't seek help ourselves unless we perceive ourselves as having a specific problem.

One resource to consider is *life coaching* in the realm of sexuality. What would it look like to develop a health-based, holistically integrative approach to sexuality? What would it look like if the conversation started from a place of health versus starting from a problem? This is what life coaching is about. What is a *life coach*? A life coach is someone who walks along in your journey toward living a life you love. Life coaching uses your experiences to help you integrate your values and goals, facilitating growth. This growth comes from insight into and understanding of your story. For more about life coaching in the realm of sexual health, please visit www.livingalifeilovecoaching.com.

SexualHealthInstitute.blogspot.com

Much of the material in this workbook was originally posted in draft form on my website via the blog, www.sexualhealthinstitute.blogspot.com. After completing the workbook, the blog became a place to add material, provide reactions and comments and a starting point for conversation. Please feel free to review the blog for new material. You are encouraged to suggest ideas, ask questions, or participate in any way you feel comfortable. For the safety of all, I moderate all posts. All posts are anonymous unless you give me explicit permission to use your name. Questions and instructions to consider:

- What has been helpful?
- What topic would you want more information about?
- Is there a missing topic?
- As you develop your sexual health, what have been your greatest struggles?
- Share examples of success.
- Describe areas where things fell apart.

Bibliography

Ackard, D & Kearney-Cooke, A. (2000) Effect of Body Image and Self-Image on Women's Sexual Behaviors. *International Journal of Eating Disorders,* 28(4), 422-429.

Amico, J. (1997) Assessing Sexual Compulsivity/Addiction in Chemically Dependent Gay Men. *Sexual Addiction and Compulsivity: The Journal of Treatment and Prevention,* 4:4.

Baird, Robert J. (2004) Clergy and cybersex: A motivational study. Ph.D. dissertation, Union Institute and University, United States -- Ohio. Retrieved March 9, 2011, from Dissertations & Theses: Full Text. (Publication No. AAT 3157507).

Bancroft, J. & Vukadinovic, Z. (2004) Sexual Addiction, Sexual Compulsivity, Sexual Impulsivity, or What? Toward a Theoretical Model. Journal of Sex Research, 41(3), 225-234.

Bean, J. (2002) Expressions of Female Sexuality. Journal of Sex & Marital Therapy. Supplement 1, 28(1), 29-38.

Berk, L & Winsler, A. (1995). "Vygotsky: His life and works" and "Vygotsky's approach to development". In Scaffolding children's learning: Vygotsky and early childhood learning. National Association for Education of Young Children. pp. 25–34

Brick, P. (1991) Fostering Positive Sexuality. Educational Leadership, 49(1), 51-53.

Bockting, W., Rosser, S. & Scheltema, K (1999) Transgender HIV prevention: implementation and evaluation of a workshop, Health Education Research, 14(2), 177-183, doi: 10.1093/her/14.2.177

Carballo-Diéguez, A., Miner, M., Dolezal, C., Rosser, S. & Jacoby, S. (2006). Sexual negotiation, HIV-status disclosure, and sexual risk behavior among Latino men who use the Internet to seek sex with other men. Archives of Sexual Behavior, 35, 473-481.

Carnes, P. (1992) Out of the shadows. Center City, MN: Hazelden.

Carnes, P. (1997) Sexual anorexia. Center City, MN: Hazelden.

Carnes, P., Delmonico, D. L. & Griffin, E. (2001) In the shadows of the net: Breaking free from compulsive online sexual behavior. Center City, MH: Hazelden Foundation Press.

Cass, V. (1984) Homosexual Identity Formation: Testing a Theoretical Model. Journal of Sex Research, 20(2), 143-167.

Clinebell, H. & Clinebell, C. (1970) The Intimate Marriage. Harper & Row.

Coleman, E. (1991) Compulsive sexual behavior: New concepts and treatments. Journal of Psychology and Human Sexuality, 4(2), 37-52.

Coleman, E. (1992) Is your patient suffering from compulsive sexual behavior. Psychiatric Annals, 22(6), 320-325.

Coleman, E. (2002) Masturbation as a means of achieving sexual health. Journal of Psychology & Human Sexuality, 14(2-3), 5-16. doi:10.1300/J056v14n02_02

Coleman, E. (1995) Treatment of compulsive sexual behavior. In R. Rosen, & S. R. Leiblum (Eds.), Case studies in sex therapy (pp. 333-349). New York, NY: Guilford Press.

Coleman, E., Raymond, N. & McBean, A. (2003) Assessment and treatment of compulsive sexual behavior. Minnesota Medicine, 86(7), 42-47.

Coleman, E. (1995) Treatment of compulsive sexual behavior. In R. Rosen, & S. R. Leiblum (Eds.), Case studies in sex therapy (pp. 333-349). New York, NY: Guilford Press.

Cooper, A., Delmonico, D. & Burg, R. (2000) Cybersex users, abusers, and compulsives: New findings and implications. Sexual Addiction & Compulsivity, 7(1-2), 5-29. doi: 10.1080/10720160008400205

Cooper, A., Delmonico, D., Griffin-Shelley, E. & Mathy, R (2004) Online sexual activity: An examination of potentially problematic behaviors. Sexual Addiction & Compulsivity, 11(3), 129-143. doi:10.1080/10720160490882642

Corley D & Schneider (2002) Disclosing Secrets: When, to Whom and How Much to Reveal Gentle Path Press.

Co-Sex Addicts Anonymous (COSA) www.cosa-recovery.org/

Cotton, M. Ball, C. & Robinson, P. (2003) Four Simple Questions Can Help Screen for Eating Disorders Journal General Internal Medicine, 18(1): 53–56.doi: 10.1046/j.1525-1497.2003.20374.x.

Daneback, K., Cooper, A. & Månsson, S. (2005) An Internet study of cybersex participants. Archives Of Sexual Behavior, 34(3), 321-328.

Deacon, S. & Minichiello, V. (1995) Sexuality and older people: Revisiting the assumptions. Educational Gerontology, 21(5), 497-513.

Dekker, A & Schmidt, G. (2002) Patterns of Masturbatory Behaviour: Changes Between the Sixties and the Nineties. Co-published simultaneously in Journal of Psychology & Human Sexuality. 142/3, 35-48; and: Masturbation as a Means of Achieving Sexual Health (ed: Walter O. Bockting and Eli Coleman) The Haworth Press, Inc., 35-48.

Demarest, J. & Allen, R. (2000) Body Image: Gender, Ethnic, and Age Differences Journal of Social Psychology, 140(4), 465-472.

Dube SR et al. Long-term consequences of childhood sexual abuse by gender of victim. American Journal of Preventive Medicine 28(5).

Easton, D. & Liszt, C. (1997) The Ethical Slut: A Guide to Infinite Sexual Possibilities Greenery Press CA.

Edwards, E. (1993) Development of a New Scale for Measuring Compulsive Buying Behavior Financial Counseling and Planning, 4, 67-85.

Edwards, W. (2012a) Using a Sexual Health Model to conceptualize cybersex treatment. Journal of Sexual Compulsivity & Addiction, manuscript accepted for publication.

Edwards, W. (2012b) Cybersex and the EA Professional. Journal of Employee Assistance, manuscript accepted for publication

Edwards, W. (2012c) The Overlap of Sex, Drugs and the Internet. *Addiction Professional* manuscript accepted for publication

Edwards, W. (2009) Living a Life I Love: Healing from Sexual Compulsivity, Sexual Addiction, Sexual Avoidance and other Sexual Health Concerns. CreateSpace:Seattle

Edwards, W. (2009) Sexual Health and the EA Professional. Journal of Employee Assistance, 39:2, 114.

Edwards, W. (2004) Measuring Sexual Health: Development Of The Sexual Health Inventory. A Dissertation Submitted To The Faculty Of The Graduate School Of The University Of Minnesota.

Edwards, W. & Coleman E. (2004) Defining sexual health: A descriptive overview. Archives of Sexual Behavior, 33(3), 189-195.

Edwards, W., Delmonico, D and Griffin E. (2011) Cybersex Unplugged: Finding Sexual Health in an Electronic World. CreateSpace:Seattle

Elliott, D., Mok, D. & Briere, J. (2004) Adult Sexual Assault: Prevalence, Symptomatology, and Sex Differences in the General Population, Journal of Traumatic Stress, 17(3), 203-211.

Facing facts: Sexual health for America's adolescents. (1995) D. W. Haffner (Ed.), New York: Sexuality Information and Education Council of the United States (SIECUS).

Feldman, M. & Meyer, I (2007) Eating Disorders in Diverse Lesbian, Gay, and Bisexual Populations International Journal of Eating Disorders, 40, 218–226, doi: 10.1002/eat.20360

Ferree, M. (2001) Females and Sex Addiction: Myths and Diagnostic Implications. Sexual Addiction & Compulsivity, 8(3/4) 287-300.

Fisher, B., Cullen, F. & Turner M. (2000) The Sexual Victimization of College Women. National Institute of Justice.

Fisher, W. & Barak, A. (2001) Internet pornography: A social psychological perspective on Internet sexuality. Journal of Sex Research, 38(4), 312-323. doi:10.1080/00224490109552102

Illinois Institute for Addiction Recovery (2008) What behaviors indicate compulsive shopping and spending? www.addictionrecov.org/spendwhat.htm

Goodman, A. (2001) What's in a Name? Terminology for Designating a Syndrome of Driven Sexual Behavior. Sexual Addiction & Compulsivity, 8(3/4), 191-213.

Gottman, John M., and Nan Silver. (1999). How I predict divorce," in *The Seven Principles for Making Marriages Work* (Chapter Two, 25-46). New York: Three Rivers Press (Random House, Inc.).

Gudelunas, D. (2005) Talking taboo: Newspaper advice columns and sexual discourse. Sexuality & Culture: An Interdisciplinary Quarterly, 9(1), 62-87.

Hammack, P. (2005) The Life Course Development of Human Sexual Orientation: An Integrative Paradigm, Human Development, 48(5), 267-290.

Hays, P. (2008) Addressing Cultural Complexities in Practice: Assessment, Diagnosis, and Therapy (2nd edition). Washington, D.C.: American Psychological Association.

Hedgepeth, E. (2000) From Margin to Center: Sexuality Education As a Model for Teaching in a Democracy, Journal of Sex Education & Therapy, 25(2/3), 137-146.

Mallon, S. (2002) Developing a Positive Sexuality Education in the Churches, British Journal of Theological Education, 12 (2), 133-144.

Maltz, W. & Maltz, L (2010) The Porn Trap: the essential guide to overcoming problems caused by pornography. Harper Paperback

Meyer, M. (2005) Drawing the sexuality card: Teaching, researching, and living bisexuality. Sexuality & Culture: An Interdisciplinary Quarterly, 9(1), 3-13.

Miller, W.R. and Rollnick, S. (2002) Motivational Interviewing: Preparing People to Change. NY: Guilford Press.

Money, J. (1993) Lovemaps. Prometheus Books, New York.

Morin, J. (1996) The Erotic Mind: Unlocking the Inner Sources of Passion and Fulfillment. Harper Paperbacks

Kaminski, P., Chapman, B., Haynes, S. & Own, L. (2005) Body image, eating behaviors, and attitudes toward exercise among gay and straight men. Eating Behaviors, 6(3), 179-187.

Kalichman, S. (2005) The Other Side of the Healthy Relationships Intervention: Mental Health Outcomes and Correlates of Sexual Risk Behavior Change, AIDS Education & Prevention; Supplement A, 17, 66-75.

Kasl, C. (1991) Women, Sex, and Addiction: A Search for Love and Power, Harper Perennial

Kelly, M., Strassberg, D. & Turner, C. (2004) Communication and Associated Relationship Issues in Female Anorgasmia. Journal of Sex & Marital Therapy, 30(4) 263-276.

Klausner JD, Wolf ,W., Fischer-Ponce L, Zolt I, Katz MH. (2000) Tracing a syphilis outbreak through cyberspace. Journal of American Medical Association, 284, 447-9.

Koch, P., Mansfield, P., Thurau, D. & Carey, M.(2005) Feeling Frumpy: The Relationships Between Body Image and Sexual Response Changes in Midlife Women. Journal of Sex Research, 42(3), 215-223.

Kim, A., McFarland, W., Yu, F. & Klausner, J. (2000) Cybersex.net: Sexual networks over the Internet, Silicon Valley, 1999-2000. Abstracts of the XIII international AIDS conference, Durban, South Africa, 9-14 July.

Kinsey, A. (1948) Sexual behavior in the human male. Philadelphia: W.B. Saunders Company.

Kinsey, A. (1953) Sexual behavior in the human female. Philadelphia: W.B. Saunders Company.

Lesieur, H. & Blume, S. (2008) The South Oaks Gambling Screen (SOGS) located at: www.addictionrecov.org/southoak.htm

Leiblum, S. (2003) Sex-starved marriages sweeping the US. Sexual & Relationship Therapy, 18(4), 427-428.

Maltz, W. (2003) Treating the Sexual Intimacy Concerns of Sexual Abuse Survivors. Contemporary Sexuality, 37(7), i-vii.

Mellody, P., Wells-Miller, A., Miller, J. Keith (2003) Facing Co Dependency. HarperOne

Mellody, P., Wells-Miller, A., Miller, J. Keith (2003) Facing Love Addiction. HarperOne

Melby, T. (2001) Childhood Sexuality. Contemporary Sexuality, 35(12), 1-3.

Meston, C. & Buss, D. (2007) Why Humans Have Sex. Archives of Sexual Behavior, 36, 477–507, doi: 10.1007/s10508-007-9175-2

Meyer, C. & Blissett, J. (2001) Sexual Orientation and Eating Psychopathology: The Role of Masculinity and Femininity, International Journal of Eating Disorders, 29(3), 314-318.

National Institute on Alcohol Abuse and Alcoholism. (1995) Assessing alcohol problems: A guide for clinicians and researchers (NIH No. 95-3745). Bethesda, MD: National Institute of Health.

Nusbaum, M. (2002) Erectile dysfunction: prevalence, etiology, and major risk factors. The Journal of the American Osteopathic Association, 10(12), 1-6.

Nusbaum, M., Lenahan, P. & Sadovsky, R (2005) Sexual health in aging men and women: Addressing the physiologic and psychological sexual changes that occur with age. Geriatrics, 60(9), 18-23.

OSHO (1999) Emotions: Freedom from Anger, Jealousy and Fear. OSHO International: New York.

Patrick, M. E., & Maggs, J. L. (2009). Does drinking lead to sex? Daily alcohol–sex behaviors and expectancies among college students. Psychology of Addictive Behaviors, 23(3), 472-481. doi:10.1037/a0016097

Peplau, L., Frederick, D., Yee, C., Maisel, N., Lever, J. & Ghavami, N. (2009) Body Image Satisfaction in Heterosexual, Gay, and Lesbian Adults, Archives of Sexual Behavior, 38, 713–725, doi: 10.1007/s10508-008-9378-1

Prevalence of Eating Disorders found at: www.eatingdisorderscoalition.org/reports/statistics.html

Prochaska, JM; Prochaska, JO; Levesque, DA. A (2001) A transtheoretical approach to changing organizations. Administration and Policy in Mental Health, 28(4), 247–61.

Robinson, B.E., Bockting, W. O. & Harrell, T. (2002) Masturbation and sexual health: An exploratory study of low income African American women. Journal of Psychology & Human Sexuality, 14(2/3), 85-102. Co-published simultaneously in Masturbation as a means of achieving sexual health (Eds.). W. O. Bockting & E. Coleman. Binghamton, N.Y.: The Haworth Press, Inc.

Robinson, B. E., Bockting, W. O., Rosser, B., Miner, M., & Coleman, E. (2002). The Sexual Health Model: application of a sexological approach to HIV prevention. Health Education Research, 17(1), 43-57. doi:10.1093/her/17.1.43

Robinson, B., Munns, R., Weber-Main, A., Lowe, M. & Raymond, N (2011) Application of the Sexual Health Model in the Long-Term Treatment of Hypoactive Sexual Desire and Female Orgasmic Disorder. Archives of Sexual Behavior, 40:2, 469-478, doi: 10.1007/s10508-010-9673-5

Rosen R., Riley A., Wagner G. Osterloh I., Kirkpatrick J. & Mishra A. (1997) The International Index of Erectile Function (IIEF): a multidimensional scale for assessment of erectile dysfunction. Urology, 49, 822-830.

Rosenthal, A.M., Sylva, D., Safron, A. & Bailey, J.M (2011) Sexual arousal patterns of bisexual men revisited. Biological Psychology doi:10.1016/j.biopsycho.2011.06.015

Rosser, B., Dwyer, M, Coleman, E., Miner, M., Metz, M., Robinson, B. & Bockting, W. (1995) Using sexually explicit material in sex education: an eighteen year comparative analysis. Journal of Sex Education and Therapy, 21, 117–128.

Rosser, B., Hatfield, L., Miner, M., Ghiselli, M., Lee, B., Welles, S. & the Positive Connections Team. (2010). Effects of a behavioral intervention to reduce serodiscordant unsafe sex among HIV positive Men who have Sex with Men: The Positive Connections randomized controlled trial study. Journal of Behavioral Medicine, 33(2), 147-158, doi: 10.1007/s10865-009-9244-1.

Rosser, S., Bockting, W., Ross, M., Miner, M. & Coleman, E. (2008) The Relationship Between Homosexuality, Internalized Homo-Negativity, and Mental Health in Men Who Have Sex with Men. Journal of Homosexuality, 55, 1-29, doi: 10.1080/00918360802129394.

Rosser, S., Gobby, J. & Carr, P (1999) The Unsafe Sexual Behavior of Persons Living with HIV: An Empirical Approach to Developing Interventions for Persons Living with HIV. Journal of Sex Education and Therapy, 24(1/2), 18-28.

Rust, P. (2002) Bisexuality: The state of the union. Annual Review of Sex Research, 13, 180-240.

Savin-Williams, R. (2005) The New Gay Teen: Shunning Labels. Gay & Lesbian Review Worldwide, 12(6), 16-19.

Scarce, M (2001) Male on Male Rape: The hidden toll of stigma and shame. Basic Books

Schneider, J. (2005) Back From Betrayal, Third Edition, Chapin

Schwartz, M. F. & Southern, S. (2000) Compulsive cybersex: The new tea room. Sexual Addiction & Compulsivity, 7(1-2), 127-144. doi: 10.1080/10720160008400211

Sex Addicts Recovery Resources www.sarr.org/coaddicts/default.htm

Sheils, A. & Caruso, J. (2004) A Reliability Induction and Reliability Generalization Study of the Cage Questionnaire. Educational and Psychological Measurement, 64(2), 254-270 doi: 10.1177/0013164403261814

Shively M. & DeCecco, J. (1977) Components of Identity, Journal of Homosexuality 3(1), 41-48.

Shulman, J. & Home, S. (2003) The Use of Self-Pleasure: Masturbation and Body Image among African American and European American Women. Psychology of Women Quarterly, 27(3), 262-269.

Singer, M. (2002) Childhood Sexuality: An Interpersonal-Intrapsychic Integration. Contemporary Sexuality, 36(11).

Smolak, L. & Murnen, S. (2002) Meta-Analytic Examination of the Relationship Between Child Sexual Abuse and Eating Disorders. International Journal of Eating Disorder, 31(2), 136-15

Stern, S. E. & Handel, A. D. (2001). Sexuality and mass media: The historical context of psychology's reaction to sexuality on the Internet, Journal of Sex Research, 38(4), 283-291 doi: 10.1080/00224490109552099

Turner, C., Villarroel, M., Chromy, J., Eggleston, E. & Rogers, S. (2005) Same-Gender Sex Among U.S. Adults. Public Opinion Quarterly, 69(3), 439-462.

Treur, T., Koperdák, M., Rózsa, S. & Füredi, J. (2005) The impact of physical and sexual abuse on body image in eating disorders. European Eating Disorders Review, 13(2), 106-111.

Tripodi, C. (2006) Long Term Treatment of Partners of Sex Addicts: A Multi-Phase Approach. Sexual Addiction & Compulsivity, 13, 269-288.

U.S. Department of Health and Human Services (2001) The surgeon general's call to action to promote sexual health and responsible sexual behavior. Rockville, MD.

West, S., Vinikoor, L. &, Zolnoun, D. (2004) Systematic Review of the Literature on Female Sexual Dysfunction Prevalence and Predictors. Annual Review of Sex Research, 15, 40-172.

Wingood, G., Diclemente, R., Harrington, K. & Davies, S. (2002) Body Image and African American Females' Sexual Health. Journal of Women's Health & Gender-Based Medicine, 11(5), 433-439.

Violence against women (2008) located at: www.4woman.gov/violence/types/sexual.cfm

Welcome to the Drug Abuse Screening Test (DAST) (2008) www.counsellingresource.com/quizzes/drug-abuse/index.html.

World Association of Sexology's declaration of sexual rights. (1999) First declared at the 13th World Congress of Sexology, 1997, Valencia, Spain. Revised and approved by the General Assembly of World Association for Sexology on August 26, 1999, during the 14th World Congress of Sexology, Hong Kong, People's Republic of China.

World Health Organization (2002) Gender and reproductive rights, glossary, sexual health. Retrieved on July 11, 2003, from www.who.int/reproductive-health/gender/glossary.html.

Endnotes

[1] OSHO (1999) Emotions: Freedom from Anger, Jealousy and Fear. OSHO International: New York.

[2] National Institute on Alcohol Abuse and Alcoholism. (1995). *Assessing alcohol problems: A guide for clinicians and researchers* (NIH No. 95-3745). Bethesda, MD: National Institute of Health

[3] Cotton, M. Ball, C., & Robinson, P (2003) Four Simple Questions Can Help Screen for Eating Disorders *Journal General Internal Medicine*, 18(1): *53–56*.doi: 10.1046/j.1525-1497.2003.20374.x.

[4] From *www.addictionrecov.org/twenty_question.aspx*, accessed 11/20/2011.

[5] At *www.addictionrecov.org/southoak.htm* accessed on 11/20/2011

[6] Edwards. E. (1993) Development of a New Scale for Measuring Compulsive Buying Behavior Financial Counseling and Planning, 4, 67-85.

[7] Adapted from http://www.hinduonnet.com/jobs/0011/05080033.htm

[8] If you want to read additional resources, please read *Slowing Down to the Speed of Life* by Carlson and Bailey, *Flow: The Psychology of Optimal Experience* by Csikszentmihalyi, and *Blink: The Power of Thinking Without Thinking* by Gladwell, and The *Power of Now* by Tolle.

[9] If you want to read additional resources, please read *Slowing Down to the Speed of Life* by Carlson and Bailey, *Flow: The Psychology of Optimal Experience* by Csikszentmihalyi, and *Blink: The Power of Thinking Without Thinking* by Gladwell, and The *Power of Now* by Tolle.

[10] adapted from : http://www.karpmandramatriangle.com accessed 9/27/2011

[11] To watch the scene: http://www.youtube.com/watch?v=NHWjlCaIrQo)

[12] Prochaska, JM; Prochaska, JO; Levesque, DA. A (2001) A transtheoretical approach to changing organizations. *Administration and Policy in Mental Health, 28(4),* 247–61.

[13] Robinson, B. E., Bockting, W. O., Rosser, B., Miner, M., & Coleman, E. (2002). The Sexual Health Model: application of a sexological approach to HIV prevention. *Health Education Research, 17(1),* 43-57. doi:10.1093/her/17.1.43

[14] Meston, C. & Buss, D. (2007) Why Humans Have Sex. *Archives of Sexual Behavior* 36, 477–507. DOI 10.1007/s10508-007-9175-2

[15] Adapted from Hays, P. (2008) *Addressing Cultural Complexities in Practice: Assessment, Diagnosis, and Therapy (2nd edition).* Washington, D.C.: American Psychological Association.

[16] Bradshaw, John (1998) Healing the Shame that Binds You. HCI

[17] Shively M. & DeCecco, J. (1977) Components of Identity, *Journal of Homosexuality 3(1),* 41-48.

[18] See World Professional Association of Transgender Health at WPATH.ORG for a copy of these protocols.

[19] Facing facts: Sexual health for America's adolescents. (1995) D. W. Haffner (Ed.), New York: Sexuality Information and Education Council of the United States (SIECUS).

[20] Kinsey, et al. 1948. Sexual Behavior in the Human Male. pp. 639, 656 (http://en.wikipedia.org/wiki/Kinsey_scale#References 11/25/11 10:50am CST)

[21] (http://www.iub.edu/~kinsey/research/ak-hhscale.html#what , 11/25/11 10:41 am CST).

[22] Cass, V. (1984) Homosexual Identity Formation: Testing a Theoretical Model. *Journal of Sex Research, 20(2),* 143-167.

[23] Rust, P. (2002) Bisexuality: The state of the union. *Annual Review of Sex Research, 13,* 180-240.

[24] Adapted from Body Love: Learning to Like Our Looks and Ourselves, Rita Freeman, Ph.D.

[25] Fisher, Cullen & Turner, 2000

[26] Dube, 2005.

[27] Scarce, 2001

[28] Adapted from Body Love: Learning to Like Our Looks and Ourselves, Rita Freeman, Ph.D.

[29] Clinebell and Clinebell, 1970.

[30] Gottman, John M., and Nan Silver. (1999). How I predict divorce," in *The Seven Principles for Making Marriages Work* (Chapter Two, 25-46). New York: Three Rivers Press (Random House, Inc.).

[31] Campbell, J. (1976) *Vol, 4: Creative Mythology: The Masks of God.* New York: Penguin.

[32] (Adapted from *http://virtuescience.com/virtuelist.html accessed 9/27/2011*.)

CPSIA information can be obtained
at www.ICGtesting.com
Printed in the USA
LVHW101613160419
614375LV00001B/9/P